With All Deliberate Speed

With All Deliberate Speed: Civil Rights Theory and Reality

Edited by
John H. McCord

University of Illinois Press · Urbana · Chicago · London

© 1969 by the Board of Trustees of the University of Illinois
Manufactured in the United States of America
Library of Congress Catalog Card No. 69-44445

252 00030 7

Foreword

The Civil Rights Movement was announced at Philadelphia on July 4, 1776. A group of self-styled representatives of a people which enjoyed unequal station declared that they were free and "that all men are created equal, that they are endowed by their Creator with certain inalienable Rights, that among these are Life, Liberty and the pursuit of Happiness." After freedom was won, an organic civil rights act, the Bill of Rights, was a first order of business.

Nearly a century later, a constituent people, accidentally black, also were declared to be free and the organic law of civil rights was extended to this constituent minority. The symposium appearing in this volume* is devoted, principally, to discussion of the role of the legal institutions in securing the civil rights of the black minority. However, we think it important initially to note that freedom and human aspiration, government and civil rights, and the integrity of society and of its legal institutions do not comprehend essentially different things when considered in the context of different classes of people. All civil rights movements are one in principle and one in realization. The distortion of a principle or the denial of aspiration affects all society, not merely the individual or class deprived. In this light, the Negro Civil Rights Movement is not unique; it is a contemporary expression of the Civil Rights Movement of 1776.

The authors of the Declaration of Independence, students of Rousseau and Locke, asserted that certain broad human aspirations were, in fact, rights. Modern legal theory is somewhat less willing to elevate interests or aspirations to the category of "rights" unless it can be shown that they have been recognized by and can be enforced by the various legal institutions of a society. The Civil Rights Movement, at its inception and in its contemporary articulation, contemplates both orders of rights: the classical order of "human rights" is the moral foundation for demands that society recognize and enforce as legal rights certain particulars derived therefrom. In the articles that follow, our contributors attend to this derivation of particulars. In the main, however, our attention is focused upon the process of legitimatizing human aspirations and also upon the question, discussed in terms of particular instance as well as legal theory, of the practical and inherent limits of our legal institutions in fully securing civil rights.

The process by which basic human aspirations of individual freedom and dignity and equality of opportunity are recognized and realized in society is certainly broader than the legal process. But legal process and legal institutions play an important role. The function of definition is the first and most obvious. Equally important is the function of education — much more so than that of enforcement. For while legal institutions can, within limits, coerce behavior by attaching sanctions to violations of announced norms, our society depends, for the most part, upon voluntary compliance with laws. Securing voluntary com-

* This symposium was first published in the *University of Illinois Law Forum*.

pliance is a function of education: it is necessary that the imprimatur of prestigious legal institutions should lead to social acceptance of the principles announced as right.

The articles in this symposium suggest that the recent contribution of legal institutions to the definition of civil rights has been substantial, albeit made with much deliberation and sometimes unimpressive speed. However, legal institutions have been much less successful in securing acceptance of these principles of right and in securing the realization of civil rights in fact. This failure may cast some doubt upon the ability of these institutions to convert legal definition into practical reality, and this doubt, suggests Dean Lenoir, has generated suspicion of traditional institutions, "spawned a new breed of activists and militants," and precipitated the crisis which now grips our country.

There is, certainly, reason to be somewhat discouraged. Our contributors, however, remain optimistic. All see a further need for extension and elaboration of civil rights by legal institutions and are hopeful that these activities will continue. But more important is the hope that the men who administer laws may do so with increasing sensitivity and imagination. The importance of the human element and the increasing awareness of this importance is becoming evident. It is reflected in a recent statement of William T. Gossett, President of the American Bar Association. Addressing himself to the problems of due process, Mr. Gossett urged lawyers to become "crusaders" and "public teachers." He admonished the Bar that it had "a continuing responsibility to enlighten the public about the necessity and utility of decency and fairness in the law's attitude and in the conduct of public officials toward the individual and his fundamental rights."

We have been most fortunate to enlist the participation of contributors who have long been crusaders and public teachers for civil rights. Their analyses, insights, and views are those of lawyers who have combined scholarly observation with active involvement. We are most grateful to them for making this symposium possible. We should also like to thank the Board of Student Editors of the *University of Illinois Law Forum* and our Associate Editor, Mrs. Marilee W. Brukman, for their assistance in the preparation of this volume.

J. H. M.
Champaign, July, 1969

Contents

"...WITH ALL DELIBERATE SPEED"

BY THE BOARD OF STUDENT EDITORS*

I. INTRODUCTION

INDIVIDUALS BELONGING TO MAJORITY GROUPS need seldom fear the loss of their civil liberty, and consequently are seldom aware of its loss by other groups. The battle for individual freedoms has been fought largely by minorities of race, color, religion, or national origin. In the United States the largest minority group, and the minority least assimilated into the community, is the Negro race. Other minorities, such as the Chinese and Japanese of the Pacific coast, the American Indian, and immigrants in general, have achieved important advances in the civil rights movement. But for many the struggle for equal rights is synonymous with the term "Negro rights." This by no means is meant to suggest that civil rights has relevance only for Negroes. Mr. Justice Harlan's words of almost 100 years ago are still persuasive: "Today it is the colored race which is denied, by corporations and individuals wielding public authority, rights fundamental in their freedom and citizenship. At some future time it may be some other race that will fall under the ban."[1] Today's civil rights movement scores victories not only for the Negro, but for all men.

Concern for individual liberty has always been the preoccupation of American political planners. In 1787 this concern delayed the ratification of the Constitution until the addition of a bill of rights was promised. So well was the promise kept that it may be asked whether any abstract issue of individual liberty can be conceived which does not fit under the broad interpretation of the Bill of Rights. For two reasons, however, the Bill of Rights has not been a perfect guardian of liberty. First, the founders feared government as the enemy of freedom; the Bill of Rights was directed against government action, not the activities of individuals. Second, it was only the federal government which was limited by the Bill of Rights; state governments were not affected. In reference to these two limitations one author has stated that the Bill of Rights provided a shield, but not a sword.[2] Individuals were shielded against oppressive government action (that is, against federal government action) but there was no means by which the federal government could take the initiative.

After the Civil War, the fourteenth amendment attempted to cast a shield against state action, and the civil rights acts of 1866-75 were passed to forge a sword for the federal government to employ against those who violated individuals' civil liberties. That program is examined in this article, followed by an account of the emasculation of the early civil rights acts by

With the special assistance of Messrs. Robert W. Cook, Douglas A. Ingold, James B. Jurgens,* and Fredric J. Zepp.*

[1] The Civil Rights Cases, 109 U.S. 3, 62, 3 S. Ct. 18, 57 (1883) (dissenting opinion).
[2] R. K. CARR, FEDERAL PROTECTION OF CIVIL RIGHTS 5-7 (1947).
(*since graduated).

1

decisions of the Supreme Court, Congressional repeal, and inactivity on the part of the Executive. The restrictive interpretation first placed on the fourteenth amendment by the Supreme Court is described, and a survey of Supreme Court cases from the Civil War to the present is given to show the Court's increasing concern with civil rights in general, and its particular concern with a more expansive reading of the amendment. Also included is a general history of civil rights, the civil rights movement, and the agitation for new federal civil rights legislation. Finally, a summary of the 1957 Act, the 1960 Act, the 1964 Act, the 1965 Voting Rights Act, and the abortive 1966 Act serves as a prelude for the more expansive treatment of these acts in the subsequent articles of this symposium.

II. CIVIL RIGHTS IN THE FEDERAL LEGISLATURE 1866-1875

Northern victory in the Civil War resolved the most serious question ever to threaten the Constitution: the nature of the Union. Victory in turn raised the problem of how the Confederate states were to rejoin the Union, if indeed they had ever left it.[3] Lee's surrender on April 9, 1865, Lincoln's death on April 15, and the fact that Congress was not in session at the moment thrust immediate responsibility for reconstruction upon President Andrew Johnson. Lincoln had insisted that "loyal" state governments erected in Tennessee, Arkansas, and Louisiana under his proclamation of December 8, 1863,[4] were constitutionally correct despite Congress' refusal to seat them. Johnson followed this reconstruction theory which Lincoln had developed during the war.[5] Accordingly, most former Confederates were to be pardoned upon taking a loyalty oath,[6] and constitutional conventions of loyal delegates were called in each Southern state.

[3] As a starting point for reconstruction thought, several theories were proposed regarding the position of the Southern states. Lincoln held that secession was impossible; the states were still in the Union, and on suppression of rebellion and creation of loyal governments they would automatically resume normal relations with the federal government. Congress proposed two theories disagreeing with Lincoln's, the "conquered provinces" and "state suicide" theories. According to these theories the South was to be under direct congressional control as unorganized territory. A more moderate theory, the "forfeited rights" or "dead states" theory, ultimately won congressional approval. It declared that by withdrawing their representatives in Congress and levying war against the United States, the seceded states had forfeited all political rights incident to the Union. This theory also allowed Congress to control reconstruction, since only Congress could restore the "dead states" to full membership in the Union. A. H. KELLY & W. A. HARBISON, THE AMERICAN CONSTITUTION 451, 455, 463-64 (3d ed. 1963). This well-written text is one of the finest works available on constitutional history and is relied on heavily in this article.

[4] Text is found in 6 MESSAGES AND PAPERS OF THE PRESIDENTS 213-15 (J. D. Richardson ed. 1897).

[5] Lincoln's final public address gives, at least to those who look for it, some indication that Lincoln might have agreed to stricter readmission terms once the war was over. The war reconstruction terms may have been offered as an inducement to the South to lay down its arms; as the offer was not accepted, stricter terms became a possibility. Lincoln's last address may be found in 1 DOCUMENTS OF AMERICAN HISTORY 448-50 (5th ed. H. S. Commager 1949).

[6] For a discussion of difficulties with the "ironclad test oath," see H. M. HYMAN, TO TRY MEN'S SOULS; LOYALTY TESTS IN AMERICAN HISTORY 225-57 (1959).

When Congress assembled in December 1865, presidential reconstruction was immediately attacked. "Radical Republicans" were against the Johnson program because it did not guarantee Negro civil rights, because it was too lenient, because it excluded Congress from any participation in reconstruction, and because it did not cope with the threat that former Confederates would vote with Northern Democrats to overthrow the Republicans.[7] Therefore the Radicals refused to seat the new Southern congressmen and created a Joint Committee on Reconstruction which was to formulate a congressional plan to replace that of the President. Popular support was with the Radicals. Lincoln's assassination (believed by many to be of Southern design) following so closely upon the long years of war strengthened Northern purpose not to abandon the causes for which the war had been fought. Nor did the South help its own cause. "Black Codes" adopted by the presidentially reconstructed states in 1865 and 1866 "bore a suspicious resemblance to the ante-bellum slave codes," and Southern election of former prominent Confederates to high state and national office was also taken as a sign of Southern bad faith.[8]

Congress instituted its own reconstruction plan with the passage of the Freedmen's Bureau Bill of 1866.[9] The bill was to extend the life of the Freedmen's Bureau, created during the war in 1865, and to enlarge the Bureau's powers within those States "in which the ordinary course of judicial proceedings has been interrupted by the rebellion." Johnson apologetically vetoed the bill.[10] One of his objections was to a section which provided for military jurisdiction over persons charged with depriving a freedman of "any civil rights or immunities belonging to white persons." "I cannot reconcile a system of military jurisdiction of this kind," said Johnson, "with the words of the Constitution . . . . [the fifth and sixth amendments]." Johnson further declared the bill unnecessary in that the freedman could and should fend for himself. Since the eleven states most directly affected by the bill were not represented at its passage, Johnson felt it his duty as the only truly national official to represent their interests. A closing plea requested Congress to agree with Johnson that the Southern states were fully restored. Congress sustained this veto, but within six months passed essentially the same legislation over a veto.[11] During this time the Civil Rights Act of 1866 was passed, the first reconstruction measure to be passed over the veto. With defeat on the Civil Rights Act, the President lost all control over reconstruction; Congress now was to pass legislation over his veto almost at will.[12]

[7] A. H. KELLY & W. A. HARBISON, *supra* note 3, at 454.

[8] *Id*. at 457-58.

[9] *See generally* M. R. KONVITZ & T. LESKES, A CENTURY OF CIVIL RIGHTS 43-48 (1961).

[10] Text of the veto message is found in 6 MESSAGES AND PAPERS OF THE PRESIDENTS 398-405 (J. D. Richardson ed. 1897).

[11] The Freedmen's Bureau Act of July 16, 1866, 14 Stat. 173, discussed in M. R. KONVITZ & T. LESKES, *supra* note 9, at 46-48.

[12] A. H. KELLY & W. A. HARBISON, *supra* note 3, at 460.

The Civil Rights Act of 1866 was the federal government's first move into the area of direct protection of individual freedom. The Act declared that "all persons born in the United States and not subject to any foreign power, excluding Indians not taxed" were citizens of the United States.[13] Such citizens, of every race and color, were to have the same rights in every state to make contracts, use the courts, hold and transfer property, benefit from all laws, and be subject to the same punishments and penalties. Any person who "under color of any law, statute, ordinance, regulation, or custom" deprived any person of such right was guilty of a federal misdemeanor. Federal courts were given exclusive jurisdiction of cases arising under the act, fines and imprisonment were provided for its violation, and the President was empowered to use the land and naval forces to secure its enforcement. Where federal law was "not adapted to the object" or was "deficient in the provisions necessary to furnish suitable remedies," the federal court was to apply "the common law, as modified and changed by the constitution and statutes of the State."

President Johnson preferred federal court jurisdiction to military jurisdiction, and therefore preferred the Civil Rights Act of 1866 to the Freedmen's Bureau Act.[14] Still, Johnson vetoed the Civil Rights Act in a message which some historians have viewed as an appeal to prejudice.[15] He felt that the act was illogical in providing immediate citizenship for the Negro, while "intelligent, worthy, and patriotic foreigners" were made to pass through a period of probation before enjoying the rights of citizens. Johnson felt the provision against deprivation of rights "under color of law" was meant to apply to state judges, and therefore invaded the judicial power of the State.[16] Also, allowing the federal courts to apply state common law was a grant of

[13] Civil Rights Act of April 9, 1866, 14 Stat. 27 (now 42 U.S.C. §§ 1982, 1989-93).

[14] Veto to Freedmen's Bureau Act of July 16, 1866, 6 MESSAGES AND PAPERS OF THE PRESIDENTS 425 (J. D. Richardson ed. 1897).

[15] Johnson warned how broad the act was:

"This provision comprehends the Chinese of the Pacific States, Indians subject to taxation, the people called gypsies, as well as the entire race designated as blacks, people of color, negroes, mulattoes, and persons of African blood. Every individual of these races born in the United States is by the bill made a citizen of the United States."

Declaring that the act was a dangerous intrusion into the internal police and economic affairs of the states, Johnson pointed, ad horrendum, to the type of state law Congress might repeal in the future:

"In the exercise of State policy over matters exclusively affecting the people of each State it has frequently been thought expedient to discriminate between the two races. By the statutes of some of the States, Northern as well as Southern, it is enacted, for instance, that no white person shall intermarry with a negro or mulatto."

6 MESSAGES AND PAPERS OF THE PRESIDENTS 405 & 407 (J. D. Richardson ed. 1897).

[16] Such an interpretation of § 1 of the Third Enforcement Act of April 20, 1871, 17 Stat. 13 (now 42 U.S.C. § 1983), which contained essentially the same language, was recently rejected by the Supreme Court in Pierson v. Ray, 386 U.S. 547, 87 S. Ct. 1213 (1967).

jurisdiction not within the article III judicial power of the United States.[17] Some of the constitutional objections to the Freedmen's Bureau Bill of 1866 were repeated. Johnson's most serious objection, however, was to the political theory of the act; the act was "another step, or rather stride, towards centralization, and the concentration of all legislative powers in the national Government."[18]

Johnson's veto, coupled with congressional doubts over the constitutionality of the Civil Rights Act, led the Radicals to press for a new constitutional amendment.[19] Two months after the Civil Rights Act was passed over the President's veto, the Senate passed the fourteenth amendment; a few days later, on June 13, 1866, the amendment was passed by the House. Section one of the amendment, in language similar to that of the Civil Rights Act, stated that "all persons born or naturalized in the United States and subject to the jurisdiction thereof, are citizens of the United States and of the State wherein they reside." The three remaining clauses of section one, the famous "privileges and immunities" clause, the "due process" clause, and the "equal protection" clause, gave a federal guarantee of private rights against state interference.[20] These provisions were intended to remove all doubt regarding Congress' constitutional power to make the Civil Rights Act binding on the states.

With the admission of Nebraska to the Union on March 1, 1867, there were thirty-seven states in the United States. Twenty-eight of these would constitute the three-fourths necessary to ratify the amendment. If the Northern and border states had solidly voted to ratify—which was not in fact the case[21]—at least one Southern state would still have been needed for ratification. If the Southern states had ratified, Congress probably would have recognized their so-called Johnson governments and allowed them representation.[22] This in fact occurred with Tennessee, which on July 19, 1866, became the third state to ratify; it was readmitted to the Union on that same date. But by March 1, 1867, only twenty states, with Tennessee as the sole

---

[17] U.S. CONST. art. III, § 1.

[18] "In all our history, in all our experience as a people living under Federal and State law, no such system as that contemplated by the details of this bill has ever before been proposed or adopted. They establish for the security of the colored race safeguards which go infinitely beyond any that the General Government has ever provided for the white race. In fact, the distinction of race and color is by the bill made to operate in favor of the colored and against the white race. They interfere with the municipal legislation of the States, with the relations existing exclusively between a State and its citizens, or between inhabitants of the same State—an absorption and assumption of power by the General Government which, if acquiesced in, must sap and destroy our federative system of limited powers and break down the barriers which preserve the rights of the States."
6 MESSAGES AND PAPERS OF THE PRESIDENTS 412-13 (J. D. Richardson ed. 1897).

[19] A. H. KELLY & W. A. HARBISON, supra note 3, at 458-61; M. R. KONVITZ & T. LESKES, supra note 9, at 51. See generally H. E. FLACK, THE ADOPTION OF THE FOURTEENTH AMENDMENT 55-136 (1908).

[20] U.S. CONST. amend. XIV, § 1.

[21] M. R. KONVITZ & T. LESKES, supra note 9, at 53.

[22] A. H. KELLY & W. A. HARBISON, supra note 3, at 464.

Southern state, had ratified. Many Southerners felt that their present uncertain position was preferable to that which they would occupy after the
amendment became a part of the Constitution.[23] Besides, if the congressional
elections of 1866 went against the Radicals, the South could hope for more
favorable readmission on President Johnson's terms.

The Radicals won an overwhelming victory in the November elections.[24]
Enjoying more than a two-thirds majority in both Houses, the Radicals
advanced upon a far more extreme program than that of the previous June.[25]
A series of four Reconstruction Acts were passed in 1867 and 1868.[26]
Through these acts Congress repudiated the Johnson government. Declaring
that no adequate state governments existed in the South, the acts placed "the
rebel states" under military jurisdiction. The military was to be responsible
for all local law enforcement and for the registration of voters. As did the
proposed fourteenth amendment, the acts declared that no person could vote
or hold office who previous to the war had taken an oath as a state or federal
official to support the Constitution and had subsequently engaged in rebellion.
Readmission of each state was conditioned upon the state's calling a constitutional convention to form a constitution guaranteeing the franchise to the
freedman and to ratify the fourteenth amendment. In all ten of the unrecon-
structed states political control quickly passed from the conservative white
population to "carpetbaggers," "scalawags," and Negroes.[27] In five states
registered Negro voters outnumbered the whites; in the others the two were
nearly equal.[28] These reconstructed states all ratified the amendment by
1870.[29] Enough had ratified for the amendment to be certified as a part of
the Constitution by Secretary of State Seward on July 28, 1868. Because of

[23] Section 3 of the amendment would have denied the right to hold state or federal
office to anyone who had taken an oath as a pre-war state or federal officer to support
the Constitution and had then engaged in rebellion. Southern attitude toward this section
is illustrated by Governor D. S. Walker of Florida:

> "Look around you and see how few persons will be left in office after this Amend-
> ment is adopted, and you will see that to vote for it is to vote for the destruction
> of your State Government. After taking out all the proscribed officers, there will
> not be enough left to order elections to fill the vacancies, and a Military Govern-
> ment will become necessary."

U. S. Comm'n on Civil Rights, Freedom to the Free 41 (1963).

[24] This important congressional election of 1866 was the occasion for Johnson's
famous "swing around the circle," a series of stump speeches around the Middle West
characterized by their immoderation. 2 S. E. Morison & H. S. Commager, The Growth
of the American Republic 31 (5th ed. 1962).

[25] A. H. Kelly & W. A. Harbison, supra note 3, at 465-66.

[26] First Reconstruction Act of March 2, 1867, 14 Stat. 428; Second Reconstruction
Act of March 23, 1867, 15 Stat. 2; Third Reconstruction Act of July 19, 1867, 15 Stat. 14;
Fourth Reconstruction Act of March 11, 1868, 15 Stat. 41. The acts, together with ap-
propriate vetoes by President Johnson, may be found in 2 Documents of American
History 30-35, 38-42, 49 (5th ed. Commager 1949).

[27] Johnson vetoed the acts, but when Congress promptly re-enacted them, Johnson
put them into operation. A. H. Kelly & W. A. Harbison, supra note 3, at 468-69.

[28] Id. at 468-69.

[29] M. R. Konvitz & T. Leskes, supra note 9, at 52.

its ratification history, some still feel that the fourteenth amendment was unconstitutionally placed in the Constitution.[30]

Section 2 of the fourteenth amendment provides for suffrage, but the provision is negative; representation is to be reduced in proportion to denial of the right to vote.[31] Attempts to make a positive provision for suffrage had been defeated in debate.[32] Northern voters were against any provision which would require Negro suffrage in the North, although the Radicals were able to impose suffrage in the District of Columbia, in the Nebraska territory, and in the South. The fourteenth amendment's approach was acceptable because it avoided the Negro voting issue in the North while exerting indirect pressure on the South.[33] Even the limited suffrage gains made by the Radicals were halted by the rout of Republican tickets and suffrage amendments in the state elections of 1867. For the presidential election of 1868 the Republicans were forced to draft a moderate suffrage plank and nominate General Grant instead of the champion of Negro suffrage, Chief Justice Salmon P. Chase.[34] Grant won by only 300,000 votes. Southern Negro voters, in excess of 450,000, gave Grant his popular majority, but were not necessary for an electoral victory.[35] Three Southern states did not take part in the election; six others, voting under carpetbag rule, denied the

---

[30] *Id.* at 53-57. As late as 1955 Maryland refused to ratify the amendment after originally rejecting it in 1867. *Id.* at 53-54. For a recent study of the arguments pro and con, see Fernandez, *The Constitutionality of the Fourteenth Amendment*, 39 So. CAL. L. REV. 378 (1966).

[31] "But when the right to vote at any election for the choice of electors for President and Vice President of the United States, Representatives in Congress, the Executive and Judicial officers of a State, or the members of the Legislature thereof, is denied to any of the male inhabitants of such State, being twenty-one years of age, and citizens of the United States, or in any way abridged, except for participation in rebellion, or other crime, the basis of representation therein shall be reduced in the proportion which the number of such male citizens shall bear to the whole number of male citizens twenty-one years of age in such state."

U.S. CONST. amend. XIV, § 2. Henry Cabot Lodge in 1890 introduced a "Force Bill" to enforce the amendment by reducing representation, but a political bargain with Southern Democrats shelved the proposal. "Since that time, an occasional Northern congressman, usually one seeking support from Negro constituents, has introduced legislation to effect a reduction in Southern representation in accordance with the amendment, but these measures have never been taken seriously." A. H. KELLY & W. A. HARBISON, *supra* note 3, at 494.

[32] *See generally* H. E. FLACK, *supra* note 19, at 97-127.

[33] "This compromise, the best amendment that congressmen could devise, and still get an amendment passed and ratified, was a modest but incomplete step toward Negro suffrage, in allowing southerners to continue excluding Negroes from voting at the possible risk of taking the unpleasant penalty of roughly fifteen less seats in the House of Representatives and thus the equivalent votes in the electoral college. Most congressmen apparently did not intend to risk drowning by swimming against the treacherous current of racial prejudice and opposition to Negro suffrage. They therefore designed a measure that would avoid the Negro issue in the North, yet exert indirect pressure on the South to accept Negro suffrage."

W. GILLETTE, THE RIGHT TO VOTE 24-25 (1965).

[34] *Id.* at 36 & 45.

[35] *Id.* at 40.

vote to many whites. A small shift in the vote of a few key states could have resulted in a Democratic victory.[36]

"Defeat in postwar state referendums, disaster in 1867 state elections, and danger signals in the federal elections of 1868 taught Republicans that something must be done . . . done by this final session of the Fortieth Congress, before the Democrats arrived in force."[37] Immediately after the presidential election, Republican support grew in favor of a new amendment to guarantee Negro suffrage and thus strengthen the party, both in the North and South.[38] Republicans preferred the bolder method of amending the Constitution as an easier and more permanent method than direct vote in each state. "Republicans had traveled a hard road long enough, and therefore agreed that the longest way around was the shortest way home."[39]

In contrast to the fourteenth amendment, little difficulty was experienced in the passage and ratification of the fifteenth amendment. Congress proposed the amendment on February 26, 1869, and on March 3, 1870, Secretary of State Fish certified that it had become a part of the Constitution. Enfranchisement of the Negro resulted in Negroes holding important posts in the governments formed under the four Reconstruction Acts of 1867 and 1868. Between 1869 and 1901, twenty-two Negroes were sent to Congress from the South. Hiram R. Revels and Blanche K. Bruce served in the Senate representing Mississippi.[40] Nevertheless, the white population soon re-entered the political conflict. By sending more whites to the polls, by seeking the support of Negroes dissatisfied with the Radicals, and through the terrorism of the Ku Klux Klan, the whites once more asserted their power. "The Radicals fought back with their principal weapons: the Negro vote, white disfranchisement, corruption, and appeals to Washington."[41] Two months after the ratification of the fifteenth amendment, Congress enacted a new civil rights act, the First Enforcement Act of May 31, 1870.[42]

The First Enforcement Act was the first real civil rights act since the Civil Rights Act of 1866. The Reconstruction Acts of 1867 and 1868 gave federal protection to Negro rights, but they did so through the temporary expedient of military jurisdiction. In contrast, the Civil Rights Act of 1866

[36] *Id*. at 40-41.

[37] *Id*. at 45.

[38] "As Thaddeus Stevens put it, [referring also to the fourteenth amendment] the Southern states 'ought never to be recognized as capable of acting in the Union, or of being counted as valid states, until the Constitution shall have been so amended . . . as to secure perpetual ascendancy to the party of the Union. . . .'

"If all this seems narrow and ungenerous, we should ask ourselves what other nation in history has ever turned over control of the government and of the spoils of victory to the leaders of a defeated rebellion?"

2 S. E. MORISON & H. S. COMMAGER, *supra* note 24, at 22.

[39] W. GILLETTE, *supra* note 33, at 52.

[40] U.S. COMM'N ON CIVIL RIGHTS, FREEDOM TO THE FREE 45 (1963).

[41] A. H. KELLY & W. A. HARBISON, *supra* note 3, at 483.

[42] First Enforcement Act of May 31, 1870, 16 Stat. 140 (now 18 U.S.C. §§ 241-42; 42 U.S.C. §§ 1971, 1981, 1989-91, 1993).

and 1870 were meant to provide continuing protection through the federal courts. Under the First Enforcement Act, all qualified citizens of the United States were to be allowed to vote at state elections without racial discrimination. Voting tests were to be administered uniformly; violations constituted federal misdemeanors warranting fine or imprisonment. Similar penalties were provided for persons who by force or intimidation prevented a citizen from qualifying or voting. An anti-Ku Klux Klan section made it a felony "if two or more persons shall band or conspire together, or go in disguise upon the public highway, or upon the premises of another . . . with intent to prevent or hinder his free exercise and enjoyment of any right or privilege granted or secured to him by the Constitution or laws of the United States . . . ." Federal courts were given exclusive jurisdiction of all cases arising under the act. Provisions were made for the removal of certain former Confederates from state and federal offices. Besides voting rights, the act placed a federal guarantee on the right of all persons to make contracts, use the courts, and enjoy full and equal protection of the laws. Along the same lines the Civil Rights Act of 1866 was re-enacted, apparently to give it the constitutional support of the fourteenth and fifteenth amendments which did not become part of the Constitution until after the Civil Rights Act's original enactment.

In December 1870, President Grant declared that "a free exercise of the elective franchise has by violence and intimidation been denied to citizens in exceptional cases in several of the States lately in rebellion and the verdict of the people has thereby been reversed."[43] Determined to secure the benefits of the fifteenth amendment, Congress passed the Second Enforcement Act of February 28, 1871.[44] Among other things, the act provided direct federal supervision of congressional elections by federal election supervisors. Before this law could be tested, a new session of Congress convened, and reports of violence in the South increased sentiments for stronger federal legislation.[45] Accordingly, the most drastic of the Enforcement Acts, the Third Enforcement Act or "Ku Klux Klan Act," was passed on April 20, 1871.[46] The law provided heavy penalties for any person who "under color of any law, statute, ordinance, custom, or usage of any State," deprived any person of rights secured by the Constitution. Similar penalties were provided against persons conspiring to rebel against the United States, interfering with duties of federal officers or enforcement of federal law, conspiring "to go together in disguise" in order to deprive any person of "the equal protection of the laws," or preventing a citizen from supporting a candidate in a congressional

---

[43] The message is found in 7 MESSAGES AND PAPERS OF THE PRESIDENTS 96 (J. D. Richardson ed. 1898).

[44] Second Enforcement Act of February 28, 1871, 16 Stat. 433.

[45] U.S. COMM'N ON CIVIL RIGHTS, FREEDOM TO THE FREE 48-50 (1963).

[46] Third Enforcement Act of April 20, 1871, 17 Stat. 13 (now 10 U.S.C. § 333; 18 U.S.C. § 372; 28 U.S.C. § 1343; 42 U.S.C. §§ 1983, 1985-86; 50 U.S.C. § 203).

election. In the areas where the President found that insurrection existed, he was authorized to suspend the writ of habeas corpus and employ the armed forces of the United States to suppress the conspiracy. Under the Ku Klux Klan Act, federal troops were dispatched to suppress literally hundreds of disturbances throughout the South.[47]

Despite the presence of federal troops and the inability of many ex-Confederates to vote and hold office, Southern whites, with the support of 90 per cent of the white population, made steady progress in regaining control of their states.[48] Disgust with certain aspects of Radical reconstruction brought support from the North. In 1871 and 1872, Congress modified the Test-Oath requirement, thus restoring voting and office-holding rights to many ex-Confederates.[49] "Liberal Republicans," disagreeing sharply with Radical policies, bolted the party in 1872 and nominated Horace Greeley for the presidency. Greeley lost, but the Radicals thereafter hesitated to pass legislation interfering too deeply in the internal affairs of the South. "It was evident that public opinion in the North was becoming weary of the attempt to impose a new social order on the South . . . ."[50] By 1874 seven states had come under the control of the Southern conservatives, now mainly operating through the Democratic Party. Radical reconstruction continued only in South Carolina, Florida, Mississippi, and Louisiana, and there only for another two years.

One last, great step was left for the Radicals in the field of civil rights before their house crumbled. On March 1, 1875, Congress enacted the most far-reaching civil rights legislation it had ever considered. The Civil Rights Act of 1875 declared:

> "That all persons within the jurisdiction of the United States shall be entitled to the full and equal enjoyment of the accomodations, advantages, facilities, and privileges of inns, public conveyances on land or water, theaters, and other places of public amusement; subject only to the conditions and limitations established by law, and applicable alike to citizens of every race and color, regardless of any previous condition of servitude."[51]

Any violation of the act was a misdemeanor, over which federal courts were given jurisdiction. Another section of the act guaranteed that no citizen should be disqualified as a juror on account of race, color, or previous con-

---

[47] "In October 1871, when Klan activity became particularly violent in South Carolina, President Grant issued a proclamation declaring nine counties in that state to be in rebellion, suspended the writ of habeas corpus, and sent in federal troops to restore order." A. H. KELLY & W. A. HARBISON, *supra* note 3, at 484.

[48] *Id.* at 484-85.

[49] An excellent discussion of Reconstruction loyalty oaths is found in H. M. HYMAN, *supra* note 6, at 251-66.

[50] A. H. KELLY & W. A. HARBISON, *supra* note 3, at 485.

[51] Civil Rights Act of March 1, 1875, 18 Stat. 335 (now 18 U.S.C. § 243; 42 U.S.C. § 1984).

dition of servitude. This proved to be the last congressional enactment to protect the Negro in his civil or political rights until Congress adopted the Civil Rights Act of 1957, eighty-two years later.

The disputed election and the "Compromise of 1877" marked the end of Radical reconstruction.[52] The Republicans had already lost control of the House. The new President Hayes was a moderate who immediately withdrew federal troops from the three remaining Radical-controlled Southern states. Hayes did veto legislation passed by a Democratic Congress in 1877 designed to repeal much of the federal Enforcement Act program.[53] In 1894, however, a bill "to repeal all statutes relating to supervisors of elections and special deputy marshals, and for other purposes,"[54] passed both Houses and was signed by President Cleveland. The act repealed thirty-nine sections of the federal Enforcement Acts which had already been scattered under various chapter headings in the Revised Statutes of 1873. In the preparation of the Criminal Code of 1909,[55] the remaining provisions of the original legislation were reduced still further.

Historical judgment on the Radical Republicans and their program has varied. Some have seen the civil rights acts of 1866-1875 only as a part of a harsh reconstruction imposed by a bitter North upon a defeated South.[56] As late as 1945, Justices Roberts, Frankfurter, and Jackson were able to say: "It is familiar history that much of this legislation was born of that vengeful spirit which to no small degree envenomed the Reconstruction era. Legislative respect for constitutional limitations was not at its height and Congress passed laws clearly unconstitutional."[57] More recent historical study, doubtlessly influenced by today's concern with civil rights, has been more kind to the Radicals. The current view acknowledges the Radicals' preoccupation with the importance of the Negro vote, but at the same time recognizes their genuine concern for the Negro.[58]

Whatever the Radicals' motives, the civil rights program of 1866-1875

---

[52] See generally C. V. WOODWARD, REUNION AND REACTION (1951).

[53] See R. K. CARR, FEDERAL PROTECTION OF CIVIL RIGHTS 46 (1947).

[54] Act of February 8, 1894, 28 Stat. 36.

[55] Act of March 4, 1909, 35 Stat. 1088.

[56] E.g., 3 C. WARREN, THE SUPREME COURT IN UNITED STATES HISTORY 322-43 (1922). In referring to the Supreme Court decisions which declared much of the civil rights program unconstitutional, Warren says:

"Viewed in historical perspective now, however, there can be no question that the decisions in these cases were most fortunate. They largely eliminated from National politics the negro question which had so long embittered Congressional debates; they relegated the burden and the duty of protecting the negro to the States, to whom they properly belonged; and they served to restore confidence in the National Court in the Southern States."

Id. at 330.

[57] Screws v. United States, 325 U.S. 91, 140, 65 S. Ct. 1031, 1054 (1945) (dissenting opinion).

[58] See A. H. KELLY & W. A. HARBISON, THE AMERICAN CONSTITUTION 454 (3d ed. 1963); M. R. KONVITZ & T. LESKES, supra note 9, at 65; C. P. MAGRATH, MORRISON R. WAITE 113 (1963); 2 S. E. MORISON & H. S. COMMAGER, supra note 24, at 22, 28.

ended in failure. Within thirty years the statutes were brought down by Supreme Court invalidation of several key provisions and the Congressional repeal of other sections described above. Administrative reluctance to enforce the remaining provisions completed the picture.[59]

III.   CIVIL RIGHTS IN THE COURTS AND BEFORE THE PEOPLE 1866-1956

In the decade following the Civil War, the Supreme Court walked a careful road of neutrality. When the Court threatened to waver from the path[60] and question the Congressional program, the Radicals brought it back into line by devices[61] such as preventing President Johnson from appointing any new justices and by withdrawing its grant of jurisdiction in a case before the Court.[62] Although the Supreme Court at first passed up several opportunities to rule on the civil rights legislation, it ultimately held much of it unconstitutional in a series of six decisions between 1876 and 1906.[63] A change in the attitude of the country explains how the Court was able to hand down decisions in the 1870's and early 1880's which would have provoked congressional outrage a decade earlier.[64] Despite his humanitarian feelings, the average Northerner had never considered the Negro his equal. Times were changing in the years after the war, and the cause of the Negro took a second place as the focus of the Nation shifted to industrial expansion and the internal harmony necessary for it.[65]

Three principal reasons were given by the Court for declaring the civil rights acts unconstitutional.[66] First, the Court felt that much of the legislation attempted to regulate individuals directly, instead of regulating state action, and therefore could not be justified by the fourteenth and fifteenth amendments.[67] On this basis the Supreme Court invalidated the Civil Rights Act

---

[59] R. K. CARR, *supra* note 53, at 46-47.

[60] The Court did stray in deciding *The Test Oath Cases:* Ex parte Milligan, 71 U.S. (4 Wall.) 2 (1866); Cummings v. Missouri, 71 U.S. (4 Wall.) 277 (1867); Ex parte Garland, 71 U.S. (4 Wall.) 333 (1867). An able discussion is found in H. M. HYMAN, TO TRY MEN'S SOULS; LOYALTY TESTS IN AMERICAN HISTORY, 259-61 (1959).

[61] *See* A. H. KELLY & W. A. HARBISON, *supra* note 58, at 477-81.

[62] The case, Ex parte McCardle, 74 U.S. (7 Wall.) 506 (1869), has been a sore point with federal courts scholars. See H. M. HART & H. WECHSLER, THE FEDERAL COURTS AND THE FEDERAL SYSTEM 290-94, 312-40 (1953).

[63] United States v. Reese, 92 U.S. 214 (1876), holding §§ 3 and 4 of the First Enforcement Act of May 31, 1870, unconstitutional; United States v. Harris, 106 U.S. 629, 1 S. Ct. 601 (1883), holding § 2 of the Third Enforcement Act of April 20, 1871, unconstitutional; *The Civil Rights Cases*, 109 U.S. 3, 3 S. Ct. 18 (1883), holding §§ 1 and 2 of the Civil Rights Act of March 1, 1875, unconstitutional; Baldwin v. Franks, 120 U.S. 678, 7 S. Ct. 656 (1887), holding § 2 of the Third Enforcement Act of April 20, 1871, unconstitutional; James v. Bowman, 190 U.S. 127, 23 S. Ct. 678 (1903), holding § 5 of the First Enforcement Act of May 31, 1870, unconstitutional; Hodges v. United States, 203 U.S. 1, 27 S. Ct. 6 (1906), holding § 16 of the First Enforcement Act of May 31, 1870, unconstitutional.

[64] *See* C. P. MAGRATH, *supra* note 58, at 130.

[65] *Id.* at 112-15.

[66] R. K. CARR, *supra* note 53, at 40-47.

[67] The fourteenth amendment says, "No State shall. . . ." U.S. CONST. amend. XIV,

of 1875 in *The Civil Rights Cases*,[68] holding that the fourteenth amendment did not authorize Congress to pass a statute penalizing private persons operating hotels, theaters, or railroads for refusing to allow Negroes to enjoy their services. On the same ground the Court held section 2 of the Ku Klux Klan Act of April 20, 1871, unconstitutional in *United States v. Harris*,[69] where members of a mob were prosecuted for attacking four prisoners in the custody of a deputy sheriff. A second, more tenuous, ground for holding the acts unconstitutional was that the fifteenth amendment protected the right to vote in federal and state elections against state interference only if the interference were based upon the race, color, or previous condition of servitude of the voter. Thus, in *United States v. Reese*,[70] sections 3 and 4 of the First Enforcement Act of May 31, 1870, were held unconstitutional because they were not directed exclusively against state interference motivated by race or color, even though the voters involved in the case were Negroes. The statute was held unconstitutional on its face, although a properly drawn statute might have been successful in the immediate case. Third, while the thirteenth amendment was held to work against private action as well as state action, the right to be free of slavery was narrowly defined so as not to include any right to be free from mere acts of discrimination based upon color. Thus in *Hodges v. United States*,[71] section 16 of the First Enforcement Act of May 31, 1870, was held unconstitutional, the Court asserting that interference with a man's right to contract did not force him into slavery or involuntary servitude.

Of broader significance than its reaction to the civil rights acts was the attitude of the Court presented toward the postwar constitutional amendments. The thirteenth, fourteenth, and fifteenth amendments were meant to revolutionize federal-state relations.[72] However, in a series of cases from *The Slaughter-House Cases* in 1873[73] to *Plessy v. Fergusen* in 1896,[74] the Court severely limited the scope of those amendments. By 1900 the "priv-

§ 1. The fifteenth amendment says, "The right of citizens of the United States to vote shall not be denied or abridged . . . by any State . . . ." U.S. Const. amend. XV, § 1.

[68] 109 U.S. 3, 3 S. Ct. 18 (1883). The first Mr. Justice Harlan, in a famous dissent, put forth a view which was to have more acceptance seventy-five years later:

"If the constitutional amendments be enforced, according to the intent with which as I conceive, they were adopted, there cannot be, in this republic, any class of human being in practical subjection to another class, with power in the latter to dole out to the former just such privileges as they may choose to grant. The supreme law of the land has decreed that no authority shall be exercised in this country upon the basis of discrimination, in respect of civil rights, against freemen and citizens because of their race, color, or previous condition of servitude."
Id. at 62, 3 S. Ct. at 57 (dissenting opinion).

[69] 106 U.S. 629, 1 S. Ct. 601 (1883).

[70] 92 U.S. 214 (1876).

[71] 203 U.S. 1, 27 S. Ct. 6 (1906).

[72] R. K. Carr, *supra* note 53, at 9-11; H. E. Flack, The Adoption of the Fourteenth Amendment 277 (1908); *See* C. P. Magrath, *supra* note 58, at 112.

[73] 83 U.S. (16 Wall.) 36 (1873).

[74] 163 U.S. 537, 16 S. Ct. 1138 (1896).

ileges and immunities" clause of the fourteenth amendment had been interpreted to place almost no restriction on the states; the "due process" clause protected only railroads; and "equal protection of the laws" meant "separate but equal."

Slaughter-House, the Court's first opportunity to rule on the fourteenth amendment, did not involve Negroes; it dealt with a monopoly granted a New Orleans slaughterhouse by the legislature of Louisiana. Rival butchers argued that the monopoly interfered with their right to do business and was thus a violation of the privileges and immunities clause of the fourteenth amendment which states that "no state . . . shall abridge the privileges and immunities of citizens of the United States."[75] The Court emphasized the words "citizens of the *United States*," and declared that the butchers' property rights were rights which accrued to them only by virtue of their *state* citizenship.[76] For all practical purposes the states remained in charge of all essential rights of their citizens. This theory of dual citizenship enabled the conservative Court to deny that a radical change had taken place in the American constitutional system.[77] In *Slaughter-House* the Court also rejected the argument that the Louisiana statute deprived the butchers of their property without due process of law, in violation of the fourteenth amendment.[78] In time due process was held to be a limitation upon state power. The original beneficiaries of due process, however, were not Negroes, but the newly formed giant corporations which sought to avoid state police power regulation of business.[79]

Despite this unpromising start, the Negro won a minor victory in one area. In *Strauder v. West Virginia,*[80] a West Virginia statute which barred Negroes from jury service was invalidated as contrary to the equal protection clause of the fourteenth amendment. Unfortunately, the Court during the same term ruled in *Virginia v. Rives*[81] that in showing a denial of due process the accused had the burden of proving that Negroes were deliberately excluded from his jury on the basis of race. Such proof was often unobtainable.

Supreme Court action in declaring the Civil Rights Act of 1875 unconstitutional in *The Civil Rights Cases,*[82] had a beneficial effect in the Northern states. Between 1883 and 1900, fifteen state civil rights acts similar to the invalidated federal act were adopted in the North.[83] The acts prohibited any

[75] U.S. Const. amend. XIV, § 1.
[76] Slaughter-House Cases, 83 U.S. (16 Wall.) 36, 76-79 (1873).
[77] A. H. Kelly & W. A. Harbison, *supra* note 58, at 505.
[78] Slaughter-House Cases, 83 U.S. (16 Wall.) 36, 80-81 (1873). Later cases followed the dissenting opinion of Mr. Justice Field, *supra* at 83 (dissenting opinion).
[79] An excellent discussion of "the revolution in due process of law" may be found in A. H. Kelly & W. A. Harbison, *supra* note 58, at 496-520.
[80] 100 U.S. 303 (1880).
[81] 100 U.S. 313 (1880).
[82] 109 U.S. 3, 3 S. Ct. 18 (1883).
[83] M. R. Konvitz & T. Leskes, *supra* note 58, at 155-57.

kind of discrimination in places of public accommodation, assemblage, or amusement; they were held constitutional both in the state courts[84] and, after a lengthy period, in the Supreme Court.[85] Because the statutes were in derogation of common law and because they were often penal, they were construed strictly and their effect was limited.[86] For example, one case held that an ice cream parlor did not come within a civil rights statute dealing with eating-houses; eating-houses could not discriminate, but ice cream parlors could.[87] Lack of enforcement also limited the effectiveness of the acts. Private litigation was expensive, and while some statutes did provide criminal sanctions, civil rights cases generally were not popular with district attorneys. Fines were small and often were looked upon as a license fee paid for the privilege to discriminate.[88]

In the South the overruling of the early civil rights acts had an opposite effect: states began to pass legislation requiring racial segregation in public places. Although the first "Jim Crow" law was adopted in Tennessee in 1881,[89] the movement did not gain impetus until *The Civil Rights Cases* were decided in 1883.[90] Typical provisions of the Jim Crow laws were miscegnation statutes, taboos in personal contacts, church and school segregation, segregation in public accomodations, inequality in politics, inequality in the administration of justice, and inequality in employment opportunities.[91] By 1907 such segregation laws had been enacted throughout the South.[92] In *Hall v. De Cuir (1878)*,[93] the Court had declared a Louisiana statute prohibiting racial discrimination in public carriers to be invalid as a burden upon interstate commerce.[94] Consistency would seem to demand that a statute requiring racial discrimination would also be a burden on interstate commerce. But in the landmark decision of *Plessy v. Ferguson*,[95] the Court de-

---

[84] *E.g.*, Picket v. Kuchan, 323 Ill. 138, 153 N.E. 667 (1926); Rhone v. Loomis, 74 Minn. 200, 77 N.W. 31 (1898).

[85] Railway Mail Ass'n v. Corsi, 326 U.S. 88, 65 S. Ct. 1483 (1945).

[86] *See* M. R. KONVITZ & T. LESKES, *supra* note 58, at 159-68.

[87] Cheches v. Burden, 74 Ind. App. 242, 128 N.E. 696 (1920).

[88] *See* M. R. KONVITZ & T. LESKES, *supra* note 58, at 177-80.

[89] U.S. COMM'N ON CIVIL RIGHTS, FREEDOM TO THE FREE 61 (1963).

[90] 1 G. MYRDAL, AN AMERICAN DILEMMA 579-580 (1944).

[91] M. R. KONVITZ, THE CONSTITUTION AND CIVIL RIGHTS 132-39 (1947).

[92] C. V. WOODWARD, THE STRANGE CAREER OF JIM CREW 81-82 (1957).

[93] 95 U.S. 485 (1878).

[94] *Hall*, which invalidated a statute prohibiting racial discrimination, ironically was latter used as a precedent for invalidating a statute which required racial discrimination in Morgan v. Virginia, 328 U.S. 373, 66 S. Ct. 1050 (1946). If the Court were consistent, all laws either prohibiting or requiring discrimination should be unconstitutional as an infringement on interstate commerce, Morgan v. Virginia, *supra*, at 390, 66 S. Ct. at 1060 (dissenting opinion of Mr. Justice Burton), but two years after *Morgan* the Court in Bob-Le Excursion Co. v. Michigan, 333 U.S. 28, 68 S. Ct. 358 (1947), upheld a state statute prohibiting discrimination on public carriers. One may conclude from this that the Court in the late 1940's was not aiming so much at legal consistency as it was at ending segregation in transportation. *See* A. H. KELLY & W. A. HARBISON, *supra* note 58, at 928-29.

[95] "We consider the underlying fallacy of the plaintiff's argument to consist in

clared a Louisiana Jim Crow statute to be constitutional, and thereby acknowledged Southern power to maintain a caste society. Because the statute
required facilities for Negroes which were "separate but equal" to those for
whites, the majority found that the statute did not deprive Negroes of equal
protection of the laws.[96] Mr. Justice Harlan alone dissented, protesting that
"[o]ur Constitution is color-blind, and neither knows nor tolerates classes
among citizens."[97]

Public accommodations was only the first of many areas in which the
Supreme Court applied the separate but equal doctrine. In *Cumming v.
County Board of Education*,[98] the Court accepted the constitutionality of
state laws requiring separate schools for whites and Negroes. Similarly, in
Berea College v. Kentucky,[99] a Kentucky statute prohibiting private schools
from admitting whites and Negroes to the same institution was held
constitutional.

Through a variety of devices Southerners were also able to avoid the
fifteenth amendment and effectively disfranchise the Negro. An important
first step was *United States v. Reese*,[100] where parts of the Enforcement Act
of 1870 were declared unconstitutional. Judicial and congressional repeal of
the Enforcement Acts, and the consequent removal of federal election officials from the South, removed any hope of continued Negro voting.[101] With
only nominal restraints reamining, the South looked for devices which on
their face were non-discriminatory but in practice excluded Negro voters.
Four such devices were found: the literacy test; the poll tax; the "grandfather
clause;" and the "white primary."[102]

the assumption that the enforced separation of the two races stamps the colored
race with a badge of inferiority. . . . The argument also assumes that social prejudices may be overcome by legislation, and that equal rights cannot be secured to
the negro except by an enforced commingling of the two races. We cannot accept
this proposition. If the two races are to meet upon terms of social equality, it must
be the result of natural affinities, a mutual appreciation of each other's merits, and
a voluntary consent of individuals. . . . Legislation is powerless to eradicate racial
instincts, or to abolish distinctions based upon physical differences, and the attempt to do so can only result in accentuating the difficulties of the present
situation."
Plessy v. Ferguson, 163 U.S. 537, 551, 16 S. Ct. 1138, 1143 (1896).

[96] Dick Gregory described "separate but equal" this way:
"I went to one of those separate but equal schools down South. I don't know
how old the textbooks were, but they sure kept me out of the Navy. If people
wanted to sail off the edge of the earth—I sure wasn't gonna be one of them! . . .
And those Southern history books! Do you realize I was twenty-two before I
learned that Lincoln freed the slaves? I always figured Jefferson Davis had us out
on probation. . . . "
D. GREGORY, FROM THE BACK OF THE BUS 51 (1962).

[97] Plessy v. Ferguson, 163 U.S. 537, 559, 16 S. Ct. 1138, 1146 (1896) (dissenting
opinion).

[98] 175 U.S. 528, 20 S. Ct. 197 (1899).

[99] 211 U.S. 45, 29 S. Ct. 33 (1908).

[100] 92 U.S. 214 (1876). A more complete discussion may be found *supra* at notes
63-70.

[101] U.S. COMM'N ON CIVIL RIGHTS, FREEDOM TO THE FREE 55 (1963).

[102] *See generally* A. H. KELLY & W. A. HARBISON, *supra* note 58, at 492-94.

Literacy tests were upheld by the Supreme Court in *Williams v. Mississippi*[103] as permissable under the equal protection clause of the fourteenth amendment. Although not apparent on their face the obvious purpose of such laws was the disfranchisement of Negroes since local officials in their discretion could administer difficult tests to "undesirable" voters. Poll taxes as a requirement for voting were likewise held to be constitutional in the *Williams* case.[104] Poll taxes again had the practical effect of excluding Negroes, especially when the taxes were made cumulative. The Supreme Court did refuse to accept "grandfather clause" laws, which for all purposes granted the right to vote only to those whose ancestors had had the right to vote in 1866.[105] In *Guinn v. United States*[106] the Supreme Court said that disfranchisement of the Negro was the only possible purpose of such a law, resulting in a deliberate evasion of the fifteenth amendment. White primary laws, on the other hand, were allowed to stand until 1927,[107] and modifications of the arrangement were not struck down by the Court until 1944;[108] these laws resulted in mass disfranchisement for the Negro. Thus, in the thirty-five years following Appomatox, the Negro had witnessed the full cycle of the rise and fall of his individual rights. At the beginning of the twentieth century the American Negro was physically free from slavery, but he had no political power; and his social position was in many ways identical to that experienced under the "Black Codes" which had so angered the Radical Republicans immediately after the Civil War.

Major race riots in both the North and South marred the first decade of the twentieth century. Violence erupted in Greenwood, South Carolina, and Wilmington, North Carolina, in 1898; in Springfield, Ohio, in 1904; in Stateboro and Atlanta, Georgia, in 1904 and 1906; in Greensburg, Indiana, and Brownsville, Texas, in 1906; and in Springfield, Illinois, in

---

103 170 U.S. 213, 18 S. Ct. 583 (1898). A typical literacy test was that of Louisiana: "[The voter] shall be able to read and write, and shall demonstrate his ability to do so when he applies for registration, by making, under oath administered by the registration officer or his deputy, written application therefor. . . ." LA. CONST. art. 197, § 3 (1898).

104 Williams v. Mississippi, 170 U.S. 213, 18 S. Ct. 583 (1898).

105 A typical "grandfather clause" was that of Louisiana: "No male person who was on January 1st, 1867, or at any date prior thereto, entitled to vote under the Constitution or statutes of any State of the United States, wherein he then resided, and no son or grandson of any such person not less than twenty-one years of age at the date of the adoption of this Constitution, and no male person of foreign birth, who was naturalized prior to the first day of January, 1898, shall be denied the right to register and vote in this State by reason of his failure to possess the educational or property qualification prescribed by this Constitution." LA. CONST. art. 197, § 5 (1898). The Louisiana Constitution allowed a person to vote if any one of three provisions were met: the education requirement, the property requirement, or the grandfather clause.

106 238 U.S. 347, 35 S. Ct. 926 (1915).

107 Nixon v. Herndon, 273 U.S. 536, 47 S. Ct. 446 (1927).

108 Smith v. Allwright, 321 U.S. 649, 64 S. Ct. 757 (1944).

1908.[109] Inaction on the part of both state and federal governments convinced Negroes that only through their own efforts could their rights be secured.[110] The school of thought fostered by Booker T. Washington, that eocnomic independence must be won before social or political equality could be gained, was challenged by the young W.E.B. Du Bois.[111] Du Bois argued that only by demanding his rights as a citizen could the Negro move toward equality.

In 1905 Du Bois and his followers met at Niagra Falls and, in what came to be called the Niagra Movement, proposed a new solution to the Negro problem.[112] Four years later, in 1910, with the aid of distinguished reformers such as Mary White Ovington, Jane Addams, John Dewey, William Lloyd Garrison, Lincoln Steffens, and Rabbi Stephen S. Wise, the Niagra group founded the National Association for the Advancement of Colored People, which for the next half-century spearheaded the struggle for Negro rights.[113] Originally the N.A.A.C.P.'s major objective was the abolition of lynchings,[114] but it had broader objectives as well.[115] In the *Guinn* case,[116] which declared the "grandfather clause" unconstitutional, the N.A.A.C.P. made its first appearance before the Supreme Court by filing an amicus brief. This was only the beginning; the current constitutional position of civil rights owes much to the N.A.A.C.P.'s "march on the Supreme Court,"[117] which by 1952 had resulted in victory in 34 of the 38 cases which the N.A.A.C.P. had argued before the court—and which promised more victories in the future.[118] A year after the birth of the N.A.A.C.P. the other early civil rights organization, the National Urban League, was founded as a coalition of three existing groups. The League's objectives were to advance the well-being of Negroes in four major areas: employment; education and youth incentives; health and welfare; and housing.[119]

[109] U.S. COMM'N ON CIVIL RIGHTS, FREEDOM TO THE FREE 74-75 (1963).

[110] *Id.* at 75-78.

[111] 2 S. E. MORISON & H. S. COMMAGER, THE GROWTH OF THE AMERICAN REPUBLIC 471-73 (5th ed. 1962).

[112] *Id.*

[113] *See Id.;* U.S. COMM'N ON CIVIL RIGHTS, FREEDOM TO THE FREE 79-81 (1963); L. HUGHES, FIGHT FOR FREEDOM, THE STORY OF THE NAACP 17-25 (1962).

[114] 69 Negroes were lynched in 1909, 67 in 1910, and 50 in 1911. The number dropped below 50 for the first time since 1883 in 1917, and for the second time in 1923. Between 1950 and 1959, six Negroes were lynched. U.S. COMM'N ON CIVIL RIGHTS, JUSTICE; 1961 UNITED STATES COMMISSION ON CIVIL RIGHTS REPORT 267-68.

[115] "The NAACP works along four main lines. It uses the State and Federal courts to secure justice and level Jim Crow barriers. It works for enactment of laws at national, state, and local levels to protect civil rights and ban racial discrimination. It carries on an educational program to create a climate of opinion in favor of equal rights. It engages in selective buying campaigns, picketing, and direct action programs."
U.S. COMM'N ON CIVIL RIGHTS, FREEDOM TO THE FREE 162 (1963).

[116] Discussed *supra*, at note 106 and accompanying text.

[117] A. H. KELLY & W. A. HARBISON, THE AMERICAN CONSTITUTION 926 (3d ed. 1963).

[118] L. HUGHES, supra note 113, at 126.

[119] U.S. COMM'N ON CIVIL RIGHTS, FREEDOM TO THE FREE 162-64 (1963).

Woodrow Wilson appealed for the Negro vote in the 1912 presidential campaign, and many Negro leaders supported him.[120] Once elected, however, Wilson put political peace above the Negro cause. Under Wilson, segregation for the first time took over the District of Columbia. The Post Office Department and the Treasury Department instituted segregation in offices, restrooms, and lunchrooms.[121] When World War I came, Negroes desiring to serve in the Armed Forces faced a situation similar to that in the national capital. The Selective Service maintained separate quotas for Negro and white draftees. More than 350,000 Negroes served during the war in segregated units; of them, 42,000 saw combat. Negroes were barred from the Marine Corps, and were permitted to serve only in menial capacities in the Navy. No provision for Negro officers was made originally, but during the war a segregated training camp was established at Fort Des Moines, Iowa, where Negro army officers were trained.[122]

Negro migration to the North during the war triggered racial strife, often related to competition for employment, as in the 1917 riot in East St. Louis, Illinois.[123] When the war ended, "international peace did not bring domestic tranquility."[124] In 1919 some 25 race riots took place, in different parts of the country, including the Nation's capital.[125] In answer to numerous requests for federal action the Department of Justice replied that under the existing law, murder and lynching was subject to the jurisdiction of the states, not the federal government.[126] The riots at Hoop Spur and Elaine, Arkansas, which resulted in the death of several Negroes and one white man, and in a trial in which 12 Negroes were sentenced to death and 80 Negroes were sentenced to from twenty years to life in prison,[127] was the occasion of the Supreme Court case of *Moore v. Dempsey*.[128] In *Moore* the court reiterated a previously taken position holding that a state, in attempting to carry into execution a judgment of death or imprisonment based upon a verdict produced by mob domination, deprives an accused of life or liberty without due process of law.[129]

Another result of Negro migration North during and after World War I was dispute over housing resulting in the passage of statutes in both the North and the South designed to keep housing segregated. The N.A.A.C.P.'s court struggles in this area produced one of the first major inroads on the

---

120 *Id.* at 83-84.
121 *Id.* at 84-86.
122 *Id.* at 88.
123 *Id.* at 88-89.
124 *Id.* at 91.
125 *Id.*
126 *Id.* at 90-91.
127 None of those accused was acquitted.
128 261 U.S. 86, 43 S. Ct. 265 (1923).
129 Id. at 91, 43 S. Ct. at 266. The Court quoted from its decision in Frank v. Magnum, 237 U.S. 309, 335, 35 S. Ct. 582, 590 (1915).

"separate but equal" doctrine which foreshadowed[130] the celebrated *Brown v. Board of Education* decision in 1954.[131] City and state legislation designed to keep blocks white was declared to constitute state action and thus violate the fourteenth amendment.[132] To avoid these decisions, property owners came up with the device of private, racially restrictive covenants which bound each property owner in a particular neighborhood to sell only to other "members of the Caucasion race." The Supreme Court in *Corrigan v. Buckley*[133] held that these covenants were mere private agreements and did not constitute state action within the fourteenth amendment.[134] *Corrigan* stood as good law until 1948 when the Court declared in *Shelly v. Kraemer*[135] that judicial enforcement of the private covenants constituted state action and thus was within the fourteenth amendment's limitations.[136] The next year the Federal Housing Authority, which had previously encouraged "homogeneous" neighborhoods, said that race would no longer be a factor in determining whether a mortgage would be insured.[137]

Many Negroes who migrated North after World War I found that for the first time they had some semblance of voting power. In many northern cities both major parties recognized the importance of the Negro vote. Some cities began to enact civil rights statutes.[138] In the South, however, the Negro remained effectively disenfranchised. After *Guinn*,[139] "grandfather clauses" were replaced by "white primary laws" which prevented Negroes from voting in primary elections, an effective method of disenfranchisement under what was essentially a one-party system. N.A.A.C.P. action[140] resulted in the decision of *Nixon v. Hernden*[141] in which the Supreme Court found that the white primary laws violated the equal protection clause as an obvious

---

[130] A. H. KELLY & W. A. HARBISON, *supra* note 117, at 926-27.

[131] 344 U.S. 1, 73 S. Ct. 1 (1954). A year later the Court handed down a second *Brown* decision, dealing with the enforcement of the first opinion, Brown v. Board of Education, 349 U.S. 294, 75 S. Ct. 753 (1955).

[132] Harmon v. Tyler, 273 U.S. 668, 47 S. Ct. 471 (1926); Buchanan v. Warley, 245 U.S. 60, 38 S. Ct. 16 (1917).

[133] 271 U.S. 323, 46 S. Ct. 521 (1926).

[134] *See generally* A. H. KELLY N W. A. HARBISON, *supra* note 117, at 927-29.

[135] 334 U.S. 1, 68 S. Ct. 836 (1948).

[136] The state action argument, of course, would not work in the District of Columbia, but in a companion case to *Shelley* which arose in the District, Hurd v. Hodge, 334 U.S. 24, 68 S. Ct. 847 (1948), the Court declared that allowing a federal court to enforce a clause which could not be enforced in the state courts because of the equal protection clause would be against the public policy of the United States. Also the Court held that judicial enforcement of such covenants in the District of Columbia would violate section 1 of the Civil Rights Act of April 9, 1866: "All citizens of the United States shall have the same right . . . to inherit, purchase, lease, sell, hold, and convey real and personal property." *Id.* at 30-31, 34, 68 S. Ct. at 851, 852.

[137] U.S. COMM'N ON CIVIL RIGHTS, FREEDOM TO THE FREE 140 (1963).

[138] *Id.* at 99-100.

[139] Discussed *supra*, at note 106 and accompanying text.

[140] *See* L. HUGHES, *supra* note 113, at 110-13.

[141] 273 U.S. 536, 47 S. Ct. 446 (1927).

instance of state action. The Court in *Nixon v. Condon*[142] also struck down a statute giving each political party the power to prescribe voting qualifications for its own members. A "private club" expedient was temporarily upheld in *Grovey v. Townsend*,[143] holding that the private organization utilized was not subject to the limitations on state action imposed by the fourteenth and fifteenth amendments. However, in *United States v. Classic*[144] as expanded in *Smith v. Allwright*,[145] the Court found that since the state had delegated the right to fix qualifications to the "private clubs," the action of the clubs was "state action within the meaning of the Fifteenth Amendment."[146] In *Terry v. Adams*,[147] the Court held that private primaries by the completely unofficial "Jaybird Party," whose nominees always received local Democratic nominations, also constituted state action.

Depression during the thirties hit the Negro harder than the rest of the country.[148] Emergency measures of the Roosevelt administration exhibited the same federal attitude toward race that had prevailed during World War I. Both A.A.A. and N.R.A. gave Negroes a second place; T.V.A. hired Negroes only for unskilled jobs and excluded them from the T.V.A. training program and the T.V.A. town of Norris, Tennessee. The Federal Housing Authority gave aid to many Negro families, but encouraged the use of racial and religious covenants to retain "neighborhood stability."[149] Nevertheless, federal concern for the welfare of the Negro showed itself in other aspects of the Roosevelt administration. Many Negroes were appointed to administrative positions in the government, among them Robert L. Vann, Special Assistant to the Attorney General; William H. Hastie, assistant solicitor for the Department of the Interior and then judge of the District Court of the Virgin Islands; and Robert C. Weaver, racial adviser to the Department of the Interior.[150] Another important step taken during the Roosevelt administration was the creation in 1939 by Attorney General Frank Murphy of a Civil Rights Section in the Department of Justice.[151] The Section viewed its purpose as twofold—clarifying what remained of the post Civil War federal legislation on civil rights, and proceedings to carry forth that law before the Supreme Court.[152] In the first few years of its life the Section handled relatively few cases; however, its existence pointed up the need for new federal legislation, and 18 years later the

[142] 286 U.S. 73, 52 S. Ct. 484 (1932).
[143] 295 U.S. 45, 55 S. Ct. 622 (1935).
[144] 313 U.S. 299, 61 S. Ct. 1031 (1941).
[145] 321 U.S. 649, 64 S. Ct. 757 (1944).
[146] *Id.* at 664, 64 S. Ct. at 765.
[147] 345 U.S. 461, 73 S. Ct. 809 (1953).
[148] U.S. COMM'N ON CIVIL RIGHTS, FREEDOM TO THE FREE 104 (1963).
[149] *Id.* at 104-05.
[150] *Id.* at 106-07.
[151] *Id.* at 107-08. An excellent book, by a participant, on the early history of the Civil Rights Section is R. K. CARR, FEDERAL PROTECTION OF CIVIL RIGHTS (1947).
[152] R. K. CARR, *supra* note 151, at 56-57, 84.

Attorney General established a Civil Rights Division in the Department of Justice in implementation of the Civil Rights Act of 1957.[153]

At the beginning of World War II, Negroes were excluded from the Marine Corps, the Army Air Corps, and the Tank, Signal, Engineer, and Artillery Corps of the Army. In the Navy and Coast Guard, Negroes were restricted to menial jobs.[154] Despite a nondiscrimination clause in the Selective Service Act of 1940,[155] the War Department on October 9, 1940, reaffirmed a segregation policy[156] and continued to operate separate units in each branch of the service. During the war itself, discrimination eased. Several Negroes achieved high posts; one attained the rank of brigadier general, another became civilian aide to the Secretary of War, and a third became executive assistant to the Director of Selective Service. The Army, Air Force, and Marines began to take Negroes. In 1942 the Navy accepted Negroes for general service and as noncommissioned officers, and in 1944 as commissioned officers. Except for the officer candidate schools, however, all military units remained segregated. At the Battle of the Bulge in 1944 Negroes and whites for the first time served in the same companies, although in separate platoons.[157]

As during World War I, employment unrest stirred at home during World War II.[158] A march on Washington scheduled by A. Phillip Randolph for 1941 was called off when President Roosevelt issued an executive order that "there shall be no discrimination in the employment of workers in defense industries or government because of race, creed, or national origin."[159] Also by executive order, a Fair Employment Practices Committee was set up in the Executive Office of the President.[160] During the war years a new rash of state civil rights acts, dealing mostly with fair employment, were passed in the northern states. Between 1932 and 1945, thirteen states enacted legislation which forbade discrimination in certain areas of employment, such as civil service and public work contracts.[161] In 1945 the New York legislature enacted the first state fair employment statute containing a state agency with real enforcement powers.[162]

The end of World War II brought new hope for the American Negro. Not only were the energies of the Nation released for the task of constructing a better society at home, but the consequences of the war made such betterment imperative. In 1945 the United States found itself in a

[153] U.S. Comm'n on Civil Rights, Freedom to the Free 108 (1963).

[154] Id. at 114.

[155] Act of Sept. 16, 1940, ch. 720, § 4(a), 54 Stat. 885, 887.

[156] Selective Service System Monograph No. 10, Special Groups 45-46 (1953).

[157] U.S. Comm'n on Civil Rights, Freedom to the Free 114-16 (1963).

[158] Id. at 116-17.

[159] Exec. Order No. 8802, 6 Fed. Reg. 3109 (1941).

[160] Exec. Order No. 9346, 8 Fed. Reg. 7183 (1943).

[161] M. R. Konvitz, The Constitution and Civil Rights 129 (1947).

[162] N. Y. Executive Law §§ 290-301. See generally M. R. Konvitz & T. Leskes, A Century of Civil Rights 197-201 (1961).

position of unprecedented world leadership. At a time when enemies were quick to publicize every defect in the "American Way" it became increasingly apparent that the Nation's most glaring defect, the open sore of racial injustice that festered in the deep South and spread its poison throughout the entire country, would have to be cured if the Nation were to sustain its claim as a leader of the free world. The overthrow of colonialism and the national rebirth of new countries whose populations were black accentuated the problem. "Racial segregation and discrimination, in short, now appeared to be dangerous and expensive social anachronisms which the Republic could no longer afford if it were to compete effectively in the great world struggle for the minds of men."[163]

America had fought a war to assure freedom and self-determination for the peoples of the world. If whites were willing to label those ideals "for experts only," Negroes were not. In the North after 1900, a Negro white-collar class had gradually made its appearance and marked its presence by its thirst for education, employment, and the enjoyments of a middle-class life.[164] Negro political power in northern cities also resulted in a step forward in the Negroes' position. The New Deal, labor shortages during the war, and broadened horizons for Negroes who had served in the Armed Forces were among the forces which swept in a "new tide of social, political, and constitutional change in the Negro's status."[165] Once again, the leader in the Negro's cause was the N.A.A.C.P.[166]

As in the years before the Civil War, the Supreme Court was faced with a bitter, sectional, constitutional conflict. Decisions of increasing importance had been rendered since 1900, and the pace quickened with the end of World Warr II. In the voting rights area previously discussed,[167] *Smith v. Allwright*[168] was followed by *Terry v. Adams.*[169] An important step towards destruction of the separate but equal doctrine was taken in the racially restrictive covenant cases[170] of *Shelley v. Kraemer*[171] and *Hurd v. Hedge*[172] which were handed down quickly after the war. Another blow at the separate but equal concept was struck at the same time in the area of public accomodations where the Court relied on the commerce power instead of the fourteenth amendment to end segregation. The Court had said during the war, in *Mitchell v. United States*[173] that a denial of Pullman

---

[163] A. H. KELLY & W. A. HARBISON, *supra* note 117, at 924-25.

[164] *Id.* at 925.

[165] *Id.* at 925-26. U.S. COMM'N ON CIVIL RIGHTS, FREEDOM TO THE FREE 122 (1963).

[166] A. H. KELLY & W. A. HARBISON, *supra* note 117, at 926.

[167] *Supra* notes 100-108 and accompanying text.

[168] 321 U.S. 649, 64 S. Ct. 757 (1944).

[169] 345 U.S. 461, 73 S. Ct. 809 (1953).

[170] Discussed *supra* at notes 130-137 and accompanying text.

[171] 334 U.S. 1, 68 S. Ct. 836 (1948).

[172] 334 U.S. 24, 68 S. Ct. 847 (1948).

[173] 313 U.S. 80, 61 S. Ct. 873 (1941).

facilities to a Negro when the facilities were available to whites was a violation of the Interstate Commerce Act. A Virginia statute requiring segregation on buses moving across state lines was later invalidated on the same ground in *Morgan v. Virginia*.[174] In *Bob-lo Excursion Co. v. Michigan*,[175] the Court held an equal accomodations section of the Michigan Civil Rights Act not to be a burden on interstate commerce. Again in *Henderson v. United States*[176] the Interstate Commerce Act was used to invalidate discrimination in railroad dining-car facilities. Doubtlessly as a result of these decisions, the Interstate Commerce Commission in 1955 ordered that racial segregation be ended in trains and buses which crossed state lines, and in their auxiliary facilities such as waiting rooms, rest rooms, and restaurants.[177]

Other measures were taken by federal administrators. On December 5, 1946, President Truman issued an executive order creating the President's Committee on Civil Rights "to inquire into and to determine whether and in what respect current law-enforcement measures and the authority and means possesed by Federal, State, and local governments may be strengthened and improved to safeguard the civil rights of the people."[178] The Committee's report, *To Secure These Rights*,[179] recommended among other things the reorganization and expansion of the Civil Rights Section of the Department of Justice, the establishment of a permanent Commission on Civil Rights, and federal legislation to correct discrimination in voting and the administration of justice. When the first modern civil rights act was enacted in 1957, it revived the President's Committee under the name of the United States Commission on Civil Rights.

President Truman quickly put into practice some of the recommendations his committee had made in *To Secure These Rights*.[180] On July 26, 1948, Truman directed in an executive order "that there shall be equality of treatment and opportunity for all persons in the armed services without regard to race, color, religion or national origin."[181] Another committee was formed to guarantee that the order was carried into effect. By 1962 the Armed Forces were largely desegregated. On the same day that he ordered the Armed Forces to desegregate, Truman established a Fair Employment Board within the Civil Service Commission to implement fair employment within the federal establishment.[182] During World War II and the Korean Conflict, the federal government began to require non-

---

[174] 328 U.S. 373, 66 S. Ct. 1050 (1946).

[175] 333 U.S. 28, 68 S. Ct. 358 (1948). See the discussion *supra* at note 136 and accompanying text.

[176] 339 U.S. 816, 70 S. Ct. 843 (1950).

[177] *See* A. H. KELLY & W. A. HARBISON, THE AMERICAN CONSTITUTION 929 (3d ed. 1963).

[178] Exec. Order No. 9808, 3 C.F.R. 590 (1946).

[179] PRESIDENT'S COMM. ON CIVIL RIGHTS, TO SECURE THESE RIGHTS (1947).

[180] U.S. COMM'N ON CIVIL RIGHTS, FREEDOM TO THE FREE 122-27 (1963).

[181] Exec. Order No. 9981, 3 C.F.R. 722 (1948).

[182] Exec. Order No. 9980, 3 C.F.R. 720 (1948).

discrimination clauses in all contracts with private industry. An enforcement committee was created in 1951. Another result traced back to the report, *To Secure These Rights,* was the desegregation of the District of Columbia in the early 1950's[183]

The "separate but equal" dictum of *Plessy v. Ferguson*[184] had a sweeping influence on civil rights. The rationale was applied not only in the public accommodations area on which *Plessy* was decided, but also in the fields of housing and education. The N.A.A.C.P.'s campaign to overrule *Plessy* made gains in both housing and in transportation,[185] but it was in the field of education that the landmark decision, *Brown v. Board of Education,*[186] was finally decided. *Brown* itself was the last in a chain of cases. Already in 1938 the Court had declared in *Missouri ex rel. Gaines v. Canada*[187] that Missouri had to admit a Negro applicant to the University of Missouri law school. Missouri had no law school for Negroes, and the state's policy of offering to pay the student's expenses at an out of state law school violated the equal protection clause of the fourteenth amendment. "Separate but equal" was not overruled in *Gaines;* the Court found only that the facilities provided were not equal. In response, the South attempted to improve Negro school facilities. After World War II the N.A.A.C.P. deliberately attacked higher education in the South as the logical place to insert a wedge in school segregation.[188] In *Sipuel v. Board of Regents,*[189] the Court in a per curiam opinion declared that as long as Oklahoma furnished whites with legal education, the equal protection clause of the fourteenth amendment required that Negroes be entitled to legal education afforded by a state institution. *McLaurin v. Oklahoma State Regents*[190] held that a Negro graduate student who had been admitted to the University of Oklahoma could not be restricted in his classroom, library, and cafeteria privileges. The Court said, "such restrictions impair and inhibit his ability to study, engage in discussions and exchange views with other students. . . ."[191] A more difficult situation arose in *Sweat v. Painter.*[192] There Texas had provided a separate Negro law school with five full-time professors and a 16,000 volume library. Nevertheless the Court held that the Negro plaintiff had a constitutional right to a legal education equal to that which Texas offered white students and that the Negro law school did not afford such an education. The Court mentioned that the reputation and prestige of the Uni-

[183] *See* U.S. COMM'N ON CIVIL RIGHTS, FREEDOM TO THE FREE 122-25 (1963).
[184] 163 U.S. 537, 16 S. Ct. 1138 (1896).
[185] A. H. KELLY & W. A. HARBISON, *supra* note 177, at 927-29.
[186] 347 U.S. 483, 74 S. Ct. 686 (1954).
[187] 305 U.S. 337, 59 S. Ct. 232 (1938).
[188] A. H. KELLY & W. A. HARBISON, *supra* note 177, at 931.
[189] 332 U.S. 631, 68 S. Ct. 299 (1948).
[190] 339 U.S. 637, 70 S. Ct. 851 (1950).
[191] *Id.* at 641, 70 S. Ct. at 853.
[192] 339 U.S. 629, 70 S. Ct. 848 (1950).

versity of Texas law school was far superior to its Negro counterpart and stated that anyone who had a free choice could not help but choose the former.

Brown v. Board of Education[193] was a consolidation of five cases which came before the Supreme Court in 1952. The case was immediately recognized as an important one; Thurgood Marshall, later to become United States Soliciter General and then Supreme Court Justice, prepared the briefs for the N.A.A.C.P.[194] After much deliberation a unanimous Court held that the separate but equal doctrine had no place in public education, and that segregated schools were inherently unequal and contrary to the equal protection of the laws requirement of the fourteenth amendent. One year later a second *Brown* decision remanded the cases to the federal district courts with directions that desegregation proceed "with all deliberate speed."[195]

Only in the border states was compliance with the *Brown* decision voluntary. Nine states of the deep South adopted resolutions "interposing" state authority to "nullify" the *Brown* decisions; they also called for the impeachment of the Justices of the Supreme Court and repeal of the fourteenth amendment.[196] In 1957 Governor Faubus ordered the Arkansas National Guard to prevent integration of Little Rock schools. The National Guard was withdrawn under court order,[197] but President Eisenhower was compelled to send federal troops to restore civil order.[198] Other devices were also employed to maintain segregation. Transfer programs in which white students could transfer out of their districts to schools where whites were in a majority were held unconstitutional in *Goss v. Board of Education*.[199] Prince Edward County, Virginia, had closed its public schools and provided state and county grants to white children to attend private schools. In *Griffin v. County School Board of Prince Edward County*[200] the Court held that this arrangement violated the equal protection clause. Justice Black, writing for the majority, said that "[t]he time for mere 'deliberate speed' has run out, and that phrase can no longer justify denying these Prince Edward County school children their constitutional rights to an education equal to that afforded by the public schools in the other parts of Virginia."[201]

---

[193] 347 U.S. 483, 74 S. Ct. 686 (1954).

[194] *See* L. HUGHES, FIGHT FOR FREEDOM, THE STORY OF THE NAACP 138-39 (1963); A. H. KELLY & W. A. HARBISON, *supra* note 177, at 933.

[195] Brown v. Board of Education, 349 U.S. 294, 301, 75 S. Ct. 753, 757 (1955).

[196] A. H. KELLY & W. A. HARBISON, *supra* note 177, at 935-43.

[197] Faubus v. United States, 254 F.2d 797 (8th Cir. 1958).

[198] Eisenhower's authority for sending the federal troops was 10 U.S.C. § 333 (1964), which was derived from the "Ku Klux Klan Act," the Third Enforcement Act of April 20, 1871, 17 Stat. 13. *See* A. H. KELLY & W. A. HARBISON, *supra* note 177, at 938-39.

[199] 373 U.S. 683, 83 S. Ct. 1405 (1963).

[200] 377 U.S. 218, 84 S. Ct. 1226 (1964).

[201] *Id.* at 234, 84 S. Ct. at 1234.

"The Brown decision was the signal for the swift disintegration of the legal structure supporting racial segregation in the South."[202] Despite the emphasis on the school context in *Brown*, the Court in short per curiam orders citing *Brown* either affirmed or remanded for further proceedings "not inconsistent with *Brown*" decisions involving the desegregation of other public facilities: city buses,[203] parks,[204] theatres,[205] beaches,[206] hospitals,[207] swimming pools,[208] and golf courses.[209] Some decisions attacking segregation in seemingly private contexts prompted the question whether the Court was not destroying the distinction between private and state action set out in *The Civil Rights Cases* of 1883.[210] However, in *Burton v. Wilmington Parking Authority*[211] the Court took pains to reaffirm *The Civil Rights Cases*, although finding state action in the immediate case presented. One authority has concluded from this that "the Civil Rights Cases would not be destroyed 'in principle' but the definition of what constituted state action promised to become steadily broader in the future."[212]

While *Brown* was felt most strongly in the South, it encouraged Negroes in all parts of the country to press for equality in the basic areas of education, employment, and housing. The Student Non-Violent Coordinating Committee (SNCC) was founded in 1960. Older groups such as the Congress of Racial Equality (CORE) founded in 1941, and the Black Muslims founded in 1933, found more support among Negroes in the late 1950's and challenged the N.A.A.C.P. and the National Urban League as the voice of the Negro. *Brown* and its repercussions brought increased pressure on states and municipalities for a legislative response.[213] In the period between 1954 and 1962 state legislatures responded: thirteen states adopted enforceable fair employment practice acts; ten states adopted public accomodation statutes; and five states adopted fair housing laws which applied to private housing.[214]

---

[202] A. H. KELLY & W. A. HARBISON, *supra* note 177, at 943.

[203] Browder v. Gayle, 142 F. Supp. 707, *aff'd per curiam*, 352 U.S. 903, 77 S. Ct. 145 (1956).

[204] Department of Conservation & Dev. v. Tate, 231 F.2d 615 (4th Cir.), *cert. denied*, 352 U.S. 838, 77 S. Ct. 58 (1956).

[205] Muir v. Louisville Park Theatrical Assoc., 347 U.S. 971, 74 S. Ct. 783 (1955).

[206] Dawson v. Mayor & City Council of Baltimore, 220 F.2d 386 (4th Cir.), *aff'd per curiam*, 350 U.S. 877, 76 S. Ct. 133 (1955).

[207] Simkins v. Moses H. Cone Memorial Hospital, 323 F.2d 959 (4th Cir. 1963), *cert. denied*, 376 U.S. 938, 84 S. Ct. 793 (1964).

[208] Saint Petersburg v. Alsap, 238 F.2d 830 (5th Cir.), *cert. denied*, 353 U.S. 922, 77 S. Ct. 680 (1957).

[209] Holmes v. City of Atlanta, 350 U.S. 879, 76 S. Ct. 141 (1955).

[210] 109 U.S. 3, 3 S. Ct. 18 (1883).

[211] 365 U.S. 715, 81 S. Ct. 856 (1961).

[212] A. H. KELLY & W. A. HARBISON, *supra* note 177, at 945.

[213] M. R. KONVITZ & T. LESKES, A CENTURY OF CIVIL RIGHTS 236-37, 223-35 (1961).

[214] M. R. KONVITZ & T. LESKES, A CENTURY OF CIVIL RIGHTS 237-38 (1961); U.S. COMM'N ON CIVIL RIGHTS, FREEDOM TO THE FREE 132-33, 182 (1963).

IV. THE GOVERNMENT RESPONDS; FEDERAL LEGISLATION 1957-1967

Brown was a high point in the Negro's quest for individual rights. The case illustrated an attitude on the part of the Supreme Court even more encouraging than the decision itself. However, the courts could do only so much. The process of private litigation and slow judicial expression of the fourteenth and fifteenth amendments had proved costly, time consuming and frustrating. The slow rate at which desegregation proceeded in the Southern schools under Court pressures illustrated this judicial deficiency. An alternative to private litigation was action by the Civil Liberties Unit of the Justice Department, created in 1939, but the Unit had long been crippled by the lack of any effective statutory protection of civil rights. The few remaining provisions of the Reconstruction civil rights acts were too limited in scope and too difficult of enforcement to be of any real value. It was apparent that new federal legislation was needed.

The Congress by 1956 was in a responsive mood. The Negro was rapidly finding the unity, direction, and most importantly, the tactics necessary to give voice to his demands.[215] He was becoming a political force to be reckoned with; consequently, the politicians courted his favor. Moreover, the country's increasing concern with its world status and concomitant sensitivity to charges that it was unfit to lead the free world[216] led many to believe that the time had come to eliminate the contrast between American words and American deeds. This contrast was illustrated by a comparison between the ideals of the fifteenth amendment and the realities of the 1956 voting statistics.[217]

The stage was thus set for the passage of the 1957 Civil Rights Act; the first federal civil rights legislation since 1875. The 1957 Act, whose direct lineage extended from the recommendations of Attorney General Brownell in 1956,[218] back through the congressional messages of President

---

[215] The event most frequently cited as the beginning of the modern era of Negro activism is the Montgomery, Alabama boycott of 1955-56. Triggered by the arrest of Mrs. Rosa Parks for refusing to relinquish her seat on a municipal bus to a white man, the boycott lasted a full year, until the United States Supreme Court affirmed a district court opinion striking down segregated seating in municipal buses. Gayle v. Browder, 352 U.S. 903, 77 S. Ct. 145 (1956), *affirming* 142 F. Supp. 707 (M.D. Ala. 1956). The boycott, which demonstrated the effectiveness of non-violent direct action, indirectly paved the way for the massive direct action campaigns of the 1960's. In addition, it led to a resurgence of activity by the Congress of Racial Equality (CORE, formed in 1943) and the creation of a new civil rights organization, the Southern Christian Leadership Conference (SCLC, formed in 1957) headed by a young Negro Minister who had handled publicity and communications during the Montgomery boycott—Martin Luther King, Jr. The late Dr. King was to become the symbolic and spiritual leader of the non-violent movement which swept America during the next decade. See generally, L. LOMAX, THE NEGRO REVOLT (1963).

[216] See N.Y. Times, Feb. 27, 1956, at 1, col. 2; at 17, cols. 1, 2, 4.

[217] See statistics quoted in 103 CONG. REC. 13336 (1957).

[218] Letter from Hon. Herbert Brownell Jr. to Speaker, House of Representatives, April 9, 1956, in H.R. REP. No. 291, 85th Cong., 1st Sess. 13-15 (1956).

Eisenhower,[219] to the 1947 *Report of the President's Commission on Civil Rights*,[220] was designed to provide a more effective means of enforcing existing civil rights, especially the most important of those rights—the right to vote.[221] Reaffirming its intent to assure all citizens equal access to the polls, Congress authorized the Attorney General to initiate *civil actions* for injunctive relief to protect persons in their exercise of the right to vote. Although the addition of civil actions, where in the past only criminal actions were avaialble, affected only a procedural change, it was hoped that by freeing the Attorney General from the burdens inherent in criminal actions, and by preventing rather than merely punishing voting infringements, effective voting relief might be obtained.

The House, in an attempt to extend protection beyond the area of voting rights alone, adopted a provision, Title 3, authorizing the Attorney General to seek preventive relief in *all cases* where persons were deprived of the "equal protection of the laws."[222] The Senate, fearful that this would grant unlimited powers to the Department of Justice and greatly expand substantive law, rejected the title.[223] Further diluting the effectiveness of the Act, the Senate inserted a jury trial provision applicable to criminal contempt cases arising under the Act. This provision grants a right to a de novo jury trial where, in the original nonjury action, a penalty in excess of a $300 fine or 45 days imprisonment is rendered.[224] However, to decrease instances of discriminatory jury selections, Congress declared that all residents of a judicial district who were over the age of 21 were competent to serve on federal juries unless disqualified by reason of prior criminal conviction, illiteracy, or infirmity.[225]

Surprisingly, the most significant provision of the 1957 Act proved to be Title 1 which created a Commission on Civil Rights.[226] Charged with the collection of information concerning denials of equal protection and the investigation of voting rights infringements,[227] the Commission's reports and

219 102 Cong. Rec. 143 (1956); 103 Cong. Rec. 410 (1957).
220 President's Comm. on Civil Rights, To Secure These Rights 154 (1947).
221 Title 4 retains 42 U.S.C. § 1971, *as amended*, (Supp. 1, 1965), the old voting rights statute (Act of May 1, 1870, ch. 114 § 1, 16 Stat. 140), now designated as subsection *a*, and add to it subsection *b* which provides:
"No person, whether acting under color of law or otherwise, shall intimidate, threaten, or coerce any other person for the purpose of interfering with the right of such other person to vote [for any federal official] at any general, special, or primary election. . . ."
Subsection *c* provides that the Attorney General may initiate actions for *civil relief* to prevent violations of subsections *a* & *b*. Civil Rights Act of 1957, Pub. L. No. 85-315 § 131(c)(d), 71 Stat. 634 *as amended*, 42 U.S.C. § 1971(b)(c) Supp. 1, 1965.
222 *See*, Congressional Quarterly Service, Revolution in Civil Rights, 29 (1965).
223 *Id.*
224 42 U.S.C. § 1995 (1964).
225 28 U.S.C. § 1861 (1964).
226 Civil Rights Act of 1957, Pub. L. No. 85-315 § 101-106, 71 Stat. 634, *as amended*, 42 U.S.C. § 1975 (1964).
227 "The Commission shall . . . (1) investigate allegations . . . that . . . citizens

recommendations were to play an important role in future civil rights legislation.[228]

The 1957 Act was a cautious entry into the civil rights arena; but it was an entry. Although its provisions were weak and, with the exception of Title 1, largely ineffective,[229] it served notice that Congress had cast off an 80 year tradition of inactivity and had reaffirmed its intent to secure fundamental rights for all.

The 1957 Act failed to effectuate its purpose. The Department of Justice, by January, 1959, had brought only one suit under the new act; the suit was dismissed in federal district court on the ground that the Act was unconstitutional.[230] A second suit, against the registrars of Macon County, Alabama, was initiated after Congress convened in 1959 but was dismissed when the registrars resigned their offices.[231] The Commission on Civil Rights had had little success in its investigation of voting denials and urgently needed an extension of its term.[232] No more successful than the 1957 Act, the *Brown* decision had had little effect.[233] Throughout the South the phrase "all deliberate speed" had been interpreted as "all deliberate delay." Although some desegregation had occurred in the border states, six states of the deep South had yet to desegregate a single school.[234]

At the same time, civil rights organizations, enthused by the intent, if not the effect, of the 1957 Act and the *Brown* ruling, increased in membership and intensified the scope and frequency of their demands.[235] Beginning with the Montgomery bus boycotts[236] and sporadic attempts to integrate Southern schools,[237] Negro leaders laid the basis for the coming era of

. . . are being deprived of the right to vote . . . ; (2) study and collect information concerning . . . denial[s] of equal protection . . . ; and (3) appraise the laws and policies of the Federal Government with respect to equal protection of the laws. . . ." Civil Rights Act of 1957, Pub. L. No. 85-315 § 104(a), 71 Stat. 634, *as amended*, 42 U.S.C. § 1975c(a) (1964).

[228] The Commission was to submit interim reports and a "final and comprehensive report of its activities, findings, and recommendations. . . ." in 1959. Civil Rights Act of 1957, Pub. L. No. 85-315 § 104(b,c), 71 Stat. 634, *as amended*, 42 U.S.C. § 1975c(b,c) (1964). The Commission's life has been extended ever since. *See*, 42 U.S.C. § 1975c(b,c) (1964).

[229] Writing in September, 1959, the Commission on Civil Rights was forced to report "no one has yet been registered through the civil remedies of the 1957 Act." COMMISSION ON CIVIL RIGHTS, REPORT, 140 (1959).

[230] United States v. Raines, 172 F. Supp. 552 (M.D. Ga., 1959), *rev'd*, 362 U.S. 17, 80 S. Ct. 519 (1960).

[231] United States v. Alabama, 171 F. Supp. 720 (M.D. Ala., 1959), *aff'd*, 267 F.2d 808 (5th Cir. 1959). The action was reinstated, in a decision based on the *1960* Civil Rights Act, in 362 U.S. 602, 80 S. Ct. 924 (1960).

[232] *See*, COMMISSION ON CIVIL RIGHTS, REPORT, 137 (1959).

[233] COMMISSION ON CIVIL RIGHTS, REPORT, 1-3, 39-77, 173-181 (1961).

[234] COMMISSION ON CIVIL RIGHTS, REPORT, 296 (1959).

[235] See generally, L. LOMAX, THE NEGRO REVOLT (1963).

[236] See note 215, *supra*.

[237] *E.g.*, the admission of Autherine Lucy to the University of Alabama in February of 1956 (N.Y. Times, Feb. 4, 1956, at 10, col. 2) and the initially unsuccessful at-

activism and open defiance of the segregation patterns of the South. Diehard segregationists, incensed by what they considered the Supreme Court's unconstitutional usurpation of states' rights and by the growing strength of the Negro, retaliated with a campaign of violence. Churches, schools, and homes were bombed or set afire[238] as a few persons, faced with the imminent breakdown of the legal structures of segregation, attempted to assure its continuance by the tactics of terror.

As a consequence of the failure of the 1957 Act, the impassioned resistance to and resultant ineffectiveness of the *Brown* decision, and the growing use of violence, legislative proposals leading to the 1960 Civil Rights Act were introduced in Congress early in 1959.[239] The administration proposed that the forceful obstruction of desegregation orders and flight from prosecution for the bombing of schools and churches be made federal crimes, that the preservation of voting records be made mandatory, and that such records be made available to the Attorney General.[240] In addition, the administration requested a two year extension of the life of the Commission on Civil Rights, congressional support for recent Supreme Court civil rights decisions (especially the *Brown* decision), and authorization to the Department of Health, Education and Welfare to aid communities in school desegregation.[241] Since schools in some states had been closed to avoid integration,[242] the administration proposed that provision be made for the schooling of children of military personnel stationed in such areas. Congressional advocates of stronger civil rights laws proposed that the Department of Health, Education and Welfare be authorized to devise desegregation plans for recalcitrant communities and pressed for enactment of the defeated Title 3 of the 1957 Act authorizing suits by the Attorney General in all equal protection cases.[243]

tempt to desegregate the public schools of Little Rock, Arkansas in the fall of 1957. *See,* A. Lewis & N.Y. Times, Portrait of a Decade, 46 (1964).

[238] *See,* N.Y. Times, June 15, 1959, at 1, col. 4.

[239] The principal proposals for the 1960 Act were contained in President Eisenhower's message to Congress of February 5, 1959. 105 Cong. Rec. 1922 (1959). *See also,* Senate Majority Leader Lyndon B. Johnson's proposals of January 20, 1959, 105 Cong. Rec. 875 (1959) and the proposals of Senators Douglas, 105 Cong. Rec. 1361 (1959), and Javits, 105 Cong. Rec. 785 (1959).

[240] 105 Cong. Rec. 1922 (1959) (Message to Congress from President Eisenhower).

[241] *Id.*

[242] *E.g.,* in Charlottsville and Norfolk, Virginia. Schools in both cities, under court order to integrate, were ordered closed by the Governor in 1958. The Governor's statutory authority to order such closings was later held to be in violation of the equal protection clause of the fourteenth amendment. James v. Almond, 170 F. Supp. 331 (E.D. Va., 1959), *appeal dismissed by stipulation,* 359 U.S. 1006, 79 S. Ct. 1146 (1959). In 1959 the schools of Prince Edward County, Virginia, were closed when the county failed to appropriate operational funds. The schools were not reopened until ordered to do so by the United States Supreme Court in Griffin v. Prince Edward County School Bd., 377 U.S. 218, 84 S. Ct. 1226 (1964) (violation of the fourteenth amendment).

[243] *See, e.g.,* 105 Cong. Rec. 1361 (1959) (Proposals by Senator Douglas).

Little progress towards anew civil rights act was made by either branch of Congress during the first session.[244] The only successful "civil rights" legislation to pass during that session was a bill extending the life of the Commission on Civil Rights until 1961.[245] The Commission had been slated to go out of existence shortly after the issuance of its report in September, 1959.[246]

The issuance of the Commission's *Report*,[247] an extensive document of findings and recommendations, breathed new life into the languishing civil rights bill and gave considerable support to those who demanded far more extensive legislation. In particular, the *Report* underscored the need for a more effective means of enforcing the right to vote—something which had not yet been proposed by the 1959 bills.

The Commission, finding that many citizens were still being denied the right to register to vote despite the 1957 Act,[248] recommended new legislation to provide for easier access to voting information and to require the preservation of voting records for up to five years.[249] To decrease instances of voting rights denials the Commission recommended legislation prohibiting registrars from refusing to exercise their duties or fulfill their obligations.[250] Three Commissioners recommended that all voting restrictions except those based on age, legal confinement, or length of residence be eliminated by constitutional amendment.[251] Most significantly, the Commission proposed that legislation be enacted to authorize the appointment, by the President, of temporary federal voting registrars empowered to register qualified citizens who had been denied the right to register by state officials.[252]

The administration, recognizing the need for broad relief from voting discrimination, yet reluctant to adopt the non-judicial approach proposed by the Commission, submitted a proposal for judicial enforcement of registration procedures.[253] Under this plan, which became Title 6 of the 1960 Act, the Justice Department, in a suit brought under the voting rights provisions of the 1957 Act, could request a finding by the court that the voting infringement complained of was pursuant to a pattern or practice of voting discrimination in the relevant area. If the court so found, it would be authorized to

244 *See*, CONGRESSIONAL QUARTERLY SERVICE, REVOLUTION IN CIVIL RIGHTS, 30-32, (1965).

245 The extension was accomplished by a rider to the Mutual Security Appropriation Act of 1960, Pub. L. No. 86-383, 73 Stat. 724, *as amended*, 42 U.S.C. § 1975c (b) (1964).

246 Civil Rights Act of 1957, Pub. L. No. 85-315 § 101-106, 71 Stat. 634, *as amended*, 42 U.S.C. § 1975 (1964).

247 COMMISSION ON CIVIL RIGHTS, REPORT, (1959).

248 *Id.* at 141.

249 *Id.* at 136-38.

250 *Id.* at 138-39.

251 *Id.* at 143-45.

252 *Id.* at 141-42 (Commissioner Battle dissenting).

253 106 CONG. REC. 5441 (1960).

appoint voting referees who would screen complaints of voting denials in that area and report those it found to be justified to the court. The court, after a hearing if state officials challenged the referee's findings, or after ten days if there were no challenge, could issue voting certificates to those whose complaints had been justified by the referees. One who interfered with the voting rights of a person so certified would be subject to penalties for contempt of court.[254]

Although other titles dealt, in a limited fashion, with racial violence[255] and school desegregation,[256] the voting rights provisions of Title 6 were clearly the heart of the 1960 Act.[257] Unfortunately the heart of the Act proved weak indeed. Despite increased activity by the Department of Justice, the 1960 Act was of little benefit to the disenfranchised Negro.[258] The Act's retention of the costly case-by-case method of enforcement, the reluctance of Southern judges to find a pattern or practice of discrimination or to authorize the appointment of federal referees, and the shift in disenfranchising tactics from the blatant to the more subtle negated the effectiveness of the 1960 Act and pointed up the need for still further legislation.[259]

However, the failings of the 1960 Act were not the only indicia of the need for more adequate legislation. A small occurrence in Greensboro, North Carolina, and the forces there set in motion, were to give the Nation a new awareness of the urgent need for truly effective civil rights legislation. Four months before the passage of the 1960 Act, Negro students quietly occupied all of the lunch counter seats in two segregated stores in Greensboro and

[254] Civil Rights Act of 1960, Pub. L. No. 86-449 § 601, 74 Stat. 86, 42 U.S.C. § 1971e (1964).

[255] Title 2, Civil Rights Act of 1960, Pub. L. No. 86-449 § 201-204, 74 Stat. 86, *amending* 18 U.S.C. § 837, 1074 (1964), prohibits (1) interstate travel to avoid prosecution, custody or confinement for the bombing or burning of buildings or vehicles; (2) the use of any interstate facility, *e.g.* telephones or the mails, to intimidate persons by threat of bombing; and (3) the possession of explosives with the intent to bomb or burn any building or vehicle. In addition, the Title creates a presumption that explosives used in any bombing had traveled in interstate commerce, thereby permitting investigation by the FBI.

[256] In addition to Title 1, Civil Rights Act of 1960, Pub. L. No. 86-449 § 101, 74 Stat. 86, *amending* 18 U.S.C. § 1509 (1964), which provides for preventive relief to restrain and criminal sanctions to punish interference with court orders, Title 5, Civil Rights Act of 1960, Pub. L. No. 86-449 § 501, 502, 74 Stat. 86, *as amended*, 20 U.S.C. § 241, 640 (Supp. 1, 1965), permits arrangements to be made for the education of children of military personnel stationed in areas where the public schools have been closed to avoid integration.

[257] In addition to providing for a voting referee plan, Title 6 authorized actions under the voting rights laws (generally, 42 U.S.C. § 1971) to be brought directly against the offending states. Civil Rights Act of 1960, Pub. L. No. 86-449 § 601b, 74 Stat. 86, *amending* 42 U.S.C. § 1971c (1964). This provision was passed in reaction to the decision in United States v. Alabama, 171 F. Supp. 720 (M.D. Ala., 1959), *aff'd*, 267 F.2d 808 (5th Cir. 1959), discussed *supra* note 231 and accompanying text.

[258] COMMISSION ON CIVIL RIGHTS, CIVIL RIGHTS, 22-23 (1963).

[259] *Id.* at 13-15.

requested service.[260] They were refused. Within two weeks a new phenomenon, the "sit-in," spread throughout five Southern states and the civil
rights movement entered a new phase.[261]

Compelled by a commitment and a courage that gained them immeasur-
able support, the American Negro and many white supporters took their
cause "into the streets." Committed to non-violence and armed only with
a song,[262] the civil rights activists waged a four year war against discrimination, segregation, and brutality—a war which culminated in the Civil Rights
Acts of 1964 and 1965.[263] The chief tactic of the war was "direct action;"
its rallying cry, "freedom now." Focusing attention on discrimination in
public facilities and accommodations, education, voting, and employment, the
movement spread rapidly throughout the South, and areas of the North as
well. Hundreds of thousands of persons from all walks of life engaged in
sit-ins, freedom rides, voter registration programs, marches, and school
integration campaigns.[264] Only occasionally were their efforts successful.[265]
Often they were met with violence and brutality;[266] yet they persevered.

[260] The students were protesting a local policy of serving only standing Negroes.
N.Y. Times, Feb. 3, 1960, at 22, col. 4.

[261] Useful books on the civil rights "revolution" of the early 1960's are: FREEDOM
NOW (A. Westin, ed. 1964): A. LEWIS & N.Y. TIMES, PORTRAIT OF A DECADE (1964); L.
LOMAX, THE NEGRO REVOLT (1963).

[262] Although many songs, usually patriotic or religious in nature, were sung by
civil rights activists, the most popular song soon became "We Shall Overcome," the
lyrics to which were frequently changed to reflect new developments in the civil rights
struggle.

[263] The Civil Rights Act of 1964, Pub L. No. 88-352, 78 Stat. 241, (codified in
scattered sections of U.S.C.); The Voting Rights Act of 1965, Pub. L. No. 89-110, 79
Stat. 437, 42 U.S.C. §§ 1971, 1973 (Supp. 1, 1965).

[264] No attempt to set forth the myriad events of the period 1960-64 is wholly
satisfactory. Brief summaries are no more satisfactory than endless enumerations of
every occurrence, large and small, significant and meaningless. A balance between these
extremes may be found in CIVIL RIGHTS 1960-63, (L. Sobel, ed. 1964), which chronicles
most of the significant events, from sit-ins to employment demonstrations, which paved
the way for the 1964 Act.

[265] E.g.: lunch counters in San Antonio, Texas were peacefully desegregated
March 16, 1960, in accordance with an agreement between Negroes and store owners.
San Antonio was the first large southern city to integrate its lunch counter facilities
(see, N.Y. Times, March 17, 1960, at 37, col. 8); four high schools were peacefully
integrated in Atlanta, Georgia on August 30, 1961 after a widespread public acceptance
campaign (see, N.Y. Times, Aug. 31, 1961, at 1, col. 3); the Southern Regional Council
reported on December 1, 1962, that almost 30,000 Negroes had been registered in key
southern areas during the Council's voter registration drives (N.Y. Times, Dec. 2, 1962,
at 73, col. 1).

[266] E.g.: fire hoses and tear gas were used to disperse Negroes protesting lunch
counter segregation (see, N.Y. Times, March 16, 1960, at 1, col. 2); freedom riders
were kicked and beaten and their bus destroyed by a fire bomb (see, Chicago Sun
Times, May 15, 1961, at 1, col. 1); tear gas and police dogs were used to end a demonstration protesting the arrest of sit-in participants (see, N.Y. Times, Dec. 16, 1961, at 1,
col. 1); two Negro churches were devastated by fire in retaliation for registration
efforts (see, N.Y. Times, Sept. 10, 1962, at 1, col. 3); continued violence of all forms

The student suspended from college for participating in a sit-in,[267] the parents of school children jeered and threatened for allowing their children to attend an integrated school,[268] the freedom rider beaten for requesting service in a public restaurant,[269] the youth shot for aiding Negro registration,[270] the James Merediths[271] and William Moores[272]—all these and many more[273] had one thing in common. That was a belief that direct action and personal involvement, whatever the individual cost, were necessary to make their dream of "freedom now" a reality.

The civil rights activists of the early '60's had a tremendous impact. For the first time, the average American citizen became aware of the plight of his darker skinned fellow citizen and began to understand the urgency of his demands. He had, via television, newsreels, and news magazines, seen the events of Oxford and Birmingham[274] and had witnessed the frightening juxtaposition of voter registration drives and burning churches.[275] The crackle of the cattle prod and the thud of the billy club were heard far beyond the streets of Plaquemine[276] and Danville.[277] They could no more be

culminated in the bombing of a Negro church and the death of four Negro girls (see, N.Y. Times, Sept. 16, 1963, at 1, col. 6).

[267] Following lunch counter sit-ins and a peaceful protest rally, eighteen students from Southern University, Baton Rouge, Louisiana, were suspended. N.Y. Times, March 31, 1960, at 27, col. 4.

[268] Mrs. James Gabrielle and her six year old daughter, Yolanda, were assaulted and jeered by a mob of segregationist women on November 29 and 30, 1960, as they returned from the recently integrated New Orleans, Louisiana grade school which Yolanda attended. N.Y. Times, Nov. 30, 1960, at 1, col. 3.

[269] Deprived of police protection, five Negro youths were attacked and beaten in McComb, Mississippi when they sought service at the ticket window and lunch counter of a Greyhound bus terminal. N.Y. Times, Nov. 30, 1961, at 1, col. 1.

[270] On February 28, 1963, a twenty year old Negro, James Travis, was shot and wounded by three white men in Greenwood, Mississippi. Travis had engaged in a local voter registration drive. CIVIL RIGHTS, 1960-63, (L. Sobel, ed. 1964).

[271] On October 1, 1962, after two days of mob violence which necessitated the use of federal marshalls, National Guardsmen, and federal combat troops, James Meredith became the first Negro to enroll at the University of Mississippi. N.Y. Times, Oct. 1, 1962, at 1, col. 8; Oct. 2, 1962, at 1, col. 8; Oct. 3, 1962, at 1, cols. 6.

[272] William Moore, a white Post Office employee, was shot and killed outside Attalla, Alabama while on a personal protest walk to Mississippi. N.Y. Times, April 25, 1963, at 20, col. 4.

[273] E.g., the six Negroes and one white woman who were beaten while attempting to integrate a skating rink in Cairo, Illinois during the summer of 1962. See, Chicago Sun Times, Aug. 19, 1962, at 6, col. 1.

[274] See notes 271 & 266 supra.

[275] See note 266 supra.

[276] Protesting the gerrymandering of Negro districts and requesting the integration of schools, jobs, and public facilities, 500 Negroes marched on the Plaquemine, Louisiana, City Hall on August 31, 1961. The march was dispersed by mounted police armed with electric cattle prods and tear gas. N.Y. Times, Sept. 1, 1963, at 41, col. 1.

[277] After being trapped in an alley and sprayed with high pressure fire hoses, Negro demonstrators were then clubbed by Danville, Virginia police. N.Y. Times, June 11, 1963, at 22, col. 1; June 12, 1963, at 28, col. 3.

forgotten than the news-pictures of the burning buses in 1960[278] and snarling
police dogs in 1963.[279]

By late summer, 1963, when over 200,000 Negroes staged a peaceful
march in Washington, D.C.,[280] it was clear that the Nation was ready, as
never before, to consider the passage of strong, sweeping civil rights legislation. But although the events of the preceeding years had provided a catalyst
for the Nation's emotional support, they had not been able to provide the
more elemental basis of legislation—the facts and figures, findings and
recommendations so clearly necessary if an intelligent legislative response
were to be fashioned. These essential ingredients were provided by the Commission on Civil Rights, whose *Reports* of 1961 and 1963 delineated the
scope of racial discrimination and made numerous recommendations for its
elimination. These recommendations led to, and in some cases were incorporated into, the most comprehensive civil rights act in the Nation's history—
the Omnibus Civil Rights Act of 1964.[281] Designed to take the civil rights
movement "out of the streets,"[282] the eleven titles of the act sought, by a wide
variety of means, to eliminate the worst excesses of discrimination as practiced
by the federal and state governments and by private individuals.[283] All but

---

[278] See note 266 *supra*.

[279] *E.g.*, in Birmingham, Alabama. *See*, N.Y. Times, May 4, 1963, at 1, col. 2.

[280] The March on Washington, one of the largest peaceful demonstrations in the
nation's history, was staged to gain congressional and public support for the then pending 1964 Civil Rights Act. Coupled with the recurrent violence and frequent brutality
then rife in Birmingham, Alabama, and the shocking murder of four Negro girls in a
church bombing in that city two weeks after the March, it marked one of the high
points in public sympathy for the civil rights movement. *See*, N.Y. Times, Aug. 26,
1963, at 1, col. 2; Aug. 27, 1963, at 23, col. 1; Aug. 28, 1963, at 1, col. 3; Aug. 29, 1963,
at 1, col. 4; Aug. 30, 1963, at 1, col. 2.

[281] The Civil Rights Act of 1964, Pub. L. No. 88-352, 78 Stat. 241, (codified in
scattered sections of U.S.C.).

[282] CONGRESSIONAL QUARTERLY SERVICE, REVOLUTION IN CIVIL RIGHTS, 84 (1964).

[283] In addition to the titles dealing with voting rights, public accommodations,
school integration, and equal employment opportunity, which will be discussed *infra*,
the act contained the following titles:
"Title 3, 42 U.S.C. § 2000b (1964), which permits the Attorney General, upon
    complaint by an aggrieved party, to bring suit to secure desegregation of pub-
    lic facilities owned, operated or managed by or on behalf of state or local
    governments;
"Title 5, 42 U.S.C. § 1975a-d (1964), which extends the life of the Commission on
    Civil Rights through January 31, 1968, authorizes the Commission to serve as
    a clearing house for civil rights information and to investigate voting frauds,
    and delineates procedural requirements for the Commission's activities;
"Title 9, which permits intervention by the Attorney General in equal protection
    cases of "public importance", 42 U.S.C. § 2000h(2) (1964), and provides for
    review of federal district court actions remanding civil rights cases to state
    courts, 28 U.S.C. § 1447(d) (1964);
"Title 10, 42 U.S.C. § 2000g(1-3) (1964), which creates a Community Relations
    Service to aid communities in resolving civil rights disputes;
"Title 11, 42 U.S.C. § 2000h (1964), which continues the jury trial provision of the
    1957 Act (*see supra* note 224, and accompanying text with regard to voting
    rights cases and provides for jury trial upon demand in all other criminal con-
    tempt cases arising under the 1964 Act."

two of the act's major provisions were directly related to the Commission on Civil Rights' findings and recommendations.

The first of those so related was Title 1, the third congressional attempt to secure the right to vote in seven years.[284] The Commission's *Reports* indicated that 90 years after the passage of the first voting rights legislation, and despite the 1957 and 1960 voting rights provisions, voting denials were still a common feature of American life. These denials were effectuated by such diverse official tactics as subjectively applying literacy tests, rejecting applicants for minor errors in their applications, and purging voter registration lists in order to require re-registration.[285] In addition to these more subtle devices, the Commission found that economic reprisals and official arrest and intimidation were also frequently employed to deter the Negroes' voting and registration efforts.[286] The Commission was quick to point out that the situation could not be rectified by existing voting rights laws.[287] Stating that the policy of the 1957 and 1960 Acts had been "frustrated,"[288] the Commission recommended new voting legislation even more comprehensive than that which it had recommended in 1959. It called upon Congress to prohibit the denial of the right to register and vote in *both* federal and state elections for reasons other than age, residence, mental disability, conviction of a felony, or failure to complete six grades of public education.[289] Again, the Commission requested the enactment of a federal registrar plan whereby registrars appointed by the President would administer state law and register qualified voters in states from which valid complaints have been received.[290] Finally, the Commission recommended that if the first two recommendations proved ineffective, Congress should act under section 2 of the fourteenth amendment to reduce the representation in the House of those states where voting denials based on race, color, or national origin continued.[291]

Congressional response to the Commission's recommendations was much weaker than civil rights proponents had hoped. Although the administration had proposed a plan for increasing the effectiveness of the federal referees,[292]

---

[284] Civil Rights Act of 1964, Pub. L. No. 88-352 § 101, 78 Stat. 241, *amending* 42 U.S.C. § 1971 (1964).

[285] COMMISSION ON CIVIL RIGHTS, REPORT, BOOK 1, VOTING, 135-38 (1961); COMMISSION ON CIVIL RIGHTS, CIVIL RIGHTS, 22, 23 (1963).

[286] *Id.*

[287] COMMISSION ON CIVIL RIGHTS, CIVIL RIGHTS, 28 (1963).

[288] *Id.* at 16.

[289] *Id.* at 28.

[290] *Id.* at 28-29.

[291] *Id.* at 29.

[292] The proposal would have authorized federal courts, in voting rights cases where a finding of pattern or practice was requested, to appoint temporary voting referees in any county where less than fifteen per cent of the qualified Negroes were registered. *See*, H.R. Doc. No. 124, 88th Cong. 1st Sess. (1963). *See also*, H. Norris, *The Civil Rights Act of 1964*, in LEGAL ASPECTS OF THE CIVIL RIGHTS MOVEMENT, 303, at 303-04 (D. King & C. Quick, eds. 1965).

Congress refused to strengthen existing enforcement procedures. Still reluctant to inject federal control into the registration process, Congress instead made one last attempt to compel state registrars to deal equitably with all applicants. Adopting the principle of the Commission's recommendation that subjective voting qualifications be prohibited, Congress required that registration qualifications be identical for all persons within a given political subdivision[293] and prohibited the rejection of registration applications for immaterial errors or omissions.[294] To eliminate the worst abuses of the literacy test, oral tests of the ability to read, write, understand, or interpret *any matter* were abolished,[295] and a presumption of literacy for any person with a sixth grade education (in an English language school) was created.[296]

The enforcement provisions of the 1957 and 1960 Acts were retained but, in recognition of the hostility of some Southern judges to civil rights cases, Congress authorized the Attorney General to request a three-judge district court in pattern or practice cases.[297] Although the House Judiciary Committee's Subcommittee Number 5 had extended the coverage of Title 1 to state as well as federal elections,[298] the Title as passed was limited to federal elections.[299]

Although the restricted nature of Title 1 doomed it to failure,[300] it represented a final attempt by Congress to compel Southern compliance with the fifteenth amendment without imposing active federal control over the registration process. Those who could not see the direction in which Congress was moving had only to look to Title 8 for a forecast of the legislation to come. That Title directed the Secretary of Commerce to compile registration and voting statistics by race, color and national origin in areas selected by the Commission on Civil Rights.[301] Such compilations were the necessary prerequisites both to enable Congress to formulate the presumption of voting denials that was to become the heart of the 1965 federal registrar plan, and to enable it to reduce the representation in the House of those states which continued to practice racial voting discrimination.

As with voting rights, Congress had previously dealt in a limited manner

[293] 42 U.S.C. § 1971(a)(2)(A) (1964), *as amended*, (Supp. 1, 1965).

[294] 42 U.S.C. § 1971(a)(2)(B) (1964), *as amended*, (Supp. 1, 1965).

[295] 42 U.S.C. § 1971(a)(2)(C) (1964), *as amended*, (Supp. 1, 1965); 42 U.S.C. § 1971(a)(3)(B) (1964). Oral tests could be conducted where necessary if agreed to by the Attorney General. 42 U.S.C. § 1971(a)(2)(C) (1964), *as amended*, (Supp. 1, 1965).

[296] 42 U.S.C. § 1971(c) (1964).

[297] Civil Rights Act of 1964, Pub. L. No. 88-352 § 101(d), 78 Stat. 241, 42 U.S.C. § 1971h (1964), *as amended*, 42 U.S.C. § 1971g (Supp. 1, 1965).

[298] *See*, U.S. CONG. CODE & AD. NEWS, 2409, 88th Cong., 2d Sess. (1964) (additional views of Hon. Robert W. Kastenmeier).

[299] Civil Rights Act of 1964, Pub. L. No. 88-352 § 101(c), 78 Stat. 241 (repealed 1965).

[300] *See*, COMMISSION ON CIVIL RIGHTS, THE VOTING RIGHTS ACT, 1 (1965); CONGRESSIONAL QUARTERLY SERVICE, REVOLUTION IN CIVIL RIGHTS, 75 (1965).

[301] 42 U.S.C. § 2000f (1964).

with the problems of school segregation,[302] and, as with voting rights, there had been little improvement since Congress had last acted. The Commission on Civil Rights reported that three states still had no desegregated schools,[303] and in many others compliance with the *Brown* decision was token at best.[304] Voluntary compliance was rare in the South. Where schools desegregated, they more often than not did so only under threat of court order.[305] Finding that by 1963 only 979 of 3,052 biracial school districts in the South had provided for desegregation,[306] the Commission concluded: "The determination of most southern school boards to employ every contrivance to evade or avoid desegregation continues to thwart implementation of [the Brown decision]."[307]

The Commission's recommendations included a proposal for legislation which would require those school boards which intentionally segregated students to adopt desegregation plans within ninety days or submit to a court ordered plan.[308] The Commission also recommended that Congress authorize it to provide technical and financial assistance to those school districts which would attempt to desegregate.[309]

The Commission's carrot-and-stick approach was adopted in principle by Congress so that the 1964 Act contained provisions designed both to compel and to assist school desegregation. Title 6 of the act required all federal agencies to issue such rules and regulations as might be necessary to insure that federal assistance available through their offices would be utilized in a non-discriminatory manner.[310] The agencies were authorized to withhold or terminate such assistance to compel compliance with their regulations.[311] Although not limited to the area of education, the provisions of Title 6 were to become a major factor in encouraging school desegregation.[312] In addition to the administrative enforcement procedures of Title 6, Congress granted limited authority to the Attorney General to initiate civil actions to compel desegregation in compliance with the *Brown* decision.[313]

---

[302] *See* note 256 and accompanying text *supra*.

[303] The states were South Carolina, Alabama, and Mississippi. COMMISSION ON CIVIL RIGHTS, CIVIL RIGHTS, 63 (1963).

[304] "Only 8 percent of the Negro pupils in the South attend schools with white children." *Id.*

[305] *Id.* at 68.

[306] *Id.* at 63.

[307] *Id.* at 68.

[308] *Id.* at 69.

[309] *Id.*

[310] 42 U.S.C. § 2000d (1964).

[311] *Id.*

[312] "Under Title VI . . . significant progress has been made. . . . [C]ommunities . . . began desegregation . . . where the prospect of school desegregation previously had seemed remote." COMMISSION ON CIVIL RIGHTS, SURVEY OF SCHOOL DESEGREGATION IN THE SOUTHERN AND BORDER STATES, 51 (1967).

[313] Title 4 provides that the Attorney General may, upon receipt of a meritorious complaint from an aggrieved party unable to bring or maintain an action himself, being a

To provide a positive incentive for school integration, Congress authorized the Commissioner of Education to provide technical assistance, training funds, grants and loans to school authorities to aid them in overcoming the problems attendant upon desegregation.[314]

The provisions of Titles 4 and 6 worked a major change in the patterns of school desegregation.[315] Whereas school boards had, in the past, been able to segregate with relative impunity, depending on the law of averages to protect them from the relatively infrequent private desegregation suits, they now faced a two-pronged governmental attack.[316] Title 6 was perhaps most effective in the border and middle south states where the commitment to segregation was waning. In these states, the threatened loss of federal funds was enough to offset the desire for segregation, and school authorities began renewed efforts to desegregate their schools.[317] In parts of the deep south, where hard core resistance to integration was a dominant factor, the threatened loss of funds had less effect. In these areas the court order remained the sole device capable of securing compliance with the law of the land.[318]

One of the most controverted sections of the 1964 Act was Title 7, the equal employment title.[319] Finding that "the economic plight of the Negro has its roots in segregation and discrimination . . . ," the Commission recommended that Congress, acting under its authority to regulate interstate commerce, enact legislation creating a federally protected right to equal employment, such right to be enforced by administrative procedures within the Department of Labor.[320] Title 7 entered the legislative process as a simple request for legislative approval of Executive Order No. 10925, dealing with equal employment by the federal government and its contractors.[321] It emerged as perhaps the most comprehensive and complex civil rights provision of the 1964 Act. The title creates, for all persons except communists, a right to equal opportunity in employment by prohibiting employers, unions, and employment agencies who directly or indirectly affect interstate commerce from engaging in discriminatory employment practices based

civil action to compel desegregation. However, before bringing such suit he must notify the offending school board or college and allow them a reasonable time to rectify the situation complained of. 42 U.S.C. § 2000(c-6) (1964).

314 42 U.S.C. § 2000(c-2)-(c-4) (1964).

315 COMMISSION ON CIVIL RIGHTS, SURVEY OF SCHOOL DESEGREGATION IN THE SOUTHERN AND BORDER STATES, 2, 26 (1967).

316 Id. at 2.

317 Id. at 25-28.

318 E.g., in Louisiana, where official resistance to Title 6 is most evident. Id. at 46.

319 42 U.S.C. § 2000e (1964). Despite the fact that half the states had adopted equal employment laws, see, N.Y. Times, June 7, 1964, at 44, col. 1, the possibility of Congress enacting federal equal employment legislation was considered so slight by President Kennedy that he did not include a proposal for such legislation in the administration package. See A. LEWIS & N.Y. TIMES, PORTRAIT OF A DECADE, 124 (1964).

320 COMMISSION ON CIVIL RIGHTS, CIVIL RIGHTS, 91 (1963).

321 Exec. Order No. 10925, 3 C.F.R. 448 (1964).

on color, race, sex, national origin, or religion.[322] In addition to prohibiting unfair employment practices as such, the title prohibits recriminations for opposition to such practices and the use of employment advertising which states a non-bona fide discriminatory preference.[323]

The title is enforced by civil actions brought by aggrieved parties,[324] and, in cases where he believes a pattern or practice of discrimination to exist, by the Attorney General.[325] Additionally, indirect enforcement is provided by the Equal Employment Opportunity Commission which is authorized to bring suit to compel compliance with prior court orders issued under the act.[326] In recognition of, and in deference to, existing state fair employment laws, and in hope that more such laws might be enacted, Congress required that state and local officials be notified of all unfair employment practices and be given time to correct alleged violations before a private suit could be brought under Title 7.[327]

Because it extended to the semi-private actions of a vast number of individuals and businesses, and because it was based on a congressional power only remotely related to the protection of civil rights, the provisions of Title 7 were extremely controversial.[328]

No less controversial were the provisions of Title 2, the public accommodations title and the symbolic heart of the 1964 Act.[329] They too reached the "private transactions" of a vast number of persons and relied for their authority on the commerce clause.[330] Unlike Title 7, Title 2 was not preceded by extensive findings and recommendations by the Commission on Civil Rights. It was, however, preceded by hundreds of demonstrations involving thousands of citizens demanding access to restaurants, theatres, amusement

---

[322] 42 U.S.C. § 2000e(2) (1964).

[323] 42 U.S.C. § 2000e(3) (1964).

[324] 42 U.S.C. § 2000e(5) (1964). Aggrieved parties may initiate such actions only after they have filed a complaint with the Equal Employment Opportunity Commission has been unable to secure voluntary compliance. 42 U.S.C. § 2000e(5) (a, d, e,) (1964).

[325] 42 U.S.C. § 2000e(6) (1964).

[326] 42 U.S.C. § 2000e(5) (i) (1964).

[327] 42 U.S.C. § 2000e(5) (b) (1964).

[328] H. Norris, *The Civil Rights Act of 1964*, in LEGAL ASPECTS OF THE CIVIL RIGHTS MOVEMENT, 303, at 314 (D. King & C. Quick, eds. 1965).

[329] 42 U.S.C. § 2000a (1964).

[330] Whether Title 2 was to rest on the commerce clause or the fourteenth amendment was the subject of much uncertainty during the hearings and debates on H.R. 1752, the public accommodations bill. The Attorney General repeatedly emphasized that the bill relied primarily on the commerce clause but included a fourteenth amendment basis as well. See, *Hearings on H.R. 7152 Before Subcomm. No. 5 of the House Comm. on the Judiciary*, 88th Cong., 1st Sess., at 1375-76, 1388, 1396, 1410, 1417-19 (1963). A good discussion of the relative merits of the commerce clause and the fourteenth amendment as applicable to public accommodations is contained in United States v. Heart of Atlanta Motel, Inc., 379 U.S. 241, 85 S. Ct. 348 (1964) and its companion case, Katzenbach v. McLung, 379 U.S. 294, 85 S. Ct. 377 (1964) (upholding constitutionality of Title 2).

parks, and similar facilities practicing open segregation.[331] Along with the right to vote, to an education, and to employment, the right to be treated as an equal in the market places of America was clearly of primary importance in the Negroes' quest for equality. Since 1960, they had demonstrated this priority in the most compelling fashion; ridicule,[332] beatings,[333] and even death[334] had been borne for this cause célèbre of the early 1960's.

Few cases have been more dramatically presented to the American public. Rare indeed was the person who was not aware of events in Greensboro, North Carolina, or Cambridge, Maryland, and the conditions which prompted them. Equally rare, however, was the individual who was not aware that a basic confrontation of rights was involved. Satisfaction of the Negroes' demands necessarily involved what appeared to be a distasteful encroachment upon the property rights of others. The congressional response reflected this dichotomy. Although the administration had proposed the prohibition of discrimination in *all* places of business affecting interstate commerce,[335] and although Subcommittee Number 5 of the House Judiciary Committee had extended the prohibition to all businesses licensed, authorized, or permitted by a state to conduct business in that state,[336] the final coverage of the public accommodations provisions was far less comprehensive. Only in the three classes of businesses considered to be most clearly "public accommodations" was discrimination prohibited. Covered were (1) establishments which provide lodging to transients, (2) restaurants, lunch counters and gas stations whose customers or goods move in interstate commerce or whose discrimination was supported by state action, and (3) places of entertainment whose source of entertainment moved in interstate commerce or whose discrimination was supported by state action.[337] While Title 2 was clearly keyed to the interstate commerce clause,[338] a fourteenth amendment basis was alternatively provided, the term "supported by state action" being intended to reach activities carried on under color of a custom or usage required or enforced by state or local officials.[339]

As with Title 7, Title 2 is to be enforced in the courts via civil suits by aggrieved parties[340] and, where violation is pursuant to a pattern or practice

---

[331] See, CIVIL RIGHTS 1960-63, *supra* note 264.

[332] *Id.*

[333] *Id.*

[334] Medgar Evers, Field Secretary for the NAACP, was shot in the back on June 11, 1963, two weeks after he had organized a sit-in at an F. W. Woolworth lunch counter in Jackson, Mississippi. N.Y. Times, June 13, 1963, at 1, col. 7.

[335] H.R. Doc. No. 124, *supra* note 292.

[336] The Attorney General testified against this expansive use of the fourteenth amendment. *See, Hearings on H.R. 7152, supra* note 330, at 2656, 2675-76, 2726.

[337] 42 U.S.C. § 2000a (1964).

[338] *Id.*

[339] 42 U.S.C. § 2000a(d) (1964). An additional fourteenth amendment basis prohibits discrimination in "any establishment or place" where such discrimination is required by state law. 42 U.S.C. § 2000a(1) (1964).

[340] 42 U.S.C. § 2000a(3)(a) (1964).

of discrimination, by the Attorney General.[341] Unlike Title 7, complaints need not be first submitted to a federal agency; however, courts may stay proceedings and refer suits to the Community Relations Service which is authorized to seek voluntary compliance.[342] Deferring to state law, the Title requires a plaintiff to notify state and local authorities of his complaint and allow the state thirty days in which to act before bringing suit in a federal court.[343]

The 1964 Civil Rights Act was unquestionably a major legislative accomplishment. Containing eleven titles, dealing with six major areas of racial discrimination,[344] creating or extending three agencies,[345] and requiring affirmative action from a host of federal agencies,[346] the act is the most significant civil rights legislation ever enacted by the United States Congress. Nonetheless, the effectiveness of the act was limited in two ways. First, the Act was somewhat restricted in scope; discrimination in retail businesses, in the sale and rental of housing, and in jury selection were major omissions from the act's coverage. The Act's failure to provide for these areas laid the basis for the unsuccessful 1966-67 Civil Rights Bill.[347] Secondly, the Act's compromise nature assured that it would also be deficient in depth. Thus, although it dealt with the right to vote, the Act failed to provide a truly effective means of enforcing that right. This deficiency made it necessary, one year later, for Congress to enact the Voting Rights Act of 1965.[348]

The 1964 Presidential election and the statistics it enabled the Bureau of Census to compile, made it clear that, despite the voting provisions of the 1964 Act, wholesale Negro disenfranchisement was still commonplace in many areas of the South. In addition, the election demonstrated to a Democratic administration and Congress that the "Solid South" was no longer an

---

[341] 42 U.S.C. § 2000a(5)(a) (1964).

[342] 42 U.S.C. § 2000a(3)(d) (1964).

[343] 42 U.S.C. § 2000a(3)(c) (1964).

[344] The six areas are: voting, public accomodations, public facilities, education, employment, and federally assisted programs (*e.g.*, urban renewal, anti-poverty programs, airport construction, hospital construction, public health programs, manpower training programs, highway construction, small business loans, school 'construction, public welfare, agriculture extension services, conservation projects, etc.).

[345] The term of the Commission on Civil Rights was extended until January 31, 1968. 42 U.S.C. § 1975(c) (1964). Created by the Act were the Community Relations Service, 42 U.S.C. § 2000g (1964), and the Equal Employment Opportunity Commission, 42 U.S.C. § 2000e(4) (1964).

[346] Title 6, non-discrimination in federally assisted programs, applies to "[E]ach federal department or agency which is empowered to extend federal financial assistance . . . other than a contract of insurance or guarantee [to any program or activity]. . . ." 42 U.S.C. § 2000d(1) (1964). Those agencies extending contracts of insurance or guarantee, *e.g.*, the FHA, are covered by Exec. Order No. 11063, 3 C.F.R. 652 (1962), which is retained by Title 6. *See*, 42 U.S.C. § 2000d(4) (1964).

[347] H.R. 14765, 89th Cong. 2d. Sess. (1966).

[348] Voting Rights Act of 1965, Pub. L. No. 89-110, 79 Stat. 437, 42 U.S.C. § 1971, 1973 (Supp. 1, 1965).

assured Democratic stronghold;[349] if Congress failed to insure the southern Negro's right to vote, the Democrats stood to lose some 90 crucial electoral votes. Faced with these twin realities, and moved by the renewed voting registration campaigns, demonstrations, and attendant violence,[350] Congress responded with a voting rights plan incorporating the basic features of the Commission on Civil Rights' recommendations of 1963; that is, the prohibition of all discriminatory use of registration procedures and qualifications and the use of federal personnel to administer state law and register voters where necessary.

As passed, the 1965 Act prohibits the use, by any state or subdivision, of any registration qualification, standard, procedure or practice to deny citizens the right to vote due to their race or color.[351] "To assure that the right of citizens . . . to vote is not denied or abridged on account of race or color . . . ," the act provides for the automatic suspension of all tests or devices used to qualify registrants in those states where such tests or devices are presumed to be used in a discriminatory manner.[352] In states in which such automatic suspension is in effect, federal voting examiners may be appointed to administer state law and certify the eligibility of voters.[353] Although

[349] The Republican nominee carried the southern states of Alabama, Georgia, Louisiana, Mississippi, and South Carolina.

[350] In early 1965 Dr. Martin Luther King began a major campaign to dramatize the continued disenfranchisement of the southern Negro. Selma, Alabama was selected as the focal point of the campaign. Voter registration drives, demonstrations and marches again publicized the county's need for effective voting rights enforcement. With the brutal dispersion of civil rights marchers (bound from Selma to Montgomery) by state troopers on March 7, and the slaying of a Unitarian minister, James Reeb, on March 11, public sympathy for the civil rights movement reached new heights. On March 17, President Johnson submitted his proposals for a new voting rights act to Congress. 105 Cong. Rec. 5058 (1965). See N.Y. Times, March 18, 1965, at 1, col. 5. For the events of the Selma-Montgomery march, see N.Y. Times, March 8, 1965, at 1, col. 1; March 9, 1965, at 34, col. 1 (editorial); March 10, 1965, at 1, col. 8. For an account of the beating and death of Rev. Reeb, see N.Y. Times, March 10, 1965, at 1, col. 1; March 12, 1965, at 1, col. 7.

[351] 42 U.S.C. § 1973 (Supp. 1, 1965).

[352] 42 U.S.C. § 1973b (Supp. 1, 1965). The presumption, and hence the automatic suspension, is triggered by a determination by the Attorney General that the state or subdivision maintained a test or devise on November 1, 1964, coupled with a determination by the Director of Census that less than fifty percent of the voting age residents were registered, or voted, in November, 1964. 42 U.S.C. § 1973b(b) (Supp. 1, 1965). In addition to the automatic suspension, tests or devices may also be suspended in any state by court order in a suit brought by the Attorney General to enforce the fifteenth amendment. 42 U.S.C. § 1973a(b) (Supp. 1, 1965).

[353] 42 U.S.C. § 1973d(e) (Supp. 1, 1965). Examiners may be appointed upon: (a) certification by the Attorney General that he has received twenty or more meritorious complaints of discriminatory voting denials within the relevant state or subdivision; or (b) certification by the Attorney General that such examiners are in his judgment necessary to enforce the fifteenth amendment. 42 U.S.C. § 1973d (Supp. 1, 1965). In addition, the appointment of examiners may be authorized by the federal district courts in any action brought by the Attorney General to enforce the fifteenth amendment. 42 U.S.C. § 1973a(a) (Supp. 1, 1965).

actual registration remains in the hands of local authorities, stiff penalties are provided for those who refuse to allow certified persons to vote.[354]

Ninety-five years after the adoption of the fifteenth amendment, Congress at last reversed the burden of litigation in voting rights cases. Congress noted that many southern officials would resort to every loophole, every trick, every tactic, to disenfranchise potential Negro voters. In recognition of this, the 1965 Act provided a presumption in favor of the disenfranchised and required those who would defy the fifteenth amendment, rather than those who sought its protection, to prove their cases in court.[355] Additionally, the 1965 Act sought to abolish the last bastion of official voting denials, the poll tax. Finding that poll taxes bore no reasonable relation to a state's interest in the conduct of elections, and that such taxes were often used as a means of disenfranchisement, Congress authorized the Attorney General to bring suit to enjoin the use of poll taxes as a precondition to voting in state elections.[356] Shortly thereafter the Supreme Court, in *Harper v. Virginia Board of Elections*,[357] struck down such use of the poll tax as violative of the equal protection clause of the fourteenth amendment.

V. The Implementation of the 1964 and 1965 Civil Rights Acts and Subsequent Legislation

The implementation of a law is quieter and less dramatic than the events of its passage and signing. The 1964 Civil Rights Act and its supplement in 1965 have now been the law for four and three years respectively, and while they have created few headlines, their steady implementation has led to lasting changes in some of society's major institutions. At the same time, it is obvious that the goals of those who championed the legislation have not yet been attained.

As has been mentioned, the 1965 Voting Rights Act served to shift the

[354] Penalties of up to $5000 or five years imprisonment of both are authorized. 42 U.S.C. § 1973j (Supp. 1, 1965).

[355] The constitutionality of the basic provisions of the 1965 Act was upheld in South Carolina v. Katzenbach 383 U.S. 301, 86 S. Ct. 803 (1966). The act has been quite successful. The Commission on Civil Rights, reporting on the first few months of the act's operation, found:

"In many areas of the South there is full compliance with [the act]. In most areas, tests and devices . . . have been effectively suspended."

Commission on Civil Rights, The Voting Rights Act, 3 (1965). As a consequence of the 1965 Act, the main cause of Negro nonvoting has shifted from overt disenfranchisement to social isolation and political apathy. The Commission's recent recommendations reflect this shift. For the first time since its creation eight years previously, the Commission recommended no changes in the law, but rather an intensive federal program of education and publicity to encourage Negro voting. *Id.* at 14.

[356] 42 U.S.C. § 1973h (Supp. 1, 1965). The use of poll taxes as a condition to voting in federal elections had already been prohibited by the twenty-fourth amendment, adopted by Congress in 1962 and ratified by two-thirds of the states in 1964.

[357] 383 U.S. 663, 86 S. Ct. 1079 (1966). At the time of the decision, only four states, Alabama, Mississippi, Texas, and Virginia, retained the poll tax as a pre-condition to voting.

burden from the disenfranchised Negro to the governmental unit.[358] After the Act went into effect, many jurisdictions were automatically prohibited from using any test or device to screen voter applicants. In addition, the Attorney General found it necessary in some instances to appoint federal voting examiners in order to guarantee rights which had originally been granted by the Fifteenth Amendment.[359] Other jurisdictions, while not under automatic prohibitions, were subsequently enjoined from using tests after the Attorney General had shown that their tests had been used in a discriminatory manner.[360] Such "freeze orders" have the effect of prohibiting the use of any test or device more stringent than age, residency, conviction of a disqualifying crime, insanity or idiocy.[361]

Efforts to register southern Negroes and to secure their right to vote will need to be of a continuous nature. It is clear, however, that Negroes are registering in unprecedented numbers, and that gradually black people are being elected to local positions throughout the South. It is estimated that in the past five years the number of registered Negro voters in the South has gone from 1.3 million to 3 million.[362] Before the 1965 Act there were 35,000 registered Negro voters in Mississippi; now there are 200,000.[363] In November of 1967, 22 Negroes were elected to public offices in Mississippi, and a total of 200 Negroes now hold elective positions in the South.[364]

Unfortunately, the mere registration of Negroes has not provided a final solution. In order to insure that registered Negroes will be able to vote free from intimidation, the Court of Appeals for the 5th Circuit found it necessary in 1966 to establish the power of a federal court to void state elections.[365] The right to vote unhindered by racial discrimination is so vital, said the same court, that it is not necessary to demonstrate that a different result would have occurred without the racial distinctions.[366]

---

[358] *See* note 355 and accompanying text *supra*.

[359] This power to initiate appointments is granted under 42 U.S.C. § 1973d (Supp. 2, 1965-66). The actual appointing is done by the Civil Service Commission. *See* 42 U.S.C. § 1973a, d. For a partial listing of jurisdictions so affected *see* 10 RACE REL. L. REP. 1398, 1830 (1965); 11 RACE REL. L. REP. 1587 1966).

[360] 42 U.S.C. § 1973a(b) (Supp. 2, 1965-66). Such orders are the result of cases brought by the Attorney General. United States v. Palmer, 356 F.2d 951 (5th Cir. 1966); United States v. Ramsey, 353 F.2d 650 (5th Cir. 1965); United States v. Ward, 349 F.2d 795 (5th Cir. 1965).

[361] United States v. Palmer, 356 F.2d 951, 954 (5th Cir. 1966); United States v. Ramsey, 353 F.2d 650, 659 (5th Cir. 1965); United States v. Ward, 349 F.2d 795, 805 (5th Cir. 1965).

[362] THE REPORTER, Mar. 7, 1968, at 25.

[363] *Id.*

[364] *Id.*

[365] Hamer V. Campbell, 358 F.2d 215 (5th Cir.), *cert. denied*, 385 U.S. 851, 87 S. Ct. 76 (1966). In a subsequent opinion the same court described this power as "[d]rastic, if not staggering." Bell v. Southwell, 376 F.2d 659 (5th Cir. 1967).

[366] In Bell v. Southwell, 376 F.2d 659 (5th Cir. 1967) an election for Justice of the Peace was voided because there were segregated voting booths and voting lists and

The registration of large numbers of Negroes in areas where no test could be utilized has raised questions regarding the illiterate voter. Statutes declaring that a write-in candidate's name must be inserted in the voter's own handwriting have been upheld.[367] On the other hand, a law which prohibited voter assistants from aiding more than one voter was declared unconstitutional as being unduly restrictive and in violation of the fourteenth amendment as implemented by the 1965 Voting Rights Act.[368]

The right of a person to use public accommodations free from racial discrimination was an early goal of the civil rights workers.[369] Title 2 of the 1964 Act and cases brought under it have sought to eradicate the discriminatory patterns that were brought to the nation's attention by the "sit-in's" of the early 1960's. Subsequent to 1964 many places of public accommodation have agreed to consent judgments or have been enjoined from continuing a policy of discrimination.[370]

Other cases have sought to interpret the scope of Title 2. For example, the fact that a public restaurant is suddenly labeled a "private club" does not exclude the owner from coverage under the Act.[371] Another distinction being made by some courts, but one which appears to exclude certain facilities from coverage, is that made between a place of "entertainment" and a place of "recreation." Places of entertainment are covered by the Act, but it says nothing about places of recreation. By calling facilities such as those for swimming, picnicking, and boating "recreational," rather than for "entertainment," courts have allowed them to continue to operate in a discrim-

---

because officials allowed a large crowd of white males to gather near the polls thus intimidating Negro voters. The court voided the election even though the Negro candidate could not have won had every registered Negro voter gone to the polls and voted for her. See also, Hamm v. Virginia State Bd. of Elections, 230 F. Supp. 156 (E.D. Va. 1964) (holding that separation of blacks and whites on poll tax, residence-certificate and registration lists violated the equal protection clause of the 14th Amendment).

367 Allen v. State Bd. of Elections, 268 F. Supp. 218 (E.D. Va. 1967); Morris v. Fortson, 261 F. Supp. 538 (N.D. Ga. 1966).

368 Morris v. Fortson, 261 F. Supp. 538, 541 (N.D. Ga. 1966).

369 Negro and white students "sitting in" segregated public facilities first drew the attention of many people to the unequal conditions in the south. See note 331 and accompanying text *supra*.

370 Many such cases are set out in volumes 11 & 12 of the *Race Relations Law Reporter*. For consent judgments see, e.g., Batts v. Dublin Gen. Hosp., Inc., 11 Race Rel. L. Rep. 1427 (E.D. N.C. 1966); Little v. Sedgefield Inn, Inc., 11 Race Rel. L. Rep. 1495 (M.D.N.C. 1966). For examples of the use of the injunction see, e.g., United States v. Northwest La. Rest. Club, 256 F. Supp. 151 (W.D. La. 1966) (club with 90 restaurants as members enjoined); United States v. Gulf-State Theaters, Inc., 256 F. Supp. 549 (N.D. Miss. 1966).

371 United States v. Jack Sabin's Private Club, 265 F. Supp. 90 (E.D. La. 1967) (owner changed name of restaurant and lounge to "private club" on July 2, 1964, held to be covered); Kyles v. Paul, 263 F. Supp. 412 (W.D. Ark. 1967); United States v. Northwest La. Restaurant Club, 256 F. Supp. 151 (W.D. La. 1966). It is not clear just what would constitute a private club but obviously the classification for membership would have to be something other than just race.

inatory manner.[372] This represents a clear attempt to avoid the intent of the Act.[373] If the distinction between recreation and entertainment remains valid, those seeking to integrate recreational establishments will have to rely on other sections of the act. The most successful approach may be to argue that they are principally engaged in the sale of food and thus are covered by section 201(b)(2).[374]

Along the same general lines it has been held that drive-in restaurants are covered, even though a substantial portion of the food is not actually consumed on the premises.[375] By contrast, a bar which does not sell food is not within the scope of the Act and therefore can discriminate.[376] However, if a bar owner wants to integrate, he can utilize section 200[377] to strike down local ordinances or rules which prevent him from integrating.[378] In the same manner, segregation which is encouraged by custom or usage and enforced by state or local officials[379] can be struck down even though the facility is not itself covered by the Act.[380]

It has been the law since 1954 that public schools should be desegregated, but the implementation has been very slow.[381] Titles 4 and 6 of the 1964 Act have expanded the powers of the federal government in an attempt to speed desegregation.[382] Title 6 prevents the allocation of public funds to segregated facilities.[383] Operating in conjunction with the Elementary and Secondary Education Act of 1965,[384] Title 6 paved the way for the Guidelines for school desegregation set up by the Department of Health, Education and Welfare.[385] To be eligible for federal funds, a school must either be operating within the H.E.W. Guidelines or under a final school desegregation order from a court.[386] Efforts have been made to avoid the conse-

---

[372] Kyles v. Paul, 263 F. Supp. 412 (E.D. Ark. 1967); Miller v. Amusement Enterprises, Inc., 259 F. Supp. 523 (E.D. La. 1966).

[373] See note 337 and accompanying text *supra*.

[374] Adams v. Fazzio Real Estate Co., 268 F. Supp. 630 (E.D. La. (1967).

[375] Newman v. Piggie Park Enterprises, Inc., 377 F.2d 433 (4th Cir. 1967) (court stating that the important fact is that the food sold was ready for consumption on the premises and not that it was actually eaten there).

[376] Tyson v. Cazes, 363 F.2d 742 (5th Cir. 1966); Ceuvas v. Sdrales, 344 F.2d 1019 (10th Cir. 1965); Pania v. New Orleans, 262 F. Supp. 651 (E.D. La. 1967).

[377] See note 337 and accompanying text *supra*.

[378] Pania v. New Orleans, 262 F. Supp. 651 (E.D. La. 1967).

[379] See note 339 and accompanying text *supra*.

[380] Robertson v. Johnston, 376 F.2d 43 (5th Cir. 1967) (holding that if a white women can show that her arrest on vagrancy charges while sitting in a Negro bar was carried out under color of a custom or usage which discourages white women from frequenting places that are predominately Negro, she will be entitled to relief).

[381] See note 302 and accompanying text *supra*.

[382] See note 315 and accompanying text *supra*.

[383] 42 U.S.C. § 2000d (1964). See note 310 and accompanying text *supra*.

[384] 20 U.S.C. §§ 236 et seq. (Supp. 2, 1965-66).

[385] 45 C.F.R. § 181 (1968) [Department of Health, Education and Welfare hereinafter referred to as H.E.W.].

[386] 45 C.F.R. § 181.2 (1968).

quences of the Guidelines,[387] but in *United States v. Jefferson County Board of Education*,[388] the Court of Appeals for the 5th Circuit held that all final school desegregation orders rendered in that circuit would have to be substantially the same as the H.E.W. Guidelines.[389] This requirement is, of course, applicable to school systems whether or not they are applying for federal assistance.[390] The Guidelines call for an end to all de jure segregation.[391] They condone "freedom of choice" plans[392] for desegregation, but these must provide for annual choices, and the choices cannot be denied except for overcrowding.[393] The Commissioner of Education recognizes that freedom of choice plans place the burden of desegregation on the Negro[394] and therefore scrutinizes with special care any school system utilizing such a plan.[395] Desegregation applies to staff and faculty as well as to students, and, therefore, the racial composition of the professional staff is another factor which will be considered when evaluating desegregation plans.[396]

---

[387] In 1966 the Alabama Legislature passed a statute which declared the H.E.W. Guidelines to exceed the authority of the 1964 Civil Rights Act. The statute contained a provision whereby a school board which was denied funds by the federal government would receive equivalent payments from the state. 12 RACE REL. L.R.—(1967).

[388] 372 F.2d 836 (5th Cir. 1966), cert denied, 389 U.S. 840, 88 S. Ct. 77 (1967).

[389] United States v. Jefferson County Bd., 372 F.2d 836, 848 (5th Cir. 1966). The court said that where exceptions are necessary, they should not defeat the policies of H.E.W. In an earlier opinion the court had stated that "great weight" should be given to the Guidelines. Singleton v. Jackson Municipal Separate School Dist., 348 F.2d 729, 731 (5th Cir. 1965).

[390] *"The national policy is plain: formerly de jure segregated school systems based on dual attendance zones must shift to unitary, nonracial systems—with or without federal funds."* United States v. Jefferson County Bd., 372 F.2d 836, 850 (5th Cir. 1966), *cert. denied*, 389 U.S. 840, 88 S. Ct. 77 (1967).

[391] 45 C.F.R. § 181.3 (1968). De jure segregation is the product of an intentional policy of race separation as opposed to de facto segregation which results in a unitary school system not by plan but because of geographical groupings.

[392] 45 C.F.R. § 181.41 (1967). Such a plan allows every parent to choose that school in the district he wants his child to attend. These programs which have become very popular in the south are criticized in *Jefferson County Bd.* "When such plans leave school officials with a broad area of uncontrolled discretion, this method of desegregation is better suited than any other to preserve the essentials of the dual system while giving paper compliance with the duty to desegregate." United States v. Jefferson County Bd., 372 F.2d 835, 888 (5th Cir. 1966), *cert. denied*, 389 U.S. 840, 88 S. Ct. 77 (1967). It is recognized that freedom of choice plans are at best a temporary means useful at this stage of school desegregation. *Id.* at 889, Kemp v. Beasley, 352 F.2d 14 (8th Cir. 1965).

[393] In the event that too many students have chosen the same school, assignments are made on the basis of proximity of school to parents' home. 45 C.F.R. § 181. 49 (1968). Factors such as requirements for health or birth records, academic or physical examinations or operation of the transportation system can not be considered in making assignments. 45 C.F.R. § 181.51 (1968).

[394] 45 C.F.R. § 181.54 (1968).

[395] "The single most substantial indication as to whether a free choice plan is actually working to eliminate the dual school structure is the extent to which Negro or other minority group students have in fact transferred from segregated schools." 45 C.F.R. § 181.54 (1968).

[396] 45 C.F.R. § 181.13 (1967). *See e.g.* Yarbrough v. Hulbert-West Memphis

Those seeking to resolve the problem of de facto school segregation have less legal support. The 1965 Act says that desegregation "shall not mean the assignment of students to public schools in order to overcome racial imbalance."[397] Although at this time there is no federally imposed duty to eliminate de facto segregation in the schools,[398] school systems may take steps to reduce racial imbalance if they so desire.[399] A more difficult question is whether a state can require school boards to take affirmative action to reduce racial imbalance. The constitutionality of an Illinois statute[400] to this effect was recently upheld by the Illinois Supreme Court over the contention that it improperly used race as a means of classification.[401] Previously, the Supreme Judicial Court of Massachusetts held that a similar statute did not violate the Fourteenth Amendment.[402] The Massachusetts court found that there was no denial of equal protection since there was no showing that a pupil was excluded from a school because of his race.[403]

Title 7 of the 1964 Act, though probably the most controversial at the time of passage,[404] has caused very little disturbance since its enactment. The Title is administered by the Equal Employment Opportunity Commission[405] which generally operates in an investigatory and conciliatory manner, encouraging voluntary compliance. As a result little information on the Commission's activities is available. However, it is known that the E.E.O.C. was greatly overburdened with complaints during the first years of its operation and has only recently begun to eliminate its backlog.[406] As an example of its efforts, the E.E.O.C. completed 68 conciliations in September and October of 1967, 38 of which were at least partially successful.[407]

The E.E.O.C. works closely with state and local employment organiza-

---

School Dist., 380 F.2d 962 (8th Cir. 1967); Franklin v. County School Bd., 360 F.2d 325 (4th Cir. 1966); Rockley v. School Dist., 258 F. Supp. 676 (D.S.C. 1966). Recently the first suit ever brought by the federal government to end segregation in a northern school district was filed seeking to enjoin a Cook county school district from segregating its faculty and staff. N.Y. Times, April 26, 1968, at 19, col. 3 (city ed.).

[397] 42 U.S.C. § 2000c(b) (1964). For a recent discussion of de facto segregation see Comment, *Constitutionality of Adventitious Segregation in the Public Schools*, 1967 U. ILL. L.F. 680.

[398] The leading case is Deal v. Bd. of Educ., 369 F.2d 55 (6th Cir. 1966), *cert. denied*, 389 U.S. 847, 88 S. Ct. 39 (1967). *Accord*, Downs v. Board of Educ., 336 F.2d 988 (10th Cir. 1964), *cert. denied*, 380 U.S. 914, 85 S. Ct. 898 (1965); Bell v. School City, 324 F.2d 209 (7th Cir. 1963), *cert. denied*, 377 U.S. 924, 84 S. Ct. 1223 (1964).

[399] Mason v. Board of Educ., 149 N.W.2d 239 (Mich. Ct. App. 1967). *See also*, Offermann v. Nitkowski, 378 F.2d 22 (2d Cir. 1967).

[400] ILL. REV. STAT. ch. 122, § 34-18-7 (1967).

[401] Tometz v. Board of Educ., 39 Ill. 2d 593, 237 N.E.2d 498 (1968).

[402] School Comm. of Boston v. Board of Educ., 352 Mass. 693, 227 N.E.2d 729 (1967), *appeal dismissed*, 389 U.S. 572, 88 S. Ct. 692 (1968).

[403] *Id.*

[404] *See* note 348 and accompanying text.

[405] 42 U.S.C. § 2000e-5(a) (1964).

[406] E.E.O.C. News Release No. 68-1 (Jan. 10, 1968).

[407] *Id.*

tions. This includes financial aid to initiate affirmative action programs.[408] During the spring and summer of 1967 efforts in 13 states resulted in the creation of over 1,400 new jobs.[409] While the Commission gives priority to the resolution of individual complaints,[410] it also attempts to expose patterns of discrimination through its investigatory process.[411] When such patterns are discovered it urges the employer to take affirmative action to remedy the situation.[412] Should conciliation fail, a private individual may bring suit,[413] and where a pattern of discrimination exists, the Attorney General is authorized to commence an action.[414] Finally, the E.E.O.C. can bring suit to force compliance with prior court orders.[415]

In spite of the efforts of the E.E.O.C., it is clear that not enough is being done. While the overall unemployment rate is declining, the rate for Negroes remains double that of whites.[416] In addition to unemployment, under-employment is a continuing problem, and in spite of general prosperity, 20 per cent of all Negroes are making no significant economic gains.[417] These factors make it clear that legal equality is not enough; efforts must be directed as well toward economic equality.[418]

At the same time that some citizens and courts were working to implement the 1964 and 1965 Acts, the attitude of Congress and of the nation was changing. In the summer of 1965 the widely held belief that civil rights was a Southern problem was torched and burned to the ground in Los Angeles.[419] The Watts riot vividly demonstrated that the "Negro problem" was national and not regional,[420] that to condemn the South while ignoring the neighbor-

---

[408] E.E.O.C. News Release No. 67-93 (Oct. 17, 1967).

[409] *Id.*

[410] E.E.O.C. News Release No. 68-1 (Jan. 10, 1968).

[411] E.E.O.C. News Release No. 67-106 (Nov. 19, 1967). This release discusses discrimination in Ohio's rubber industry plants. A similar investigation was made of minority employment in white collar positions in New York City. E.E.O.C. News Release No. 68-1 (Jan. 10, 1968).

[412] Such an effort has been made in the textile industry in the Carolinas. In June and July of 1967, 10 textile mills hired 246 Negroes, or 41% of all new hires for the period. E.E.O.C. News Release No. 67-71 (Sept. 7, 1967).

[413] Foy v. Norfolk & Western Ry., 377 F.2d 243 (4th Cir. 1967), Mickel v. South Carolina State Employment Serv., 377 F.2d 239 (4th Cir. 1967).

[414] *See* footnote 348 and accompanying text *supra.*

[415] *See* footnote 349 and accompanying text *supra.*

[416] REPORT OF THE NAT'L ADVISORY COMM'N ON CIVIL DISORDERS 253 (Bantam ed. 1968).

[417] *Id.* at 252.

[418] The Poor People's Campaign which brought disadvantaged citizens from all over the country to Washington was the first major effort of the civil rights movement during the spring of 1968. Its emphasis was on jobs, food and welfare. The campaign had been designed by Martin Luther King prior to his assassination. N.Y. Times Apr. 30, 1968, at 1, col. 5 (city ed.)

[419] The Watts riot left 34 dead and 4,000 injured. *See* REPORT OF THE NAT'L ADVISORY COMM'N ON CIVIL DISORDERS 37-38 (Bantam ed. 1968).

[420] The awareness of the scope of the problem is perhaps best expressed by the Commission:

"This is our basic conclusion: Our nation is moving toward two societies, one

ing slum had been nothing more than foolish ethnocentrism. For the first time Americans heard the militant proclamations of Stokely Carmichael and H. Rap Brown. The concept of "Black Power" and the further disturbances of 1966 and 1967[421] demonstrated that Watts was not an isolated event in the Negro revolution. Violence and the threat of violence became entwined with the non-violent civil rights movement. From the point of view of many white liberals the riots threatened to undo the progress of recent years. This, coupled with the demand for open housing laws in some northern cities, disturbed many who had formerly been sympathetic to the Negro cause. Other whites began for the first time to really notice the slums of their own cities and, feeling threatened, some took steps to arm themselves.[422]

Among black Americans many hopes had been raised because much had been promised.[423] Programs such as the War on Poverty operated slowly, and relatively few in the deprived areas felt any significant effect.[424] The Negro in the crowded cities had become tired: tired of waiting, tired of being pushed around by police, tired of seeing advertisements for things he could not buy, but perhaps most of all, he was tired of waiting for "whitey" to start treating him like a man.[425]

The burning of the nation's cities did not encourage Congress to rush to the aid of Negroes. On the contrary, rising Negro militancy coupled with the financial burden of the war in Vietnam led Congress to reject legislation dealing with civil rights and poverty. The 89th Congress failed to pass the 1966 Civil Rights Bill which included provisions prohibiting discrimination in state and federal jury selection, penalizing acts of violence against a person exercising his previously guaranteed civil rights, and forbid-

---

black, one white—separate and unequal.
"Reaction to last summer's disorders has quickened the movement and deepened the division. Discrimination and segregation have long permeated much of American life; they now threaten the future of every American."
Id. at 1.

[421] In 1966 there were 43 disorders and riots reported. *Id.* at 40. In 1967 there were 150. *Id.* at 32.

[422] Gun sales increased in some cities affected by the violence. Sales were mostly to whites. N.Y. Times, Aug. 2, 1967, at 19, col. 1.

[423] The Commission labels the changes in Negro attitude as a "Revolution of Rising Expectations." REPORT OF THE NAT'L ADVISORY COMM'N ON CIVIL DISORDERS 226 (Bantam ed. 1968).

[424] Economist Vivian Henderson's testimony before the Commission concluded: "No one can deny that all Negroes have benefited from civil rights laws and desegregation in public life in one way or another. The fact is, however, that the masses of Negroes have not experienced tangible benefits in a significant way. This is so in education and housing. It is critically so in the area of jobs and economic security."
Id. at 231.

[425] The Commission listed twelve deeply held grievances common to the ghetto Negro. The three of highest intensity were police practices, unemployment and underemployment, and inadequate housing. *Id.* at 7. The most poignant illustration of the Negro's desire for respect is the inscription occasionally seen on placards during a demonstration: "I am a Man."

ding discrimination in the sale or rental of housing.[426] In the midst of the 1967 disorders, the House rejected a bill designed to exterminate rats in depressed areas.[427] Of more concern to some members of Congress was legislation designed to deal with rioters and agitators.[428] By the end of 1967 the Senate finally passed a bill requiring random selection of grand and petit juries and barring any discrimination in jury selection by reason of race, color, religion, sex, national origin or economic status.[429] The bill was limited to federal jurors.[430] Throughout this period, however, there were those members who were pushing for new civil rights legislation, and as the year ended Senator Mansfield promised that the pending Civil Rights Bill would be the first order of business when the Senate reconvened.[431]

After the Christmas recess, debate on the bill resumed and continued until March fourth when it was finally cut off by a single vote.[432] On March eleventh the Senate passed the bill and sent it to the House where its future seemed at best uncertain.[433] No action was to be taken by the House on the bill until after Easter, but on April fourth the nation was plunged into gloom and crisis when Dr. Martin Luther King was assassinated. The following week, as smoke from rioters' fires hovered over Washington, and as federal troops protected the White House, the House passed the Senate bill intact, and the next day it was signed into law.[434]

It is difficult to say what, in fact, stimulated the passage of the new Act. Certainly Dr. King's death caused the House to act sooner than would otherwise have been the case. But if Dr. King's death was decisive in securing House passage of the Act, the Senate, which had passed it prior to this event, was clearly influenced by other factors. Undoubtedly among these was the publication of the Riot Commission's Report.[435] Although the Report probably won few converts to the cause of civil rights, its publication emphasized the necessity of immediate action in order to prevent another summer of

---

[426] H.R. 14765, 89th Cong., 2d Sess. (1966).

[427] N.Y. Times, July 21, 1967, at 1, col. 1.

[428] Much of the concern seemed aimed at creating a law to deal with Stokely Carmichael. N.Y. Times, July 12, 1967, at 23, col. 2.

[429] This bill, now Pub. L. No. 90-274, was subsequently passed by the House and signed by President Johnson on March 27, 1968. N.Y. Times, March 28, 1968, at 36, col. 3 (city ed.).

[430] Pub. L. No. 90-274.

[431] N.Y. Times, Dec. 16, 1967, at 20, col. 1.

[432] N.Y. Times, March 5, 1968, at 1, col. 8 (city ed.).

[433] N.Y. Times, March 12, 1968, at 1, col. 1 (city ed.). The House had passed an open housing bill two years previously, but in the meantime had become more conservative. N.Y. Times, March 5, 1968, at 1, col. 8 (city ed.).

[434] N.Y. Times, April 12, 1968, at 1, col. 1 (city ed.).

[435] The commission made a wide range of proposals for local and state governments, for the police, for the news media, and for the federal government. Specific recommendations to the federal government included 2,000,000 new jobs over the next three years, action to eliminate de facto school segregation in the north, a guaranteed annual income, and the construction of 6 million new units of decent housing in the next five years.

violence. By passing a civil rights act Congress could show its concern for the Negro without having to appropriate large sums of money.

The Civil Rights Act of 1968 reflects Congressional concern with both the plight of the Negro and the problem of riots and civil disorders. In its civil rights aspects the Act will eventually prohibit discrimination in the sale or rental of an estimated 52.6 million housing units.[436] This is to be accomplished in three stages. As of its date of passage the Act barred discrimination in federally owned housing and in multi unit housing where mortgages were issued or underwritten by the Federal Housing Administration and the Veterans Administration.[437] On January 1, 1969, the prohibition will be extended to apartments and real estate developments,[438] but owner occupied houses with four or less units will be excluded.[439] Finally, on January 1, 1970, the sale or rental of single family houses through a broker will have to be transacted on a nondiscriminatory basis.[440] An owner will still be able to sell his home to whomever he pleases provided he does not use a broker or advertise that the sale is to be on a discriminatory basis.[441] A party who feels he has been discriminated against can register his complaint with the Department of Housing and Urban Development, and that department is authorized to attempt conciliation.[442] Should conciliation fail, a suit can be brought by the person aggrieved.[443] Where the Attorney General finds a pattern of discrimination, he may also seek enforcement through a civil action.[444]

In addition to its open housing provisions the Act protects previously guaranteed rights. Under Title 1 of the Act it is a federal crime to intimidate or injure any person exercising rights in relation to activities involving voting, employment, jury service, education, and the use of public accommodations.[445] Upon conviction, the Act provides for a fine of up to $10,000 and imprisonment for ten years, or, if death results, imprisonment for life.[446]

[436] N.Y. Times, March 12, 1968, at 1, col. 1 (city ed.).
[437] 42 U.S.C. § 3603(a)(1).
[438] 42 U.S.C. § 3603(a)(2).
[439] U.S.C. § 3603(b)(2).
[440] 42 U.S.C. § 3603(b)(1).
[441] 42 U.S.C. § 3603(b)(1).
[442] 42 U.S.C. § 3610(a).
[443] 42 U.S.C. § 3610(d).
[444] 42 U.S.C. § 3613. On June 17, 1968, the United States Supreme Court decided the case of Jones v. Alfred H. Mayer Co. — U.S. —, 88 S. Ct. 2186 (1968). The court held that an 1866 statute, 42 U.S.C. § 1982, providing that "/a/11 citizens of the United States shall have the same right . . . as is enjoyed by white citizens thereof to inherit, purchase, lease, sell hold, and convey real and personal property" bars all racial discrimination, private as well as public, in the sale or rental of property. Unlike the 1968 law, § 1982 is enforceable only by private parties. In one respect, however, § 1982 is broader than the 1968 law. Since § 1982 contains no exceptions it would appear that a private individual has a remedy against discrimination even in those areas specifically exempted under the 1968 law.
[445] 18 U.S.C. § 245.
[446] 18 U.S.C. § 245.

In an attempt to deal with the problem of riots the Act makes it a federal crime to travel from one state to another, or to use interstate communication facilities with the intent to start or further a riot, or to aid anyone in starting or furthering one.[447] Title 10 of the Act makes it a federal crime to manufacture, or transport in interstate commerce firearms, firebombs, or other explosive devices with the knowledge or intent that they will be used illegally in a civil disorder.[448] In addition, it is a federal crime to teach or demonstrate the use of such devices with the knowledge that they will be used in a civil disorder.[449] And finally, it is a federal crime to obstruct, impede, or interfere with any fireman or law enforcement officer lawfully engaged in performing his official duties during a civil disorder.[450]

Perhaps now the end has come so far as major civil rights legislation is concerned. There will be proposals of an economic and social nature, and of course, the quiet work of implementation and enforcement will continue, but what was once a Negro civil rights movement is now an American social revolution that is proceeding with breathtaking and sometimes violent speed. At this date it is by no means certain what the final result will provide; it is only certain that there is no turning back. The black man will never return to "his place."

VI.   Conclusion

This introduction has attempted to trace the history of an idea—an idea which first gained official status when Abraham Lincoln signed the Emancipation Proclamation. From there it moved to the legislatures and the courts and finally into the busses, restaurants, schools, houses, and streets of the country. If the idea is going to succeed it must now move into the hearts and minds of the people. Today no American can accurately say that this is not his problem.

[447] 18 U.S.C. § 2101.
[448] 18 U.S.C. § 231(a)(2).
[449] 18 U.S.C. § 231(a)(1).
[450] 18 U.S.C. § 231(a)(3).

EQUAL EDUCATIONAL OPPORTUNITY FOR NEGROES—ABSTRACTION OR REALITY

BY ROBERT L. CARTER*

I. INTRODUCTION

NOT LONG AGO, the noneducated man could rise to fame and fortune in the United States through the use of ingenuity and industry. Today, that era has ended. We now live not only in a highly mechanized society but in one rapidly approaching cybernetics where economic success is functionally related to education. Our economy is increasingly service-oriented. Employment in the skilled trades requires knowledge obtainable only through a fairly rigorous academic program, or to put it more precisely perhaps, the gateway to a skilled job is thorough learning in rudimentary academics— the higher the skill, the greater the necessary academic grasp. Thus, today, as never before, education is the key to employability, and meaningful employment is the passport to the bounty of our society.

A good education, therefore, is nothing short of critical for black Americans because of the very real correlation between academic skills and employment, income and anti-social conduct.[1] Black people recognize that education has traditionally been the avenue of upward mobility in American life. Thus, their rightful demand for equal educational opportunities for blacks is now so economically essential that it is not amiss to classify it as one of the "basic" civil rights.[2]

Moreover, education bears a close relationship to other public non-economic needs of a democratic society. Without it there can be no intelligent use of the franchise, and reliance cannot be placed on the first amendment to insure effective public influence on the decision-making process. In short, the United States will not be able to hold itself out as either a free or a democratic society without an educated citizenry. Due to the correlation between education and democratic institutions, the right to equal educational opportunities is, in truth "a fundamental political right, because preservative of all rights."[3] As such, it should be accorded a preferred

* *ROBERT L. CARTER, A.B. 1937, Lincoln University; LL.B. 1940, Howard University, LL.M. 1947, Columbia University; General Counsel NAACP 1956-1968.*

[1] *See* COLEMAN, EQUALITY OF EDUCATIONAL OPPORTUNITY (1966); UNITED STATES COMMISSION ON CIVIL RIGHTS, ON RACIAL ISOLATION IN THE PUBLIC SCHOOLS (1967).

[2] Skinner v. Oklahoma, 316 U.S. 535, 541, 62 S. Ct. 1110, 1116 (1942). Certainly, if the "right" to have children is a basic civil right, then the "right" of a parent to support those children must assume equal dimensions.

[3] Yick Wo v. Hopkins, 118 U.S. 356, 370, 7 S. Ct. 1064, 1075 (1886). Like the

status and given substantial, not minimal, protection. In ordering the Department of Health, Education and Welfare to conduct a survey of educational opportunites because "of the fundamental significance of educational opportunity to many important social issues today . . . ,"[4] Congress recognized the essentiality of equal educational opportunities for the underprivileged.

In this country, it has long been accepted that education is an essential public function.[5] When the United States Supreme Court decided *Brown v. Board of Education* (*Brown I*), it described education as necessary to the maintenance of a democratic society and as a requisite to personal success.[6]

Few will dispute the Negro's *right* to equal educational opportunities. Yet serious and substantial disagreement occurs in respect to attempts to spell out those incidents basic to its enjoyment by black people and to define the resulting responsibility of government for its implementation and realization.

There is substantial agreement that a racially integrated education, as opposed to a segregated one, has certain identifiable characteristics which are more consistent with the underlying philosophies and principles of this society. Most recently in this connection, Judge J. Skelly Wright in *Hobson v. Hansen* aptly caught these qualities in stating that integration "educates white and Negro students equally in the fundamentals of racial tolerance and understanding. None of the parties to this suit, indeed, oppose this formulation, and they further agree that learning to live interracially is, or in a democracy should be, a vital component in every student's experience."[7]

Supreme Court "we must consider public education in the light of its full development and its present place in American life throughout the Nation." Brown v. Board of Education, 347 U.S. 483, 492-93, 74 S. Ct. 686, 695 (1954).

[4] COLEMAN, *supra* note 1, at 1.

[5] *See* Griffin v. Prince Edward County, 377 U.S. 218, 84 S. Ct. 593 (1964). Cf. Evans v. Newton, 382 U.S. 296, 87 S. Ct. 911 (1966); Terry v. Adams, 345 U.S. 461, 73 S. Ct. 809 (1953).

[6] Brown v. Board of Education, 347 U.S. 483, 493, 74 S. Ct. 686, 691 (1954), where the Court said:

"Today, education is perhaps the most important function of state and local governments. Compulsory school attendance laws and the great expenditures for education both demonstrate our recognition of the importance of education to our democratic society. It is required in the performance of our most basic public responsibilities, even service in the armed forces. It is the very foundation of good citizenship. Today it is a principal instrument in awakening the child to cultural values, in preparing him for later professional training, and in helping him to adjust normally to his environment. In these days, it is doubtful that any child may reasonably be expected to succeed in life if he is denied the opportunity of an education. Such an opportunity, where the state has undertaken to provide it, is a right which must be made available to all on equal terms."

[7] 269 F. Supp. 401, 419 (D.D.C. 1967). Continuing at 419, the court said:

"Elementary school integration enables the very young of either race to accept each other as persons before racial attitudes and prejudices have a chance to intrude and harden. Negro and white children playing innocently together in the schoolyard are the primary liberating promise in a society imprisoned by racial consciousness. If stereotypic racial thinking does set in, it can best be overcome by the reciprocal racial exposure which school integration entails."

At 504 the court again picks up the thought:

Ninety-six years earlier, Charles Summer, in recording his views on racially integrated education, favored it for similar reasons:

> "The child is not trained in the way he should go; for he is trained under the ban of inequality. How can he grow up to the stature of equal citizenship? He is pinched and dwarfed while the stigma of color is stamped upon him. . . .
>
> "Nor is separation without evil to the whites. The prejudice of color is nursed when it should be stifled . . . the school itself must practice the lesson [of equality]. Children learn by example more than by precept. How precious the example which teaches that all are equal in rights. But this can be only where all commingle in the common school as in common citizenship. . . . There should be no separate school. It is not enough that all should be taught alike; they must all be taught together . . . nor can they receive equal quantities of knowledge in the same way, except at the common school."[8]

Judge Wisdom has probably made the most eloquent and relevant statement of the country's present day critical interest and stake in integrated education when he said in dissenting in *Broussard v. Houston Independent School District:*

> "There is a bridge under construction, resting on the Constitution, connecting whites and Negroes and designed to lead the two races, starting with young children, to a harmonious, peaceful, civilized existence. That bridge is a plan for equal educational opportunities for all in an integrated, unitary public school system based on school administrators *affirmatively finding ways to make the plan work.*
>
> "Black nationalists and white racists to the contrary, school integration is relevant. It is an educational objective as well as a constitutional imperative."[9]

Notwithstanding the importance of education today, the constitutional

---

"In addition, segregation in the school precludes the kind of social encounter between Negroes and whites which is an indispensable attribute of education for mature citizenship in an interracial and democratic society."

[8] Speech of Senator Summer, Cong. Globe, 42d Cong., 2d Sess. 384 (1872). *See* Kemp v. Beasley, 389 F.2d 178, 181-82 (8th Cir. 1968). In July 1964, the Advisory Committee on Racial Imbalance and Education appointed by the Massachusetts State Board of Education issued a report finding that racial imbalance: (1) damages the self-confidence and motivation of Negro children; (2) re-enforces racial prejudice; (3) does not prepare the children for living in a multiracial world or the Negro child for future job opportunities in a technological society; (4) results in gaps in the quality of education among schools; and (5) is in conflict with the American creed of equal opportunity. Massachusetts State Board of Education, Advisory Committee on Racial Imbalance and Education, Interim Report 11, 12 (1964); *see also* Massachusetts Advisory Committee to the United States Commission on Civil Rights, Report of Racial Imbalance in the Boston Public Schools (1965).

[9] 395 F.2d 817, 828 (5th Cir. 1968).

imperative to afford equal educational opportunities to Negroes as well as whites, and the consistency of integration in education with basic American ideals, segregation in education remains the rule of the day—and an iron-strong rule indeed.

The unhappy reality is that the constitutional guarantee of equal education is meaningless to the vast majority of black children, whether in attendance in public schools in the South or in the urban North. The question arises why what is recognized as a public and personal necessity is not yet within reach of large numbers of our citizenry. The answer to that question would require an analysis of all the complex social and political forces that shape this society—a task obviously beyond the scope of this article.

II. THE ROLE OF LEGAL INSTITUTIONS

If we gain some insight into the role the law and the courts play in the attempt to make the equal education constitutional guaranty a genuine safeguard for black Americans, perhaps the larger question may be better illuminated. Such an inquiry must start with *Brown I* where the Court questioned rhetorically the relationship of segregation to unequal education and affirmatively found a direct causal connection between the two. There it said:

> "Does segregation of children in public schools solely on the basis of race, even though the physical facilities and other "tangible" factors may be equal, deprive the children of the minority group of equal educational opportunities? We believe that it does."[10]

It is important to note that, although in all of the cases involved state laws required or permitted segregation on the basis of race, this was not the narrow issue the Court explored. Rather, the question to be decided was placed within the broader context of "segregation . . . solely on the basis of race"[11] without defining *how* such segregation occurred. Unquestionably, this was purposeful. In view of the public attention the controversy generated, the care with which the underlying questions were explained, and the Court's knowledge that its final determination would be of monumental importance, however it came out, it is impossible to assume that what was unanimously agreed upon as the central issue was framed or approved fortuitously or without meticulous attention.

In *Brown I* the Court justified its decision on two separate but inter-related grounds. First, it concluded that segregation on the basis of race was impermissible and constituted a deprivation of equal protection as well

---

[10] Brown v. Board of Education, 347 U.S. 483, 493, 74 S. Ct. 686, 691 (1954).
[11] *Id.* at 493, 74 S. Ct. at 691.

as due process of law.[12] Second, it held that the psychological harm visited upon black children denied them equal educational opportunities.[13]

This second ground is stated implicitly in the Court's language[14] and is an extension of concepts taken from *Sweatt v. Painter*[15] and *McLaurin v. Oklahoma State Regents*.[16]

In *Sweatt* part of equal education's constitutional dimension was described as intangible factors "incapable of objective measurement," including what the community thought.[17] In *McLaurin* any restrictions impairing and inhibiting a black student's "ability to study, to engage in discussion and to exchange views with other students and, in general, to learn his profession" was flatly ruled unlawful.[18] These factors were reaffirmed in *Brown I*

---

[12] *See* Brown v. Board of Education, 347 U.S. 483, 74 S. Ct. 686 (1954), and Bolling v. Sharpe, 347 U.S. 497, 74 S. Ct. 693 (1954), where a similar conclusion was reached for the District of Columbia under the due process clause of the fifth amendment. In *Bolling* the court stated:

"Segregation in public education is not reasonably related to any proper governmental objective, and thus it imposes on Negro children of the District of Columbia a burden that constitutes an arbitrary deprivation of their liberty in violation of the due process clause.

"In view of our decision that the Constitution prohibits the states from maintaining racially segregated public schools, it would be unthinkable that the same Constitution would impose a lesser duty on the Federal Government. We hold that racial segregation in the public schools of the District of Columbia is a denial of the due process of law guaranteed by the Fifth Amendment to the Constitution."

See also Hobson v. Hansen, 269 F. Supp. 401, 419 (D.D.C. 1967).

[13] In United States v. Jefferson County Board of Education, 372 F.2d 836, 871 (5th Cir. 1966), aff'd *en banc*, 380 F.2d 385 (5th Cir. 1967), Circuit Judge Wisdom warned that:

"The *Brown I* finding that segregated schooling causes psychological harm and denies equal educational opportunities should not be construed as the sole basis for the decision. So construed, the way would be open for proponents of the status quo to attempt to show, on the facts, that integration may be harmful, or the greater of two evils."

Judge Wisdom concluded "that the judgment 'must have rested on the view that racial segregation is, in principle, a denial of equality to the minority against whom it is directed.'"

[14] "To separate them from others of similar age and qualifications solely because of their race generates a feeling of inferiority as to their status in the community that may affect their hearts and minds in a way unlikely ever to be undone. The effect of this separation on their educational opportunities was well stated by a finding in the Kansas case by a court which nevertheless felt compelled to rule against the Negro plaintiffs:

"'Segregation of white and colored children in public schools has a detrimental effect upon the colored children. The impact is greater when it has the sanction of the law; for the policy of separating the races is usually interpreted as denoting the inferiority of the Negro group. A sense of inferiority affects the motivation of a child to learn. Segregation with the sanction of law, therefore, has a tendency to [retard] the educational and mental development of Negro children and to deprive them of some of the benefits they would receive in a racially integrated school system.'"

Brown v. Board of Education, 347 U.S. 483, 494, 74 S. Ct. 686, 692 (1954).

[15] 339 U.S. 629, 70 S. Ct. 894 (1950).

[16] 339 U.S. 637, 70 S. Ct. 899 (1950).

[17] Sweatt v. Painter, 339 U.S. 629, 634, 70 S. Ct. 894 (1950).

[18] McLaurin v. Oklahoma State Regents, 339 U.S. 637, 641, 70 S. Ct. 899 (1950).

and meshed into a new or enlarged standard of psychological or emotional harm.[19] The Court found that "[s]uch considerations apply with added force to children in grade and high school.[20]

In *McLaurin* and *Brown I* all of the input material factors were equal, or to put it more accurately, such equality was posited and stipulated for the purposes of the litigation, so that the constitutional prohibition was based exclusively on the relationship of separation to equal education.[21] In *Sweatt* the Court made clear that had the material facilities been up to par, it would nevertheless have reached the same result. That the educationally inhibiting effect of racial isolation is the critical factor in these decisions can perhaps be seen best in *McLaurin*. There the Negro petitioner was actually in attendance at the otherwise all white state university. Yet because the few racial restrictions imposed were found to limit his ability to interact with his white schoolmates, they were struck down.

Whether *Brown I* is viewed as prohibiting segregation—because it is an impermissible racial classification, or because it does educational damage to blacks, or because of the inherent inequality of segregated education, or because of any combination of these factors—then the how, why or what causes of segregation would appear to be immaterial. Whether the state commands the segregation, builds upon it, or merely accepts it, the same invalid classification, the injury, or inequality takes place. The fact that law ordains the segregation merely aggravates its illegality.[22]

[19] Brown v. Board of Education, 347 U.S. 483, 493-94, 74 S. Ct. 686, 692 (1954).

[20] *Id.* at 493-94, 74 S. Ct. at 692. The Court concluded that "whatever may have been the extent of psychological knowledge at the time of *Plessy v. Ferguson*, this finding is amply supported by modern authority."
In United States v. Jefferson County Board of Education, 372 F.2d 836, 870-71 (5th Cir. 1966), Circuit Judge Wisdom observed that:
"*Brown* was an inevitable, predictable extension of *Sweatt* . . . and *McLaurin*. . . . Those cases involved separate but equal or identical graduate facilities. Factors 'incapable of objective measurement' but crucial to a good graduate education were not available to segregated Negroes. These were the intangible factors that prevented the Negro graduate students from having normal contacts and association with white students. Apartheid made the two groups unequal. In *Brown I* these same intangibles were found [to] 'apply, with added force, to children in grade and high schools; educational opportunity in public schools must be made available to all on equal terms.'"

[21] In Barksdale v. Springfield School Comm., 237 F. Supp. 543, 546 (D. Mass. 1964), the court, on the basis of expert evidence, found that:
"[R]acially imbalanced schools are not conducive to learning, that is, to retention, performance, and the development of creativity. Racial concentration in his school communicates to the Negro child that he is different and is expected to be different from white children. Therefore, even if all schools are equal in physical plant, facilities, and ability and number of teachers, and even if academic achievement were at the same level at all schools, the opportunity to Negro children in racially concentrated schools to obtain equal educational opportunities is impaired. . . ."

[22] This was the finding of the court in Brown v. Board of Education, 347 U.S. 483, 494, 74 S. Ct. 686, 692 (1954):
"Segregation of white and colored children in public schools has a detrimental effect upon the colored children. *The impact is greater when it has the sanction of the law.*" (Emphasis added.)
In United States v. Jefferson County Board of Education, 372 F.2d 836, 868 (5th Cir.

A contrary conclusion can only be reached by viewing *Brown I* as rest-
ing *solely* upon the existence of a statute (as opposed to other forms of state
action) affirmatively requiring the isolation of the races without regard to
the resultant injury or inequality. Such reasoning is at odds with the underlying rationale and spirit of the *Brown* decision. *Brown* articulates a fundamental change in constitutional concepts. It held that racial segregation is
forbidden—that segregation, in and of itself, denies equal educational opportunity. As a new thrust in constitutional law which voices the country's basic
commitment to egalitarianism, *Brown* needed careful nurturing and should
have been given an expansive and generous scope by courts required to apply
its principles. As Circuit Judge Wisdom observed recently:

> "*Brown's* broad meaning, its important meaning, is its revitalization of
> the national constitutional right, the Thirteenth, Fourteenth and Fif-
> teenth Amendments created in favor of Negroes. This is the right of
> Negroes to *national* citizenship. . . ."[23]

As for education, the necessary import of *Brown* and its predecessors is that
whatever the cause of the separation, Negroes in a dominant white culture
cannot obtain equal educational opportunities within the mandate of the
Constitution in an educational environment separate and apart from white
students.[24]

1966), the court noted that:
"Although psychological harm and lack of educational opportunities to Negroes
may exist whether caused by *de facto* or *de jure* segregation, a state policy of
apartheid aggravates the harm."
[23] *Id.* at 872. Judge Kaufman expressed a similar view in Taylor v. Board of Education of City School District, 191 F. Supp. 181, 187 (S.D.N.Y. 1961):
"The *Brown* decision, in short, was a lesson in democracy, directed to the public
at large and more particularly to those responsible for the operation of the schools."
Earlier in the *Jefferson County* case the Court offered a variation on this theme adapted
to the Southern situation, yet recognizing the broader complications of *Brown:*
"The two *Brown* decisions established equalization of educational opportunities
as a high priority goal for all of the states and compelled seventeen states, which by
law had segregated public schools, to take affirmative action to reorganize their
schools into a unitary non-racial system."
Id. at 247.
[24] *See* UNITED STATES COMMISSION ON CIVIL RIGHTS, *supra* note 1, at 193:
"The central truth which emerges from this report and from all of the Commission's investigations is simply this: Negro children suffer serious harm when their
education takes place in public schools which are racially segregated, whatever
the source of such segregation may be.
"Negro children who attend predominantly Negro schools do not achieve as well
as other children, Negro and white. . . .
"Negro children believe that their schools are stigmatized and regarded as inferior
by the community as a whole. Their belief is shared by their parents and by their
teachers. And their belief is founded in fact. . . .
"Negroes in this country were first enslaved, later segregated by law, and now
are segregated and discriminated against by a combination of governmental and
private action. They do not reside today in ghettos as the result of free choice
and the attendance of their children in racially isolated schools is not an accident
of fate wholly unconnected with deliberate segregation and other forms of discrimination. In the light of this history, the feelings of stigma generated in Negro

Unfortunately, *Brown* has been read otherwise. Instead of an expansive reading, courts have sought to limit and restrict its impact. In *Briggs v. Elliott*,[25] one of the original cases involved in the *Brown* opinion, Judge Parker dwelt upon what *Brown I* did not expressly say. On the grounds that the Constitution has an impact of negation only, Judge Parker concluded in dictum that "the Constitution . . . does not require integration. It merely forbids discrimination."[26] This interpretation was quickly taken up by a host of federal courts.[27] Seizing upon Judge Parker's analysis, segregation and

children by attendance at racially isolated schools are realistic and cannot easily be overcome."

In Hobson v. Hansen, 269 F. Supp. 401, 406 (D.D.C. 1967), Circuit Judge Wright stated that:

"Racially and socially homogenous schools damage the minds and spirit of all children who attend them—the Negro, the white, the poor and the affluent—and block the attainment of the broader goals of democratic education, whether the segregation occurs by law or by fact. . . .

"The court also finds that a Negro student in a predominantly Negro school gets a formal education inferior to the academic education he would receive, and which white students receive, in a school which is integrated or predominantly white."

Id. at 419. Continuing at 504, Judge Wright stated:

"Negro schools provide their Negro students with an education inferior to that which others, white and Negro alike, receive in integrated or predominantly white education settings. This the court finds from the evidence adduced at trial. This finding is confirmed by the Supreme Court in *Brown I*, which, besides noting that "separate" schools are inherently unequal and psychologically harmful to Negro school children, approved the finding entered by the lower court explicitly stating that even unmandated segregation has a "detrimental effect" on Negroes. The court can judicially note that corroborating views can also be found in the conclusions of the federal agency commissioned by Congress to investigate racial questions; in the decisions of federal courts, and of state legislatures and education officers and committees; and in the experienced judgments of American educators and psychologists expert in race relations, who make it clear that the damage segregation causes stems from the sense of confinement it imparts, together with the low esteem which the predominantly Negro school naturally draws from the white as well as the Negro community."

[25] 132 F. Supp. 776 (E.D.S.C. 1955).

[26] *Id.* at 777.

[27] *See, e.g.,* Kelley v. Board of Education, 270 F.2d 209, 228-29 (6th Cir. 1959), *cert. denied,* 361 U.S. 924 (1959); Rippy v. Borders, 250 F.2d 690, 692-93 (5th Cir. 1957); School Board v. Atkins, 246 F.2d 325, 327 (4th Cir. 1957), *cert. denied,* 355 U.S. 855 (1957); Avery v. Wichita Falls Independent School District, 241 F.2d 230, 233-34 (5th Cir.), *cert. denied,* 353 U.S. 938 (1957); School Board v. Allen, 240 F.2d 59, 62 (4th Cir. 1956), *cert. denied,* 353 U.S. 910 (1957); Evans v. Buchanan, 207 F. Supp. 820, 823-24 (D. Del. 1962); Thompson v. County School Board, 204 F. Supp. 620, 625 (E.D. Va. 1962); Jackson v. School Board, 203 F. Supp. 701, 704 (W.D. Va.), *rev'd on other grounds,* 308 F.2d 918 (4th Cir. 1962).

Judge Zavatt, in Blocker v. Board of Education, 226 F. Supp. 208, 220 (E.D.N.Y. 1964), observed:

"One of the *Brown* cases on remand and a succession of subsequent cases contain statements as to what the Supreme Court did not decide. It is of little value in the present setting, however, to place undue emphasis upon what our highest tribunal has *not* decided; attention has been called above to what the Court did decide and to its time tested policy of drawing constitutional decisions no broader than is required by the case before it. Several post-*Brown* cases involving public schools have stated, often gratuitously, that the Constitution does not require a general mixture of the races. This doctrine, if it may be so called, has its inception in dictum found in *Briggs v. Elliott,* one of the remanded *Brown* cases which said:

integration were treated as if disparate. The message this conveyed to the public was that there was no obligation to disestablish patterns of segregation and reorganize on an integrated basis. Once again, the words of Judge Wisdom are very much to the point:

> "Many other school boards throughout the South have been willing victims of the Briggs word-magic. They embraced the chains that held them captive. The glitter of the rhetoric obscured the looseness of their bonds.
> "I doubt if many laymen understand the question-begging distinction between 'desegregation' and 'integration.' In the vernacular there is no distinction. But here, as in similar situations in other states, the lay board understood the effect of their lawyers' reading of Briggs. As stated in the Board's brief: 'There is no affirmative duty on the School District to consider race in the selection of school sites'; that would be an affirmative act leading to integration."[28]

Briggs not only totally ignores any consideration of segregation, unless affirmatively and presently mandated by statute, but it fails to give weight to the question of injury produced by racial segregation. More important, *Briggs* disregards the central constitutional issue—the legal *right* of Negroes to equal educational opportunities. Today, the *Briggs* analysis of negation is moribund and all but totally discredited. It has been rejected by the Fifth,[29] the Third,[30] the Eighth,[31] and the Tenth Circuits,[32] and by district courts in the District of Columbia,[33] the First,[34] and the Second Circuits.[35] Certainly burial is well deserved for *Briggs* "is logically inconsistent with *Brown* and subsequent decisional law on the subject,"[36] which makes clear that the

'[I]t is important that we point out exactly what the Supreme Court has decided and what it has not decided in this case. It has not decided that the federal courts are to take over or regulate the public schools of the states. It has not decided that the states must mix persons of different races in the schools or must require them to attend schools or must deprive them of the right of choosing the schools they attend. . . . The Constitution, in other words, does not require integration.'
This construction draws continuing sustenance through a process in which each case relies upon the preceding one; it would appear that the ultimate and solitary source is this dictum in *Briggs* v. *Elliott* . . . ."

28 Wisdom, J., dissenting in Broussard v. Houston Independent School District, 395 F.2d 817, 822 (5th Cir. 1968).

29 United States v. Jefferson County Board of Education, 372 F.2d 836 (5th Cir. 1966); Singleton v. Jackson Municipal Separate School District, 348 F.2d 729 (5th Cir. 1965).

30 Evans v. Ennis, 281 F.2d 385 (3d Cir. 1960).

31 Kelley v. Public School District, 378 F.2d 483 (8th Cir. 1967); Kemp v. Beasley, 352 F.2d 14 (8th Cir. 1965); Dove v. Parham, 282 F.2d 256 (8th Cir. 1960).

32 Board of Education v. Dowell, 375 F.2d 158 (10th Cir. 1967).

33 Hobson v. Hansen, 269 F. Supp. 401 (D.D.C. 1967).

34 Barksdale v. Springfield School Comm., 237 F. Supp. 543 (D. Mass. 1964).

35 Blocker v. Board of Education, 226 F. Supp. 208 (E.D.N.Y. 1964); Taylor v. Board of Education, 191 F. Supp. 181 (S.D.N.Y. 1961); Branche v. Board of Education, 204 F. Supp. 150 (E.D.N.Y. 1962).

36 See Kemp v. Beasley, 352 F.2d 14 (8th Cir. 1965).

constitutional imperative is one of equal educational opportunity regardless of the word formula employed.

Federal courts in the South are now concerning themselves with defining the constitutional *rights* of black school children to be free of the burden of school segregation, and *the duties* of state officials to transform the dual school system to a unitary system free of racial restriction.[37] Sitting en banc, the Fifth Circuit bluntly articulated the import of the changed judicial attitude as the very antithesis of the *Briggs* rationale:

"The Court holds that boards and officials administering public schools in this circuit have the affirmative duty under the Fourteenth Amendment to bring about an integrated, unitary school system in which there are no Negro schools and no white schools—just schools. Expressions in our earlier opinions distinguishing between integration and desegregation must yield to this affirmative duty we now recognize."[38]

Unfortunately, before the *Briggs* dictum was laid to rest, it gave birth to a very troublesome northern aberration. In *Bell v. School Board of the City of Gary, Indiana*,[39] a federal court in Indiana, relying upon *Briggs*, held that the Constitution did not interdict adventitious school segregation. This view was adopted by the Seventh Circuit. Since *Bell*, several other courts have refused to interfere with de facto school segregation under the theory that to do so would be to require integration.[40]

Although the imprint of *Briggs* is clear, *Bell* and its progeny have at least addressed themselves to some of the relevant issues. Where the *Bell* court went astray was in the assumption that its primary concern was to determine the extent of the duty of school officials to eliminate racial imbalance. Within the framework of their defined obligation, the rights of Negro children would then be perceived. However, the teaching of *Brown* and its predecessors is that the central issue is whether the Constitution's warrant of equal educational opportunity has been met, and the critical constitutional fact is that segregated education, however it occurs, denies Negroes what the Constitution is said to secure.

At the point when it is determined that equal education is denied, and not before, does the question of the nature, scope and extent of a school official's duty arise. *Brown I* dealt solely with determining the nature of the constitutional rights of Negroes to equal educational opportunities, with the states'

[37] See cases collected notes 29-35 *supra*.

[38] United States v. Jefferson County Board of Education, 380 F.2d 385 (5th Cir. 1967).

[39] 213 F. Supp. 819 (N.D. Ind.), *aff'd*, 324 F.2d 209 (7th Cir. 1963), *cert. denied*, 377 U.S. 924, 84 S. Ct. 1223 (1964).

[40] Deal v. Cincinnati Board of Education, 244 F.2d 572 (6th Cir. 1965); Downs v. Board of Education, 336 F.2d 988 (10th Cir. 1964), *cert. denied*, 380 U.S. 914 (1965); Webb v. Board of Education, 223 F. Supp. 466 (N.D. Ill. 1963); Lynch v. Kenston School District, 229 F. Supp. 740 (N.D. Ohio 1964).

obligation being left for resolution in *Brown II*.[41] *Brown I* did not first address itself to the question of the duties required of school officials and then resolve the rights of the Negro plaintiffs on the basis of what was found to be required of the state. On the contrary, *Brown* determined the rights of the black school children and their entitlement to constitutional protection. Then, and only then, was inquiry made concerning the duties of the school officials. This entire process is reversed by *Bell*, with the result that the nature of the school board's obligation determines the character and extent of the Negro child's right to an equal education. This is a distortion of basic values and priorities and constitutes *Bell's* underlying fallacy.

The three decisions quoted below which reject the *Bell* reasoning on this score are legally sounder in analysis, but since none was by a court of appeals, the *Bell* rationale has been accorded greater significance. *Blocker v. Board of Education of Manhasset, New York*[42] vigorously rejected the *Bell* reasoning in these words:

"In *Bell* the court concluded that there was 'no support for the plaintiffs position that the defendant has an affirmative duty to balance the races in the various schools under its jurisdiction, regardless of the residence of students involved.' *Bell v. School City of Gary, Indiana*, 213 F. Supp. 819, 831 (N.D. Ind. 1963). *The question, however, is not whether the State has an affirmative duty to balance the races, but, rather, whether it is to be enjoined from countenancing, and thereby perpetuating, a system of virtually separate elementary schools for Negro and white children.* To frame the question otherwise would, in the instant case, be delusive . . . ."

Branche v. Board of Education of Town of Hempstead relied on the following rationale:[43]

"The central constitutional fact is the inadequacy of segregated education. That it is not coerced by direct action of an aim of the state cannot, alone, be decisive of the issue of deprivation of constitutional right. . . . The educational system that is thus compulsory and publicly afforded must deal with the inadequacy arising from adventitious segre-

[42] 226 F. Supp. 208, 222 (E.D.N.Y. 1964). The court, at 223, went on to conclude that:
    "The Fourteenth Amendment does not cease to operate once the narrow confines of the Brown-type situation are exceeded; the Supreme Court has made it clear that it is the duty of the courts to interdict "evasive schemes for segregation whether attempted 'ingeniously or ingenuously'," *Cooper v. Aaron*, 358 U.S. 1, 17, 78 S. Ct. 1401, 1409, 3 L. Ed. 2d 5 (1958), and has reaffirmed that objective in a recent decision on the subject. See *Goss v. Knoxville Board of Education*, 373 U.S. 683, 83 S. Ct. 1405, 10 L. Ed. 2d 632 (1963). Viewed in this context then, can it be said that one type of segregation, having its basis in state law or evasive schemes to defeat desegregation, is to be proscribed, while another, having the same effect but another cause, is to be condoned? Surely, the Constitution is made of sturdier stuff."
[43] 204 F. Supp. 150, 153 (E.D.N.Y. 1962).

gation, it cannot accept an indurate segregation on the ground that it is not coerced or planned but accepted."

Finally, *Barksdale v. Springfield School Committee* refused to accept the *Bell* thesis on this basis:[44]

"The defendants argue, nevertheless, that there is no constitutional mandate to remedy racial imbalance. *Bell v. School City of Gary, Indiana,* 324 F.2d 209 (7th Cir. 1963). But that is not the question. The question is whether there is a constitutional duty to provide equal educational opportunities for all children within the system. While *Brown* answered that question affirmatively in the context of coerced segregation, the constitutional fact—the inadequacy of segregated education—is the same in this case, and I so find. It is neither just nor sensible to proscribe segregation having its basis in affirmative state action while at the same time failing to provide a remedy for segregation which grows out of discrimination in housing, or other economic or social factors. Education is tax supported and compulsory, and public school educators, therefore, must deal with inadequacies within the educational system as they arise, and it matters not that the inadequacies are not of their making. . . .
"I cannot accept the view in *Bell* that only forced segregation is incompatible with the requirements of the Fourteenth Amendment, nor do I find meaningful the statement that '[t]he Constitution . . . does not require integration. It merely forbids discrimination.' "

Moreover, the New Jersey and California Supreme Courts have refused to follow *Bell*.[45] Much is said today about "law address[ing] itself to actualities."[46] If that be so, then surely *Bell* was erroneously decided for it is singularly immaterial whether a denial of equal educational opportunities is characterized as "de jure" or "de facto." Still remaining is the fact of segregation with all of its resulting harm and inequality.[47]

---

44 237 F. Supp. 543, 546 (D. Mass. 1964).
45 Booker v. Board of Education, 45 N.J. 161, 212 A.2d 1 (1965); Jackson v. Pasadena City School District, 59 Cal. 2d 876, 382 P.2d 878 (1963).
46 Griffin v. Illinois, 351 U.S. 12, 23, 76 S. Ct. 585 (1956).
47 See UNITED STATES COMMISSION ON CIVIL RIGHTS, *supra* note 1, at 114:
"Racial isolation in the schools tends to lower students' achievement, restrict their aspirations, and impair their sense of being able to affect their own destiny.
"By contrast, Negro children in predominantly white schools more often score higher on achievement tests, develop higher aspirations, and have a firmer sense of control over their own destinies.
"Differences in performance, attitudes, and aspirations occur most often when Negroes are in majority-white schools. Negro children in schools that are majority-Negro often fail to do better than Negro children in all-Negro schools. In addition, the results stemming from desegregated schooling tend to be most positive for those Negro children who began their attendance at desegregated schools in the earlier elementary grades.
"An important contributing element to the damage arising from racially isolated schools is the fact that they often are regarded by the community as inferior institutions and students and teachers sense that their schools are stigmatized. This has an effect on their attitudes which influences student achievement.
"Racial isolation also appears to have a negative effect upon the job opportunities

More important, denials of equal educational opportunities do not just happen. Rather, governmental officials act or fail to act, and it is their action or nonaction that results in the deprivation. Certainly it is of little or no consolation to a Negro child to be told that his right to equal educational opportunities—a passport to participation in American society—is conditional upon some fictional distinction between "de jure" and "de facto," so remote from reality as to be understood only by a handful of lawyers.

Apparently, this was the belief even of those who dissented in the *Jefferson* case,[48] for they wanted no interpretation of constitutional rights of Negro children and of the obligation of school officials for the South which was more generous in scope in the first instance and more stringent in its proscription in the second than would be true for the North. At most the

of Negroes. Negro adults who experienced desegregated schooling tend to have higher incomes and more often hold white-collar jobs than Negro adults who attended isolated schools. These differences are traceable to the higher achievement levels of the Negroes from desegregated schools, and, in part, to the fact that association with whites often aids Negroes in competing more effectively in the job market.

"Attendance in racially isolated schools tends to generate attitudes on the part of Negroes and whites that lead them to prefer association with members of their own race. The attitudes appear early in the schools, carry over into later life, and are reflected in behavior. Both Negroes and whites are less likely to have associations with members of the other race if they attended racially isolated schools. Racial isolation not only inflicts educational damage upon Negro students when they are in school, it reinforces the very attitudes and behavior that maintain and intensify racial isolation as well.

"Moreover, the absence of interracial contact perpetuates the sense that many whites have that Negroes and Negro schools are inferior."

It is interesting to note that in every case decided in a federal court which holds or suggests that equal educational opportunities are denied by adventitious segregation, the question of whether such segregation has a damaging effect upon Negroes has been reached and decided affirmatively. *See, e.g.,* Branche v. Board of Education, 204 F. Supp. 150 (E.D.N.Y. 1962); Blocker v. Board of Education, 226 F. Supp. 208 (E.D.N.Y. 1964); Barksdale v. Springfield School Committee, 237 F. Supp. 543 (D. Mass. 1964); Hobson v. Hansen, 269 F. Supp. 401 (D.D.C. 1967); *see also* Jackson v. Pasadena City School District, 59 Cal. 2d 876, 382 P.2d 878 (1963); Booker v. Board of Education, 45 N.J. 161, 212 A.2d 1 (1965).

[48] United States v. Jefferson County Board of Education, 380 F.2d 385, 397-98 (5th Cir. 1967):

"The Negro children in Cleveland, Chicago, Los Angeles, Boston, New York, or any other area of the nation which the opinion classifies under de facto segregation, would receive little comfort from the assertion that the racial make-up of their school system does not violate their constitutional rights, because they were born into a de facto society, while the exact same racial make-up of the school system in the 17 Southern and border states violates the constitutional rights of their counterparts, or even their blood brothers, because they were born into a de jure society. All children everywhere in the nation are protected by the Constitution, and the treatment which violates their constitutional rights in one area of the country, also violates such constitutional rights in another area. The details of the remedy to be applied, however, may vary with local conditions. Basically, all of them must be given the same constitutional protection. Due process and equal protection will not tolerate a lower standard, and surely not a double standard. The problem is a national one."

distinction between segregation in education—northern or southern style—
is a question of degree and not of kind.[49] It is clear that *Bell*, like *Briggs*, will
eventually be repudiated, simply because in American constitutional law,
arid legalistic doctrine will sooner or later be overturned. However often
our courts may deviate therefrom, events require them to remember that
their role is to infuse the Constitution with life and meaning so that it is
relevant to present-day needs. The problem is whether this infused vitality
which is to come will suffice to halt the deterioration of public education and
to foster educational practice and methodology that will give the Constitution's guaranty real-life meaning to black school children in the United
States.

III.   THE EFFECT OF THE LEGAL PROCESS

Brown I is one of the peaks of American jurisprudence because in
stating the guarantee of equality as fundamental to our basic law, it expresses
the loftiest values in our society. In assuming that the system can move,
more or less routinely, in conformity with the highest of ethical considerations,
the decision uplifts the spirit for it depicts us as we like to view ourselves.
It eased, for the moment at least, deep-felt fears of an irreconcilable division
in our society along racial lines. As a hortatory appeal to conscience, *Brown*
will remain a historic statement in American law.

On the level of realism, however, *Brown* does not fare so well. Some
fourteen years later, one is forced to conclude that the decision has been a
major failure. Unequal and inferior education for black children is probably
more widespread today than was true in 1954. Segregated schools are on
the increase in the North, and very little change has been made in the pattern
of school segregation in the South. Moreover, we know now that Negro
children are being graduated from predominantly Negro public schools at
far below the level of educational attainment of children coming from
schools of white concentration. This makes the educational prospects for
Negro children appear to be far more desolate than ever.[50]

An examination of the pace of school desegregation in the South to the
point just prior to, and again just after, passage of the United States Civil
Rights Act of 1964 will give us a reasonably accurate picture of the success
of *Brown* in transforming the South from a biracial school system to one
without discrimination based on race.[51]

---

[49] *See* Carter, *De Facto School Segregation: An Examination of the Legal and
Constitutional Questions Presented*, 16 W. RES. L. REV. 502, 504 (1965).

[50] *See* PUBLIC EDUCATION ASSOCIATION, STATUS OF PUBLIC SCHOOL EDUCATION OF
NEGRO AND PUERTO RICAN CHILDREN (1955); CLARK, DARK GHETTO, 111-154 (1965).

[51] United States v. Jefferson County Board of Education, 372 F.2d 836, 854 (5th
Cir. 1966). The court provides us with a more complete analysis of the rate of change:

In the 1963-64 school year, the eleven states of the Confederacy had 1.17 per cent of their Negro students in schools with white students. In 1964-65, undoubtedly because of the effect of the 1964 Act, the percentage doubled, reaching 2.25. For the 1965-66 school year, this time because of guidelines of the U.S. Department of Health, Education and Welfare, the percentage reached 6.01 per cent. In 1965-66, the entire region encompassing the southern *and border* states had 10.9 per cent of its black children in school with white children; 1,555 biracial school districts out of 3,031 in the southern and border states were still fully segregated; 3,101,043 black children in the region attended all-black schools. Despite the impetus of the 1964 Act, the state of Alabama, Louisiana and Mississippi still had less than one per cent of their Negro enrollment attending schools with white students.

More telling perhaps is the table set forth on the opposite page:[52]

Even these figures, for the school year 1965-1966, are somewhat misleading because most of the increases recorded therein were achieved during that school year and not before.[53]

A quick canvas of the Federal Reporters since 1965 discloses that segregation in public education remains virtually intact.[54] There has been considerable activity in the southern and border states since the 1965-1966

THE RATE OF CHANGE

Percentage of Negroes in Schools with Whites

School Year	South	% Change	Border	% Change	Region	% Change
1959-60*	.160		45.4		6.4	
1960-61	.162	.002	49.0	3.6	7.0	.6
1961-62	.241	.079	52.5	3.5	7.6	.6
1962-63	.453	.212	51.8	0.7	8.0	.4
1963-64	1.17	.717	54.8	3.0	9.2	1.2
1964-65	2.25	1.08	58.3	3.5	10.9	1.7
1965-66	6.01	3.76	68.9	10.6	15.9	5.0

*First school year in which SERS began recording number of Negroes in schools with whites.

[52] *Id.* at 905.

[53] *See* Statistical Summary, Southern Educational Reporting Service, December, 1965.

[54] *See* Kelley v. Altheimer Public School District No. 22, 378 F.2d 483 (8th Cir. 1967); Raney v. Board of Education, 381 F.2d 252 (8th Cir. 1967); Monroe v. Board of Commissioners, 380 F.2d 955 (6th Cir. 1967); Board of Education v. Dowell, 375 F.2d 159 (10th Cir. 1967); United States v. Board of Public Instruction, 395 F.2d 66 (95th Cir. 1968); Coppedge v. Franklin County Board of Education, 273 F. Supp. 289 (E.D. N.C. 1967); Swann v. Charlotte-Mecklenburg Board of Education, 369 F.2d 29 (4th Cir. 1966); Singleton v. Jackson Municipal Separate School District, 348 F.2d 729 (5th Cir. 1965); Kier v. County School Board, 249 F. Supp. 239 (W.D. Va. 1966), Bell v. School Board, 249 F. Supp. 249 (W.D. Va. 1966); Davis v. Board of School Commissioners, 364 F.2d 896 (5th Cir. 1966).

STATUS OF DESEGREGATION
(17 Southern and Border States and D.C.)

| | School Districts | | | | Enrollment | | Negroes in Schools with Whites | |
	Total	With Negroes and Whites	In Compliance †	Not In Compliance †	White	Negro	No.	% ††
Alabama	118	119	105	14	559,123**	295,848**	1,250*	.43
Arkansas	410	217	400	10	337,652**	111,952**	4,900*	4.38
Florida	67	67	67	0	1,056,805*	256,063*	25,000*	9.76
Georgia	196	180	192	5	784,917*	355,950*	9,465*	2.66
Louisiana	67	67	33	34	483,941	318,651	2,187	.69
Mississippi	149	149	118	31	309,413	296,834	1,750*	.59
North Carolina	170	170	165	4	828,638**	349,282**	18,000*	5.15
South Carolina	108	108	86	21	374,007	263,983	3,864	1.46
Tennessee	152	129	149	2	714,241*	176,541*	28,801	16.31
Texas	1,325	850	1,303	7	2,136,150*	349,192*	60,000*	17.18
Virginia	130	127	124	12	757,037**	239,729**	27,550*	11.49
SOUTH	2,892	2,183	2,742	140	8,341,924	3,014,025	182,767	6.01
Delaware	58	47	59	0	86,041	20,485	17,069	83.32
Dist. or Columbia	1	1	1	0	15,173	128,843	109,270	84.81
Kentucky	200	167	204	0	713,451**	59,835**	46,891	78.37
Maryland	24	23	24	0	583,796	178,851	99,442	55.60
Missouri	1,096	212*	675	0	843,167	105,171	79,000*	75.12
Oklahoma	1,046	323	1,044	4	564,250*	45,750*	17,500*	38.25
West Virginia	55	44	55	0	425,087*	19,850	15,850*	79.85
BORDER	2,480	817	2,062	4	3,230,965	558,785	385,022	68.90
REGION	5,372	3,000	4,804	144	11,572,889	3,572,810	567,789	15.89

* Estimated.

** 1964-65.

† The sum of adding the districts "In Compliance" and "Not in Compliance" will not always equal the total number of districts because the Office of Education reports a different number of districts from that of some of the state departments of education.

†† The number of Negroes in schools with whites, compared to the total Negro enrollment.

school year as a result of the 1964 Civil Rights Act.[55] But the Civil Rights
Act, already diluted, is faced with the prospect of being stripped of its principal weapon—the power to cut off federal funds to school districts that
refuse to desegrate their facilities and personnel.[56]

Fear of losing federal funds has been the chief motivating factor which
has moved school authorities in most situations to take steps in compliance
with *Brown*. The conduct of the school board in *Green v. County School
Board of New Kent County* is typical. The Court noted that:

> "The School Board initially sought dismissal of this suit on the ground
> that petitioners had failed to apply to the State Board for assignment to
> New Kent school. However, on August 2, 1965, five months after the
> suit was brought, respondent School Board, in order to remain eligible
> for federal financial aid, adopted a 'freedom-of-choice' plan for desegre-
> gating the schools."[57]

At this point, the sad but inescapable conclusion is that *Brown* has
failed to achieve equal educational opportunities for Negro school children
in border and southern states.[58]

In the North *Brown* has recorded even less success. As already noted,

---

[55] Congress, concerned with the lack of progress in securing equal educational
opportunities for Negro school children, enacted Title VI of the Civil Rights Act of
1964 to deal with that and similar problems:
> "No person in the United States shall, on the ground of race, color, or national
> origin, be excluded from participation in, be denied the benefits of, or be subjected
> to discrimination under any program or activity receiving Federal financial assis-
> tance." 42 U.S.C. § 2000d (1964).

The Department of Health, Education and Welfare issued regulations covering racial
discrimination in federally aided school systems, as directed by 42 U.S.C. § 2000d-1,
and in a statement of policies, or "guidelines," the Department's Office of Education
established standards according to which school systems in the process of desegregation
can remain qualified for federal funds.

[56] The fear of financial loss has been the primary stimulus for providing equal
educational opportunities in the southern and border states. This is apparent from the
number of local boards which eliminated dual zones in favor of some more acceptable
method of segregation in 1965-66, the first year of the HEW enforcement program.
New York Times, Sept. 28, 1968, at 1 reports that an amendment which would forbid
the use of federal funds to force the bussing of students or to force any student to
attend a particular school, was written into the appropriation bill by House-Senate
conferees. Subsequently, this limitation was voted down. But what it does indicate is
that there will be a continuing struggle to take away from the federal government any
muscle it has in this regard.

[57] 391 U.S. 430, 88 S. Ct. 1689 (1968). *See also* Raney v. Board of Education, 391
U.S. 443, 88 S. Ct. 1697 (1968), where, as in *Green*, respondent first took steps in 1965
to abandon that policy (dual zones) to remain eligible for federal financial aid.

[58] As the court in United States v. Jefferson County Board of Education, 272 F.2d
836, 847 (5th Cir. 1966) observed:
> "A national effort, bringing together Congress, the executive and the judiciary may
> be able to make meaningful the right of Negro children to equal educational op-
> portunities. *The courts acting alone have failed.*"

Indeed, at the time the *Jefferson County* case was brought only 0.43% of the Negro
children of Alabama and 0.69% of the Negro children of Louisiana were attending
desegregated schools. *Id.* at 845.

Bell and its progeny refuse to concede that *Brown* so much as applies to northern-style school segregation—so-called de facto segregation or racial imbalance—absent contrivance,[59] on the theory that no cognizable constitutional infraction is manifested by the existence of this form of segregation. Under the *Bell* formulation, disposition of the question concerning the constitutionality of the existing de facto school segregation completes the court's responsibility. Even a specific showing of a relationship between the segregation complained of and a denial of equal educational opportunity, or a showing of inferior educational facilities is not regarded as sufficient to bring the Constitution into play. Thus, *Bell* renders both *Brown I* and *Plessy v. Ferguson*[60] inapplicable.

One of the reasons for *Brown's* failure in the South is that in *Brown II*[61] the Court gave to the local school board the primary duty of effectuating the newly defined constitutional right of black children to equal education.[62] This was a particularly unfortunate choice because, on the one hand local school authorities were the least likely to understand the impact of the law's new thrust, and on the other hand they were more prone to resent the need for change or to view the Court's decision as a personal affront.

Even where there was a desire to comply with the law, monumental political problems had to be overcome before any affirmative action could be taken. School board members are elected or appointed officials, and in local communities where resistance to the *Brown* decisions has aptly been labelled "massive," they are not free to exercise independent judgment. As the *Jefferson* court noted:

"The dead hand of the old past and the closed fist of the recent past account for some of the slow progress. There are other reasons—as obvious to Congress as to courts. Local loyalties compelled school officials and elected officials to make a public record of their unwillingness to act."[63]

---

59 See cases cited note 40 *supra*.
60 163 U.S. 537, 16 S. Ct. 1138 (1896).
61 Brown v. Board of Education, 349 U.S. 294, 75 S. Ct. 753 (1955).
62 *Id.* at 299.
63 United States v. Jefferson County Board of Education, 272 F.2d 836, 854 (5th Cir. 1966). Not untypical of the "massive resistance" offered by the South is the situation in Little Rock, Arkansas. The following history is taken from Clark v. Board of Education, 369 F.2d 661, 664 (8th Cir. 1966):
"The present case has numerous ancestors that have preceded it before this and other courts. The litigation began ten years ago with the filing of a class action seeking the desegregation of the public schools of Little Rock, Arkansas. *Aaron v. Cooper,* 143 F. Supp. 855 (E.D. Ark. 1956). The Board in that case proposed a gradual desegregation plan, to be fully implemented by 1963, based upon geographical attendance zones. We approved that plan in *Aaron v. Cooper,* 243 F.2d 361 (8th Cir. 1957), with the understanding that the District Court would retain jurisdiction to insure the effectuation of the transition to a racially non-discriminatory school system. The attempted implementation of the plan, however, resulted in the well-known difficulties at Central High School in 1957. Continued official resistance to the law resulted in the enjoining as part of the original *Aaron* case of various per-

Added to this was the not inconsequential factor that school officials had to face the fears and concerns of the white community about the impact of change in the quality of education of white children. Even in the North, where commitment to overt segregation is not as great, local school boards are similarly influenced by fears and concerns of white parents and find it difficult to embark voluntarily upon a course of action to eliminate racial imbalance. Thus, both in the North and South, local school officials are the ones least capable of taking the action which implementation of *Brown* requires.

Federal courts were ordered to play a limited and negative role in the transformation process—they were to require compliance where it was not voluntarily forthcoming. When action was undertaken leading to compliance, they were to evaluate the steps taken to determine whether what was contemplated or was being done constituted a good faith effort at implementation. By inference, the lower federal courts were to allow state officials to determine the course and pace of desegregation and to intervene only after the fact. Even then the standard of measurement—good faith—was regarded as a subjective yardstick, and this gave the courts a rationale for allowing more time when none was needed.

One could expect problems to result from giving local school boards primary responsibility for enforcing a black child's right to equal educational opportunity, particularly when a definition of that right in its constitutional dimension is at odds with their established patterns, understanding and policies. This is particularly true when the standards used to judge compliance are such vague and ephemeral yardsticks as "public interest" and "good faith." This difficulty might have been minimized if the courts had applied objective criteria to give concreteness to these rather elusive guidelines. On the contrary, however, far too many courts, even as late as today, before enjoining the delaying tactics of school officials require a showing of sub-

---

sons, including the Governor of Arkansas, from interfering with the desegregation steps. . . . We were then forced to deny an attempt to place a two and one-half year moratorium on integration. . . . An 'emergency session' of the Arkansas legislature in August 1958 resulted in the enactment of legislation under which the Governor closed the Little Rock schools for the 1958-59 school year, which closing was subsequently held unconstitutional. . . . Thereafter, the Board sought to lease the public school facilities to a private school system operating on a racially segregated basis. The Court enjoined that transfer. . . .

"The Board continued to fight on. The 1959-60 school year found the Board assigning students to schools on the basis of criteria found in an Arkansas pupil assignment law. §§ 80-1519 through 80-1547 and 80-1234 Ark. Stats., 1947, Vol. 7 (1960 Replacement). We held in *Parham v. Dove*, 271 F.2d 132 (8th Cir. 1959) that this statute was not unconstitutional on its face. Thereafter, a number of students challenged the deviation from the geographical boundaries, and we then held that since the deviations were due to racial discrimination the application of this plan was unconstitutional; and we again called the Board and its representatives' attention to the continuing injunction in the first *Aaron* case requiring them to " 'take affirmative steps, on their own initiative' to facilitate and accomplish operation of the school district on a nondiscriminatory basis." *Norwood v. Tucker*, 287 F.2d 798, 809 (8th Cir. 1961)."

jective evil intent before being willing to intervene. Thus, the spirit and intent of the school administration assumes paramount importance. The practical effect of all this was stated in a concurring opinion in *Bradley v. School Board of Richmond:*

"While we join in permitting this experiment, we are not fully persuaded that the plan will be enough to enable the Negro pupils to extricate themselves from the segregation which has long been firmly established and resolutely maintained in Richmond. *A procedure which might well succeed under sympathetic administration could prove woefully inadequate in an antagonistic environment. The procedure cannot be separated from the spirit that produced it and will motivate its application. . . .*

"*A plan of desegregation is more than a matter of words. The attitude and purpose of public officials school administrators and faculties are an integral part of any plan and determine its effectiveness more than the words employed. If these public agents translate their duty into affirmative and sympathetic action the plan will work; if their spirit is obstructive, or at least negative, little progress will be made, no matter what form of words may be used.*"[64]

In the reapportionment cases, the federal courts were given a greater affirmative responsibility for implementation, with a far more satisfactory result. There they were ordered to apply an objective standard of "one man, one vote,"[65] and most importantly, were told to insure that constitutionally-acceptable plans were in force for the next election, whether by adoption of a state legislature or by order of the federal court.[66] In addition, allowable deviations from the constitutional standard were strictly defined.[67] In *Brown*, the Supreme Court, in discussing the problems to be considered, told the lower federal courts to weigh the public interest and convenience and the good faith of the school authorities against the rights of Negro school chil-

[64] 345 F.2d 310, 321-22 (4th Cir. 1965) (Sobeloff and Bell, J.J., concurring in part and dissenting in part) (emphasis added). *See also* Swann v. Charlotte Mecklenburg Board of Education, 369 F.2d 29 (4th Cir. 1966) (Sobeloff and Bell, JJ., concurring).

[65] Reynolds v. Sims, 377 U.S. 533, 568, 84 S. Ct. 1362, 1387 (1964):
"[A]s a basic constitutional standard, the Equal Protection Clause requires that seats in both houses . . . be apportioned on a population basis. Simply stated, an individual's right to vote . . . is unconstitutionally impaired when its weight is in a substantial fashion diluted when compared with the votes of citizens living in other parts of the state."

[66] *Id.* at 585:
"Remedial techniques in this new and developing area of the law will probably often differ with the circumstances of the challenged apportionment and a variety of local conditions. It is enough to say now that, once a State's legislative apportionment scheme has been found to be unconstitutional, it would be the unusual case in which a court would be justified in not taking appropriate action to insure that no further elections are conducted under the invalid plan."

[67] *Id.*; W.M.C.A. v. Lomenzo, 377 U.S. 633, 84 S. Ct. 1418 (1964); Maryland Committee for Fair Representation v. Tawes, 377 U.S. 656, 84 S. Ct. 1429 (1964); Davis v. Mann, 377 U.S. 678, 84 S. Ct. 1441 (1964); Lucas v. Forty-Fourth General Assembly, 377 U.S. 713, 84 S. Ct. 1527 (1964); Roman v. Sincock, 377 U.S. 695, 84 S. Ct. 1449 (1964).

dren to equal educational opportunities.[68] The opinion enunciates a rather unusual principle pursuant to which implementation of admitted constitutional rights could be conditioned and delayed. Indeed, the Court concedes in *Green* that the essence of *Brown II* was to secure an opening breach in the pattern of school segregation in the South, and that it intended no urgent pressure for immediate and complete enforcement of the desegregation obligation. The Court's focus in *Brown II* on judicial statesmanship is explained in *Green* in the following words:

> "It is, of course, true that for the time immediately after *Brown II* the concern was with making an initial break in a long-established pattern of excluding Negro children from schools attended by white children. The principal focus was on obtaining for those Negro children courageous enough to break with tradition a place in the 'white' schools. See, e.g., *Cooper v. Aaron*, 358 U. S. 1. Under *Brown II* that immediate goal was only the first step, however. The *transition to a unitary, non-racial system of public education was and is the ultimate end to be brought about; it was because of the 'complexities arising from the transition to a system* of public education freed of racial discrimination' that we provided for 'all deliberate speed' in the implementation of the principles of *Brown I*."[69]

Never before had the Court allowed constitutional rights to be enforced piecemeal, and hopefully it never will again. In fact, the entire notion is inconsistent with the concept of a right, unless the Negro's right to equal educational opportunity is conditioned. If so, it would be the first conditional right recognized under the Equal Protection Clause.[70]

---

[68] Brown v. Board of Education, 349 U.S. 294, 75 S. Ct. 753 (1955).

[69] Green v. County School Board, 391 U.S. 430, 88 S. Ct. 1689 (1968) (emphasis added). Once again Judge Wisdom's statement is apposite. Dissenting in Broussard v. Houston Independent School District, 395 F.2d 817, 822 (5th Cir. 1968), he stated:
"In the years that first followed the *school desegregation* cases, apologists for token desegregation could rationalize the Delphic riddle *Briggs* found in *Brown*. *Briggs* offered a middle way in a difficult transitory period. And the lack of specific directions in the Supreme Court's mandate in *Brown* along with a district court's inherent equitable power and primary responsibility for tailoring decrees to individual cases seemingly gave inferior courts wide latitude in their handling of school desegregation plans. Later and slowly, by the case-by-case development of the law, the Supreme Court put limits on the scope of an inferior court's authority to bless token action to desegregate schools."

[70] Indeed, in United States v. Jefferson County Board of Education, 372 F.2d 836, 868 (5th Cir. 1967), the court analyzed the problem as follows:
"The gradual transition the Supreme Court authorized was to allow the states time to solve the administration problems inherent in that changeover. *No delay would have been necessary if the right at issue in Brown had been only the right of individual Negro plaintiffs to admission to a white school. Moreover, the delay of one year in deciding Brown II and the gradual remedy Brown II fashioned can be justified only on the ground that the 'personal and present' right of the individual plaintiffs must yield to the overriding right of Negroes as a class to a completely integrated public education."*
The conditional limitations placed upon right to equal education in *Brown II* is justified on the basis of the overriding class interests. But what is a class except a group of similarly situated individuals?

Unfortunately, school boards, North and South, have been something less than affirmative in making necessary changes to accord Negro children their right to equal educational opportunities. For the last fourteen years they have hidden behind the *Briggs* rationale and have refused to act with diligence to end the dual school system. For the most part, movement occurred only under court compulsion or threat of loss of federal funds; in the main, a start towards compliance has come only after years of protracted litigation,[71] and even then the change has been grudging and small. The pattern has been for school authorities to retreat from the status quo as slowly as the courts, and now HEW, will tolerate. The result to date has been a series of frustrations, all at the expense of the black child. The prospects for the future are equally dim. Realistically, there is little hope of ever undoing the past and ushering in a new era of educational equality for Negro children.[72]

School boards willing to act have encountered difficulty in ascertaining what their *current* duty is, since, by definition in *Brown II*, that duty is continually shifting. Confusion in this regard only adds to the probability of protracted litigation. Judge Tuttle has voiced, in something akin to despair, the unmanageability of the task assigned to courts under the *Brown II* yardsticks in overseeing the desegregation process:

"This is the fourth appearance of this case before this court. This present appeal, coming as it does from an order of the trial court entered nearly eighteen months ago, on March 31, 1965, points up, among other things, the utter impracticability for supervising the manner in which segregated school systems break out of the policy of complete segregation into gradual steps of compliance with the constitutional requirements of *Brown v. Board of Education.* . . .

"One of the reasons for the impracticability of this method of over-

---

71 Thus, the prior history of Warren v. County School Board, 357 F.2d 452, 453 (4th Cir. 1966), a case involving the board of Arlington County, Virginia, located just across the Potomac from our nation's capital, reads as follows: School Board v. Allen, 240 F.2d 59 (4th Cir. 1956), *cert. denied*, 353 U.S. 910, 77 S. Ct. 664 (1957), *aff'g* Thompson v. County School Board, 144 F. Supp. 239 (E.D. Va. 1956); Thompson v. County School Board, 252 F.2d 929 (4th Cir.), *cert. denied*, 356 U.S. 958, 78 S. Ct. 994 (1958), *aff'g* 159 F. Supp. 567 (E.D. Va. 1957); Hamm v. County School Board, 263 F.2d 226 (4th Cir. 1959), *aff'g in part and remanding in part*, Thompson v. County School Board, 166 F. Supp. 529 (E. D. Va. 1958); Brooks v. County School Board, 324 F.2d 303 (4th Cir. 1963), *rev'g* Thompson v. County School Board, 204 F. Supp. 620 (E.D. Va. 1962).

72 United States v. Jefferson County Board of Education, 372 F.2d 836 (5th Cir. 1967). Judge Wisdom's summary of the situation is as follows:

"Under *Briggs*' blessing, school boards throughout this circuit first declined to take any affirmative action that might be considered a move towards integration. Later, they embraced the Pupil Placement Laws as likely to lead to no more thean a little token desegregation. Now they turn to freedom of choice plans, supervised by the district courts. As the defendants construe and administer these plans . . . there is little prospect of the plans ever undoing past discrimination or of coming close to the goal of equal educational opportunities."

seeing the transitional stages of operations of the school boards involved is that, under the Supreme Court's 'deliberate speed' provisions,
it has been the duty of the appellate courts to interpret and reinterpret
this language as time has grown apace, it is now being the twelfth school
year since the Supreme Court's decision."[73]

The absence of uniform standards in *Brown II* for use in enforcing the
rights articulated in *Brown I* has also had its effect. It is not uncommon for
adjoining school boards to be under federal court orders radically different in
approach.[74] The Fifth Circuit, which carries the heaviest school desegregation
case load,[75] addressed itself in *Jefferson* to the problem of non-uniformity
and bluntly admitted the absence of "good reason" for variations in the
schedule and manner of desegregation. There is a substantial time lag between the rendition of its opinions and their implementation by the district
courts, as well as a variance by the district courts from the circuit court's
ruling which they were obligated to follow.[76]

It was in no small part the failure of federal courts to secure compliance

---

[73] Davis v. Board of School Commissioners of Mobile County, 364 F.2d 896, 898
(5th Cir. 1966). *See also*, United States v. Jefferson County Board of Education, 372
F.2d 836, 854 (5th Cir. 1967):
  "But even school authorities willing to act have moved slowly because of uncertainty as to the scope of their duty to act affirmatively. This is attributable to (a)
  a misplaced reliance on the *Briggs* dictum that the Constitution 'does not require
  integration,' (b) a misunderstanding of the *Brown II* mandate, desegregate with
  'all deliberate speed,' and (c) a mistaken notion that transfers under the Pupil
  Placement Laws satisfy desegregation requirements."
See also Kelley v. Altheimer Arkansas Public School District No. 22, 378 F.2d 483,
492 (8th Cir. 1967):
  "Undue reliance on the 'deliberate speed' language in the *Brown* case, plus adher-
  ence to the dictum in *Briggs*, has resulted in a decision which makes it more difficult to achieve a non-racially operated school system."
[74] *See* United States v. Jefferson County Board of Education, 372 F.2d 836, 860
(5th Cir. 1967):
  "Of the 99 court-approved freedom of choice plans in this circuit, 44 do not desegregate all grades by 1967; 78 fail to provide specific, non-racial criteria for denying
  choices; 79 fail to provide any start toward faculty desegregation; only 22 provide
  for transfers to take courses not otherwise available; only 4 include the *Singleton*
  transfer rule."
[75] *Id.* at 860:

	1. *Case Load*		
	District Court	Court of Appeals	Supreme Court
Number of Cases	128	42	5
Number of Orders Entered	513	76	10

2. *Frequency of Appeals to this Court*

Number of Cases with one or more appeals	42
Number of Cases with two or more appeals	21
Number of Cases with three or more appeals	8
Number of Cases with four or more appeals	4
Number of Cases with five or more appeals	2

[76] *Id.* at 860-861.

with *Brown* that led to the adoption of the HEW guidelines in 1965-1966.[77] Part of the problem, finally put to rest in *McNeese v. Board of Education for School District 187*,[78] was that some courts were refusing to allow class suits and were requiring the completion of complicated state administrative remedies prior to resort to the federal court.

From the outset, unfortunately, federal courts have allowed recalcitrant school boards to take action which negated the basic thrust of *Brown I*. School building programs have been approved notwithstanding the fact that they manifestly can only lead to further segregation.[79] Obviously discriminatory pupil transfer provisions have been approved,[80] and school bus segregation is still common throughout the South.[81] Faculty discrimination has been tolerated until recently[82] and geographical zoning plans continue to be approved regardless of the fact that they inevitably produce complete or nearly complete segregation.[83]

To sum up, blacks have not made signficant advances towards achieve-

[77] United States v. Jefferson County Board of Education, 372 F.2d 836 (5th Cir. 1967); Singleton v. Jackson Municipal Separate School District, 348 F.2d 729 (5th Cir. 1965); Price v. Denison Independent School District, 348 F.2d 1010 (5th Cir. 1965); Davis v. Board of School Commissioners, 364 F.2d 896 (5th Cir. 1966); Kemp v. Beasley, 352 F.2d 14 (8th Cir. 1965); Smith v. Board of Education, 365 F.2d 770 (8th Cir. 1966). In this vein it is interesting to note that in 1964 the schools were still completely segregated in Clarendon County, the county involved in the Briggs litigation. *See* Burnson v. Board of Trustees, 311 F.2d 107 (4th Cir. 1962).

[78] 373 U.S. 668 (1963). *See also* Armstrong v. Board of Education, 323 F.2d 333 (5th Cir. 1963) and cases cited therein; Carlson v. Walker, 238 F.2d 724 (4th Cir. 1956); Covington v. Edwards, 264 F.2d 780 (4th Cir. 1959).

[79] Kelley v. Altheimer Arkansas Public School District, 378 F.2d 483 (8th Cir. 1967); Broussard v. Houston Independent School District, 395 F.2d 817 (5th Cir. 1968); Wright v. County School Board, 252 F. Supp. 378 (E.D. Va. 1966); Wheeler v. Durham City Board of Education, 346 F.2d 768 (4th Cir. 1965); Board of Public Instruction v. Braxton, 326 F.2d 616 (5th Cir. 1964); United States v. Board of Public Instruction, 395 F.2d 66 (5th Cir. 1968); Lee v. Macon County Board of Education, 267 F. Supp. 458 (M.D. Ala. 1967).

[80] *See* Goss v. Board of Education, 373 U.S. 683 (1963).

[81] Franklin v. Barbour County Board of Education, 259 F. Supp. 545 (M.D. Ala. 1966); Harris v. County Board of Education, 259 F. Supp. 167 (M.D. Ala. 1966); Carr v. County Board of Education, 253 F. Supp. 306 (M.D. Ala. 1966); Harris v. County Board of Education, 253 F. Supp. 276 (M.D. Ala. 1966); Wright v. County School Board, 252 F. Supp. 378 (E.D. Va. 1966); UNITED STATES COMMISSION ON CIVIL RIGHTS, RACIAL ISOLATION IN THE PUBLIC SCHOOLS (1967).

[82] *See* Rogers v. Paul, 382 U.S. 198, 86 S. Ct. 358 (1965); Bradley v. School Board, 382 U.S. 103, 86 S. Ct. 224 (1965); *See also* Augustus v. Board of Public Instruction, 306 F.2d 862 (5th Cir. 1962); Mapp v. Board of Education, 319 F.2d 571 (6th Cir. 1963); Gilliam v. School Board, 345 F.2d 325 (4th Cir. 1965); Bowditch v. Buncombe County Board of Education, 345 F.2d 329 (4th Cir. 1965).

[83] Deal v. Board of Education, 369 F.2d 55 (6th Cir. 1966); Bell v. School City of Gary, 324 F.2d 209 (7th Cir. 1963); Downs v. Board of Education, 336 F.2d 966 (10th Cir. 1964); Lynch v. Kinston School District Board of Education, 229 F. Supp. 740 (N.D. Ohio 1964); Webb v. Board of Education, 223 F. Supp. 466 (N.D. Ill. 1963); Evans v. Buchanan, 207 F. Supp. 820 (D. Del. 1962); Henry v. Godsell, 165 F. Supp. 87 (E.D. Mich. 1958); Brown v. Board of Education, 139 F. Supp. 468 (D.C. Kan. 1955); Gilliam v. School Board, 345 F.2d 325 (4th Cir. 1965).

ment of actual equal educational opportunity under the *Brown* decision. Lately, realization of the extent of the failure has been brought home to the federal courts and seems to have produced shock and rumblings. There should have been no surprise, however, because the Supreme Court's approach in *Brown II* was the one best calculated to produce the results it did and to leave the Constitution's guarantee of the right of Negro children to an equal education as only a legal abstraction.

IV. FUTURE INVOLVEMENT

As the United States Supreme Court was forced to deal with evasive schemes and tactics unquestioningly aimed at frustrating the implementation of school desegregation, it became increasingly clear that its "all deliberate speed" approach had not had the intended effect.[84] Instead of growing acceptance and good faith attempts at accommodation to the new constitutional requirements, there was defiance and hostility. Negroes who had placed great reliance on the law, and particularly on the Supreme Court, became restive and evidenced lessened confidence in the law.

As time passed without the process of desegregation quickening, the Court was forced to consider stricter standards than those enunciated in *Brown II.* Two per curiam decisions, *Bradley v. School Board of Richmond*[85] and *Rogers v. Paul,*[86] marked a turning point. With those cases, a decision had been reached that desegregation plans must be evaluated on the basis of their effectiveness as tools to implement *Brown I.* The new standard articulated in *Green v. County School Board*[87] required that these plans give "meaningful assurance of prompt and effective disestablishment" of school segregation. Henceforth, the yardstick to measure compliance with the Constitution's mandate was to be its effectiveness in eliminating the dual school system. School boards were said to have the legal obligation to do all that was necessary to eradicate segregation "root and branch," and were bound by the Constitution to present a plan of school desegregation that "promises realistically to work now."[88] Local federal courts for the first time were given guidelines containing objective standards for evaluating school board compliance. Good faith was still to be a part of the evaluation, but now the courts were told to weigh the plans "in the light of the facts at hand and in the light of any alternatives which may be shown as feasible and more promising in their effectiveness."[89] The method employed was not important—only results now counted. A school board must now justify any course of action it takes on the

---

[84] Cooper v. Aaron, 358 U.S. 1 (1958); Goss v. Board of Education, 373 U.S. 683 (1963); Griffin v. County School Board, 377 U.S. 218 (1964).

[85] 382 U.S. 103, 86 S. Ct. 358 (1965).

[86] 382 U.S. 198, 86 S. Ct. 224 (1965).

[87] Green v. County School Board, 391 U.S. 430, 88 S. Ct. 1689 (1968).

[88] *Id.* at 725.

[89] *Id.* at 724.

grounds that, among the various options available, the one chosen offers superior potentiality for bringing about full desegregation at the earliest practicable time. The Fourth,[90] Fifth,[91] and Eighth Circuit[92] which had already manifested restiveness with the slow pace of desegregation, and had begun to insist upon stricter standards may respond to these guidelines, but it is still doubtful that this new sense of urgency will in fact produce any more satisfactory results than the previous doctrine.

The threshold question is whether the Court understands that its result-oriented approach will speed up the process of desegregation only if the *Green* rationale is given an overall application throughout the federal court system. *Brown* was stymied not only by southern opposition but by *Briggs v. Elliott*[93] and by the Court's acceptance of the doctrine that administrative remedies such as pupil placement laws, which were quite obviously enacted to slow the pace of desegregation, had to be exhausted before application for relief in the federal court could be made.[94] In the Fifth Circuit *United States v. Jefferson*,[95] which followed the "effective result" doctrine, has been nullified by *Broussard v. Houston*.[96] *Broussard* allows an extensive construction program of neighborhood schools in the black residential community and will reduce the effectiveness of *Brown* and *Jefferson* to mere high-sounding rhetoric in the black child's quest for equal education in Houston.

The real problem is that equal education as a constitutional standard is very difficult to enforce. In fourteen years the judiciary has been unable to make even a dent in the pattern of school segregation in half of the school districts of the southern and border states. With the more rigid yardstick enunciated in *Green*, the desegregation pace may speed up considerably. This is doubtful, however; the present climate would seem to imply continued resistance to change and grudging movement at best.

Even if the climate becomes conducive to the voluntary elimination of most segregation, this will not conclude the matter since termination of formal segregation does not mean the end of segregation in fact. *Jefferson*[97] and *Dowell v. Board of Education of Oklahoma City Public Schools*[98] sought to devise approaches to prevent school systems from changing into systems segregated in fact in the process of disestablishment of the biracial

90 *See* Coppedge v. County Board of Education, 273 F. Supp. 289 (E.D.N.C. 1967), *aff'd*, 394 F.2d 410 (4th Cir. 1968).

91 United States v. Jefferson County Board of Education, 372 F.2d 836 (5th Cir. 1967); United States v. Board of Education, 396 F.2d 44 (5th Cir. 1968).

92 Kemp v. Beasley, 389 F.2d 178, 181 (8th Cir. 1968).

93 132 F. Supp. 776 (E.D.S.C. 1955).

94 *See, e.g.*, Carson v. Warlick, 238 F.2d 724 (4th Cir. 1956), *cert. denied*, 353 U.S. 910 (1957); Shuttlesworth v. Board of Education, 162 F.2d 372 (W.D. Ala.), *aff'd*, 358 U.S. 101 (1958).

95 372 F.2d 836 (5th Cir. 1967).

96 395 F.2d 817 (5th Cir. 1968).

97 372 F.2d 836 (5th Cir. 1967).

98 244 F. Supp. 971 (W.D. Okla. 1965).

school system. *Broussard v. Houston*[99] aside, demographic problems may prove insurmountable.[100]

De facto segregation has become a national problem, and its impact on the quality of education available to black students is as deleterious as is segregation required by law. It is clear that the ending of this form of segregation will require deliberate and conscious action by local and state authorities. Color blindness is thus no longer a virtue but a constitutional menace. Racial classifications to remedy past injury must be allowable or the Constitution's mandate of equality cannot be realized. "Courts will not say in one breath that public school systems may not practice segregation and in the next that they may do nothing to eliminate it."[101] The Constitution forbids invidious discrimination, and other racial classifications are generally suspect. Where, however, they can be justified as essential for the achievement of an important governmental function, no fourteenth amendment stircture is violated.[102] Thus, educational policy deliberately designed to improve the Negro's educational status would not run afoul in constitutional proscriptions.

Brown is a commitment to the thesis that the constitutional requirement of equal education can be met only with the total elimination of segregation. Yet, it is apparent that it will become increasingly impossible to remove or even to contain de facto segregation in urban educational systems except through organization of school districts on a metropolitan-wide basis and through the interdistrict adjustment of school district boundaries. There is, of course, no legal barrier to this form of educational change except restraints and limitations imposed by reasonableness and rationality.

State power to alter the boundary limits of its geographic subdivisions is complete;[103] but it is equally clear the artificial geographic state subdivisions cannot nullify a black child's constitutional guaranty of equal education.[104] Thus, a showing that a state through school district process had denied Negro children the right to equal education would necessitate such modification as to remove all impediments to the enforcement of the constitutional guaranty. Certainly vindication of the right to equal education by elimination of dividers which made for Negro-white school separation would be no more difficult than redistricting to enforce the one-man, one-vote principle.

In addition to the districting question there is the need for the equal allocation of educational resources between schools and school districts of

99 395 F.2d 817 (5th Cir. 1968).

100 REPORT OF THE NATIONAL ADVISORY COMMISSION ON CIVIL DISORDERS 390 (1968).

101 Wanner v. County School Board, 357 F.2d 452, 455 (4th Cir. 1960).

102 *See* Loving v. Virginia, 388 U.S. 1, 87 S. Ct. 1817 (1967); McLaughlin v. Florida, 379 U.S. 184, 85 S. Ct. 283 (1964).

103 *See, e.g.,* People v. Deatherage, 401 Ill. 25, 81 N.E.2d 581 (1948).

104 *See, e.g.,* Gomillion v. Lightfoot, 364 U.S. 339, 78 S. Ct. 961 (1960).

Negro concentration and those of white concentration. The *Plessy v. Ferguson* requirement of material equality, as *Roger v. Paul* made clear, still retains its vitality as the legal basis for this approach to equal education. Thus, equalization in the distribution of such educational facilities as books, libraries, courses of study, teacher certification, and specialists, teacher-student ratios, science laboratories and per-pupil expenditures could be mandated by court order.

The basic problem is that we are ignorant as yet of what the necessary ingredients of educational practice or methodology must be to insure equal education. The classroom mix seems to be the most important factor of all, and teacher expectations seems to be as vital as teacher qualification. The latter issue has been getting a great deal of concentrated attention, since it seems to be the easiest question to resolve.

There is also a growing clamor for something called community control or decentralization. The immediate and short-range effect of this movement is to intensify patterns of de facto segregation. The stated virtue of decentralization, however, is that it gives black parents opportunity to wield influence over the education of their children. School administrators and teachers will be conscious that they will be held to accountability by the black community, and hence only those with ability to empathize with and encourage the educational aspirations of black children will find it comfortable to teach black children. In truth, such accountability does not necessitate decentralization, but it does make it simpler for groups lacking in power to influence the conduct of schools in their own communities than if they have to compete with others for such influence.

There are some observers who feel that courts should not seek to involve themselves in difficult social issues such as equal education poses. There is certainly much to support that argument. The United States Supreme Court has announced a sweeping doctrine of constitutional insurance of equal education for Negroes which has had very little impact on the educational development of the vast majority of Negro youngsters in public schools in the fourteen years since it was first enunciated. Today segregated education in the South remains solidly entrenched, and segregation in the North has become so massive that it seems irrevocable. Both forms of segregation can be solved and trends reversed if the will and desire to do are present. But that is the basic problem. Whatever desire might have existed in 1954 to end apartheid in education has receded.

Thus, the courts will have to supervise public school systems if inequality in the allocation of educational resources and guaranty of equal-education opportunity is to become effective—a task studiously avoided by the judiciary for obvious reasons. The only alternative is to leave this difficult social problem in others' hands on the grounds that courts cannot deal with the issue effectively. That solution, however, will further aggravate the non-white community and strengthen its growing conviction that the courts, the law and the Constitution are solely for the benefit of white America. If for no other reason than that not to act is to harden the growing black-white polarization of our society, courts must continue to struggle with this complex problem and attempt to bring equal education closer to reality in the lives of black children.

PUBLIC ACCOMMODATIONS

BY *LeMARQUIS DeJARMON**

I. An Historical Anomaly

WHEN AMERICA'S LEGAL HISTORY is finally written, the struggle to make public accommodations truly accommodate all members of the public will certainly be regarded as the pivotal point at which this country first took a serious look at the ideals of its heritage. Prior to the open struggle for free access of all to places of public accommodation, men of good will, honor and high qualification could, without pangs of conscience, accept the fact that certain citizens were often read out of the term "public." Although government, federal and state, regulated and controlled these businesses, it nevertheless took the position that it was powerless to secure rights of accommodation to all of its citizens. Countless examples of this approach can be cited, but one will suffice for the purpose of this article.

In *State v. Clyburn*,[1] some eight years prior to the passage of Title II of the Civil Rights Act of 1964, several black youths, all college students, were arrested on charges of trespass for attempting to buy sodas in the "white" side of an ice cream parlor. An ordinance of the city of Durham, North Carolina, where this ice cream parlor was located, required that the races be separated.[2] The proprietor in order to secure a license had incurred the added expense of having his building constructed to comply with the ordinance. The North Carolina Supreme Court held that the 14th amendment rights of the student defendants had not been violated, stating that an individual proprietor is free to discriminate against customers on the basis of race.[3] The State was powerless to do anything other than enforce its "neutral" trespass law. The fact that the ordinance compelled the proprietor to construct his building a certain way in order to enforce segregation was of no moment.

* *LeMARQUIS DeJARMON. A. B. 1939, Howard University; LL.B (J.D.) 1948, Western Reserve University; LL.M. 1962, New York University; Professor of Law, North Carolina College; Secretary, North Carolina State Advisory Committee, United States Civil Rights Commission.*

[1] 247 N.C. 455, 101 S.E.2d 295 (1957).

[2] Durham, N.C., Code ch. 13, § 42 (1947):
"In all licensed restaurants, public eating places and 'weenie shops' where persons of the white and colored races are permitted to be served with, and eat food, and are allowed to congregate, there shall be provided separate rooms for separate accommodations of each race. The partition between the rooms shall be constructed by wood, plaster, or brick or like materials, and shall reach from the floor to the ceiling. Any person violating this section shall upon conviction, pay a fine of ten dollars, and each day's violation thereof shall constitute a separate and distinct offense."

[3] State v. Clyburn, 247 N.C. 455, 101 S.E.2d 295 (1957).

The crowning irony of this episode occurred a few short years later, following the wave of lunch counter "sit-ins" which swept through the South. In *State v. Avent*[4] the United States Supreme Court remanded a "sit-in" case to the North Carolina court for a determination of the role of the Durham ordinance in the arrest and convictions. Thereafter, the city repealed this ordinance[5] and the *Avent* case was dismissed.[6] After the ordinance was repealed, a group of black citizens urged the City Council to pass a public accommodations ordinance. On advice of the city attorney the council took the position that under the state statutes it did not have the power to adopt a public accommodations ordinance. In reply to an inquiry as to why the statute empowering the council to pass the earlier ordinance requiring segregation did not empower the council to guarantee free access to places of public accommodations to all citizens, the city attorney explained that the earlier ordinance was, in fact, ultra vires. Thus for years Durham had relentlessly enforced an ultra vires ordinance to the disadvantage of one-third of its citizens[7] and at the expense to entrepreneurs of additional building and maintenance costs.[8]

The author has dealt in detail with this one ordinance because it is typical[9] of the conditions which prompted the drive for the passage of Title II of the Civil Rights Act of 1964.[10] The extent to which state and local governments employed apparently neutral laws to block black citizens' access to the marketplace is one of the anomalies of history. Their actions raise the fundamental question of whether a republican government has the power and duty to assure free access to the marketplace, or whether access to the marketplace—either as producer or consumer—is to be manipulated exclusively by the "lions" of the marketplace.

From the feudal period through the development of the "black codes" at the turn of the century the consumer's right to participate in the marketplace was a source of little legal controversy. A marketplace without consumers is, to say the least, a fruitless venture. In England the theory behind what has become known as the "giant trilogy"[11] was that the consumer should have available the best possible product or service. A review of these earlier cases shows that, where the consumer would have gained better services and goods as a result of group action forcing inefficient operators from the scene, the courts were sympathetic.[12] Conversely, where group

4 North Carolina v. Avent, 373 U.S. 375, 83 S. Ct. 1311 (1963).

5 DURHAM, N.C., CODE ch. 13, § 42 (1947).

6 State v. Avent, 253 N.C. 580, 118 S.E.2d 47 (1961).

7 Taken from the 1960 Census.

8 Shortly after the repeal of the ordinance, the ice cream parlor, built in compliance therewith, was under new management and under a new name.

9 See Pollitt, *Dime Store Demonstrations*, 1960 DUKE L.J. 315 (1960).

10 42 U.S.C. § 2000(a) (1964).

11 Mogul Steamship Co. v. McGregor, [1892] A.C. 25; Allen v. Flood, [1898] A.C. 1; Quinn v. Leatherm, [1901] A.C. 495.

12 *See* English Hop Growers, Ltd. v. Dering, [1928] 2 K.B. 174.

activities would limit or hinder the consumer's access to goods and services, the courts did not hesitate to strike down the combination.[13] In the United States our anti-trust laws have been aimed at commercial competition which would limit the consumer's participation in the free flow of goods and services in the common marketplace.[14] Thus, the "black codes"—and the laws and customs they spawned—were indeed an historical anomaly in that they were acts restricting the consumer's freedom in the marketplace, while in other areas government was seeking to expand it.

II.   Constitutionalization of the Theory of Reliance

Historically, the right to demand services appears to have been predicated on the concept of dependence. At common law the innkeeper and the common carrier could not deny their services to travellers because the latter had come to depend and rely on those services.[15] On the other hand, businessmen whose services were not directly essential to the public good were free to deal with their patrons as they might choose.[16] The innkeeper was held to a higher standard than, say, the race track operator, because the lonely wayfarer in the middle of the forest was much more dependent on the wayside inn than were the patrons of the "sport of kings" on the race track operator. In a country which is fast becoming a nation of multi-family, high-rise apartments, however, dependence on certain public accommodations for essential services becomes more acute.

Professor Berle[17] suggests that this theory of reliance and its consequent theory of legal power to demand certain activity from proprietors and business associations is in this country becoming constitutionalized:

"The Bill of Rights and the Fourteenth and Fifteenth Amendments would thus have direct application to and also throughout any corporation whose position gave it power. . . .

"This is new as a rule of law, but it is typically American in tradition. Instead of a social attack on an enterprise as an enterprise, with nationalization or socialization as the aim, this is the application of a set of general rules to the organisms and individuals who govern them, with a view to achieving a freer order of individual life. Under this theory certain human values are protected by the American Constitution; any fraction of the governmental system, economic as well as legal, is prohibited from invading or violating them. The principle is logical because, as has been seen, the modern state has set up, and come to rely on, the corporate system to carry out functions for which in modern life by community demand the government is held ultimately responsible. It is unlimited

13 *See* McEllistrim v. Ballymac Elligott Co-operative, [1919] A.C. 548.
14 Berle, *Constitutional Limitation on Corporate Activity—Protection of Personal Rights from Invasion through Economic Power*, 100 U. Pa. L. Rev. 933, 936 (1952).
15 Wood v. Leadbitter, 13 M & W 838, 153 Eng. Rep. 351 (Ex. 1845).
16 Marone v. Washington Jockey Club, 227 U.S. 633, 33 S. Ct. 401 (1913).
17 Berle, *supra* note 14.

because it follows corporate power whenever that power actually exists. It resolves the conflict between the property notion that an owner can do what he likes with his own and the governmental concept that a public agency is obliged to serve all alike within strict constitutional limitations, evenhandedly, up to the limit of its capacity. Instead of nationalizing the enterprise, this doctrine 'constitutionalizes' the operation."[18]

The Berle view not only answers the question of the appropriateness of the demand for public accommodation laws upon our present legal institutions, but also explains, to some extent, limitations in the coverage of Title II of the Civil Rights Act of 1964. It is apparent from a cursory reading of Title II that those public accommodations which are directly essential to the citizen's well-being and services or accommodations on which citizens as a community have come to rely are expressly covered while those on which such reliance is minimal or not vital are not covered, except as they are associated with a covered accommodation.

In this light the "sit-in" demonstrations of the sixties were not wholly and exclusively concerned with "civil rights" as we refer to it today, but were part of a greater political, economic and constitutional problem. In an industrialized society where the community must rely on the titans of the marketplace to furnish its needs and conveniences, the commerce clause takes on an expanded political as well as economic significance. A citizen may indeed be deprived of his rights if he cannot buy what he needs or if he cannot rest after a long trip on limited access federally financed highways. The Constitution of the United States, together with the Bill of Rights, was dedicated to the preservation of the prevalent 18th century philosophy, exemplified by Jeremy Bentham, that the individual was the chief concern and the chief integer of organized society. Thus, constitutional government's *raison d'etre* is to protect the individual from a despotic state. In this day of concentrated economic power does not the individual, the integer of organized society, need the same protection from the non-state, yet public, organism which controls the goods and services on which his livelihood and creative comforts depend?

In the period immediately preceeding the passage of Title II the judiciary recognized the merit of this view and struck down many of the legislative and political subterfuges employed to ensure that a significant portion of the American people would continually be deprived of free participation as consumers in an open marketplace.[19] Also during this period, both political parties in their quadrennial convention platforms added planks

---

[18] *Id*. at 943.

[19] *See* Edwards v. South Carolina, 372 U.S. 229, 83 S. Ct. 680 (1963); Fields v. South Carolina, 375 U.S. 44, 84 S. Ct. 157 (1963); Cox v. Louisiana, 379 U.S. 536, 85 S. Ct. 453 (1965); North Carolina v. Avent, 373 U.S. 375, 83 S. Ct. 1311 (1963). *See also* Pollitt, *supra* note 9.

calling for free access to places of public accommodation.[20] The indignity suffered by several foreign diplomats upon being denied service at places of public accommodation along the infamous Route 40 between New York and Washington had created several embarrassing incidents for the executive branch of our federal government[21] and was a compelling reason for the political pronouncements.

III.   TITLE II OF THE 1964 CIVIL RIGHTS ACT

The legislative branch finally responded, after a year and a half of debate and the shock of a presidential assassination, with Title II of the Civil Rights Act of 1964.[22] The 1964 Act, instead of being enacted as an enforcing provision of section 1982 of Title 42, United States Code,[23] was enacted pursuant to Congress' plenary power to regulate commerce between and among the several states.[24] Title II survived several attacks on its constitutionality shortly after its enactment.[25]

Once the constitutionality of the Act was settled, subsequent questions arose concerning Title II's coverage. The Act itself prohibits discrimination on grounds of race, color, or national origin in hotels, motels, theaters, places of amusement presenting entertainment which moves in interstate commerce, transient lodging facilities (with the "Mrs. Murphy" exception), restaurants, luncheon counters, and gasoline stations which sell food or goods which move in interstate commerce or which service interstate travelers. In addition, the Act covers establishments which either contain or are located within the premises of any establishment specified in the Act. Further, the statute reaches discrimination that is supported by state action or is carried on under color of law, custom, or usage, enforced by officials of the state or required by action of a state or a political subdivision thereof.

[20] *See* N.Y. News Convention Bureau, July 27, 1960.

[21] It has been suggested that these incidents hastened the completion of the "John F. Kennedy Freeway" which took most of the diplomatic interstate travel off U.S. Route 40. In addition, President Kennedy, in a message to Congress, proposed a bill, the stated purpose of which was: "to promote the general welfare by eliminating discrimination based on race, color, religion or national origin in . . . public accommodations through the exercise by Congress of the powers conferred upon it . . . to enforce the provisions of the Fourteenth and Fifteenth Amendments, to regulate commerce among the several states and to make laws necessary and proper to execute the powers conferred upon it by the Constitution." H.R. Doc. No. 124, 88th Cong., 1st Sess. 14 (1964).

[22] 42 U.S.C. § 2000(a).

[23] This section, one of the surviving sections of the Act of May 31, 1870, ch. 114, 16 Stat. 144, was exacted pursuant to the 13th amendment to the U. S. Constitution. Four years after the passage of the Title II, the Supreme Court directed Congress' attention to its all but forgotten enactment in the case of Jones v. Alfred H. Mayer Co., 392 U. S. 409, 88 S. Ct. 2186 (1968).

[24] *See* U.S. CONST. art. 1, § 8.

[25] Heart of Atlanta Motel v. United States, 379 U.S. 241, 85 S. Ct. 348 (1964); Katzenbach v. McClung, 379 U.S. 294, 85 S. Ct. 377 (1964); Willis v. Pickrick Restaurant, 231 F. Supp. 396 (N.D. Ga. 1964).

The bulk of the litigation in the area of public accommodations for the past three years has centered upon the Act's coverage. The NAACP Legal Defense and Educational Fund, as of December, 1967, had forty-five cases involving public accommodations on its docket.[26] A survey of the recent volumes of the Race Relations Law Reporter[27] will reveal a much longer list of cases dealing with individual instances of racial discrimination where the sole issue is that of coverage of the Act. It is unnecessary to review these cases in detail. Suffice it to say these numerous cases illustrate the weakness of basing Title II on the commerce clause rather than declaring free access to places of public accommodations to be a fundamental incident of federal citizenship. Since practical politics requires that the legislative branch be primarily concerned with the possible, the case-by-case approach to extending coverage of the Act may well be the price that had to be paid to secure any Congressional action. Although the case-by-case approach casts the expense of litigation upon those who have borne the brunt of discrimination for more than a century, the recent case of *Newman v. Piggie Park Enterprises*[28] lightens the burden a little by allowing the plaintiff to recover attorney's fees.

Since the statutory inclusions and exclusions of Title II appear to be patterned after the historical test of dependence—that an interstate traveler is more dependent on the hotel, motel, and various facilities contained or located within them, than he is on a barber shop, beauty parlor or bowling alley—the coverage of the Act will continue to be extended by case-by-case litigation. As America moves toward a shorter working day and its citizens have more time for recreation and relaxation, the need to re-evaluate the narrow construction of that provision[29] which bars discrimination in sports arenas and places of entertainment becomes apparent. The rapid expansion of metropolitan centers and the development of "strip cities" will increase the demand and dependence on such facilities. The law must respond to these demands and needs in a meaningful manner.

Private clubs "not in fact open to the public" are expressly exempted from the Act. Congress recognized that a bona fide private club should be able to restrict its services to its members; however, the Act is silent on

26 *See* Supplement Docket Report, NAACP Legal Defense and Educational Fund, December, 1967.

27 *See* 10 RACE REL. L. REP. (1965); 11 RACE REL. L. REP. (1966); 12 RACE REL. L. REP. (1967).

28 390 U.S. 400, 88 S. Ct. 964 (1968).

29 42 U.S.C. 2000(a)(b)(3) (1964). Any motion picture theater, concert hall, sports arena, stadium or other places of exhibition or entertainment, originally outdoor recreational facilities such as swimming, boating, picnicking, roller skating, etc. were not included. "Place of exhibition and entertainment" was construed as a place which presented performances rather than a place of enjoyment. *See, e.g.,* Robertson v. Johnson, 249 F. Supp. 618 (E.D. La. 1966); Kyles v. Paul, 263 F. Supp. 412 (D. Ark. 1967); Miller v. Amusement Enterprises, 259 F. Supp. 523 (E.D. La. 1966). *See also* Shield v. Midtown Bowling Lanes, 11 Race Rel. L. Rep. (M.D. Ga. 1966).

whether clubs can discriminate in the selection of those members. The thrust of the phrase "not in fact open to the public" was directed at the subterfuge of using the private club form to conduct a discriminatory public business. Thus, if one organized his business as a "club" but issued membership cards to all comers except Negroes, obviously he would be covered by the Act as being "in fact open to the public."[30] The future value of this section is that it is an expression of the Congressional awareness that, if Title II is to be meaningful, the enforcers and the interpreters of the Act must look beyond the mere form to the substance of the alleged discrimination.

Subsection (d) of the Act,[31] although used rather sparingly, has been narrowly and technically construed. In *Tyson v. Cazes*[32] a Negro sought service in a bar in Plaquemine, Louisiana; when he was refused service and failed to leave, he was arrested. Since Plaquemine had an ordinance prohibiting bars from selling alcoholic beverages to blacks and whites on the same premises, the plaintiff filed suit for injunctive relief under subsection (d). The district court[33] held that, even though the separate service ordinance[34] was on the books, the discrimination was the private choice of the operator and therefore the subsequent arrest was not "state action." The court of appeals noted that, while the appeal was pending, the separate service ordinance had been repealed,[35] and ruled that it was the coincidence of the prohibitory ordinance and the operator's refusal to serve the plaintiff that made the operator's conduct unlawful under subsection (d). Since the ordinance had been repealed, and was not likely to be re-enacted, the question was rendered moot and the case was dismissed.[36]

In *Tyson* the court appears to have ignored the provision condemning racial discrimination where it "is carried on under color of any custom or

---

[30] When the 18th amendment was repealed, some state laws authorized the licensing of bars, taverns and clubs. The private club license was substantially less in price than the bar and tavern licenses. Many bar owners resorted to the practice of organizing private clubs in order to take advantage of the less expensive license fee. The practice has been resurrected under Title II in order to take advantage of subsection (e) of the Act. *See* The Washington Post, Aug. 6, 1964, § A, at 6, col. 4; Wall Street Journal, Jul. 22, 1964, at 1, col. 4. *See also* United States v. Northwest Louisiana Restaurant Club, 256 F. Supp. 151 (W.D. La. 1966).

[31] 42 U.S.C. § 2000a(d) (1964).

[32] 363 F.2d 742 (5th Cir. 1966).

[33] 238 F. Supp. 937 (E.D. La. 1965).

[34] PLAQUEMINE, LA., ORDINANCES ch. 3, § 3-8:
"It shall be unlawful for any person to sell spiritous, venous or malt liquor of alcoholic content of more than 3.2 per cent by volume for consumption on the same premises to persons of the white and Caucasian race and persons of the Negro or black race. (Ord. No. 683, § 7, 11-30-61)."

[35] PLAQUEMINE, LA., ORDINANCE 723.

[36] Compare Anderson v. City of Albany, 321 F.2d 649 (5th Cir. 1963). In a similar case, Robertson v. Johnson, 376 F.2d 43 (5th Cir. 1967), the Court of Appeals held that a complaint stated a cause of action against a police officer who arrested a white woman for vagrancy because she was sitting in a predominantly Negro bar in New Orleans. The Court of Appeals cited the Black's Law Dictionary definition of "custom" and "usage" and held that the plaintiff, upon proof, would be entitled to relief.

usage required or enforced by officials of the state or political subdivision thereof." In the light of the history of Plaquemine Parish it is not unreasonable to assume that this tavern operator would have found it most difficult to secure or retain a license for his business had he not complied with the separate service ordinance. It is also fairly clear that "color of custom and usage" in Plaquemine Parish continued to exist long after the repeal of the ordinance itself, and that the officials of this political subdivision will have little hesitancy in enforcing that custom and usage. For the *Tyson* case to turn on the subsequent repeal of the prohibitory ordinance is to pay homage to form and ignore substance. The simple truth is that the Negro cannot buy what the white man can buy in Plaquemine Parish.[37]

The future effectiveness of Title II will depend in large measure upon the weight given to the requirements of custom and usage. There are numerous businesses not expressly covered by the Act which render needed and vital services to the public but whose clientele is restricted on racial grounds due to the custom of the community. Since they are not among those businesses enumerated in subsection (d), these businesses have continued operating on a racially discriminatory basis since passage of the Civil Rights Act of 1964.

Coin-operated laundromats are a prime example. Prior to the passage of the 1964 Act, coin-operated laundromats in a number of southern cities were required by law, custom and usage to separate the races. Many of these laundromats were located in shopping centers and other broadly frequented commercial areas and restricted their services solely to members of the Caucasian race. After the passage of the 1964 Act, when all the expressly covered establishments in shopping centers were required to cease discrimination, some of the laundromats persisted in their customary manner. When Negroes attempted to use these facilities, they were barred and frequently arrested. Trial courts have consistently taken the position that, since the law had changed and the local statute or ordinance was inoperative, no violation of the Act had occurred. The fact that community attitudes, as well as those of individuals, had been created and nourished by a century of life under segregation laws often enforced by violent white racists groups, has received little judicial recognition. Although the courts have shown little hesitancy since 1964 in striking down discrimination *required* by statute or ordinance, the by-product of *custom* generated by years of "legal" discrimination under these statutes and ordinances is often summarily dismissed.

In spite of these areas where the Act has been less than fully effective, the response of the public as a whole has been such that a favorable climate has been created in which even these problems may be corrected. It could well be that the social climate created by the public response to Title II contributed to the development of the law in other areas. There are many businesses, about which there may have existed a bona fide question of cover-

37 Jones v. Alfred H. Mayer Co., 392 U.S. 409, 88 S. Ct. 2186 (1968).

age, which nevertheless abandoned their former discriminatory practices when it became apparent that covered businesses in the community were not experiencing difficulty. From the standpoint of competition it was thought wise to desegregate despite the question of coverage. How widespread this reaction may be, of course, is not fully known, but it is of no little significance that the NAACP Legal Defense and Educational Fund has come to the conclusion that most of the basic legal questions under Title II have been firmly resolved.[38]

IV. State and Local Activity

Even if the Legal Defense and Education Fund is correct in its view that the legal problems on the federal level are resolved, there are still many areas in which state and local governments can work to advantage. Until recent years this has been the area of greatest neglect. It has been assumed that free access to places of public accommodation was a right which the states were bound to protect; Mr. Justice Bradley in the *Civil Rights Cases* stated:

"We have discussed the question presented by the law on the assumption that a right to enjoy equal accommodations and privileges in all inns, public conveyances and places of public amusement, is one of the essential rights of the citizen which no State can abridge or interfere with."[39]

Implicit in this statement is the assumption that the states have a duty to protect this "essential right of the citizens" as effectively as other rights of the citizens, since rights can only exist under law. The states have readily enforced and re-enforced rights of property with the full weight of the state's power, but the essential human rights of equal enjoyment and free access, which Mr. Justice Bradley assumed to be just as essential, have been both abrogated by the "black codes" in the South and ignored by the North.

Since 1964, however, several states—both northern and southern—have created state anti-discrimination commissions to supplement the Federal Act. Some cities have enacted anti-discrimination ordinances establishing Human Relations Commissions to conciliate and settle cases of discrimination in places of public accommodation. Some of these ordinances authorize the city attorney to prosecute where conciliation has failed.[40]

Other communities, however, particularly in the South, have been opposed to state and local government activity supplementing the Federal

[38] Letter from NAACP Legal Defense and Educational Fund to all cooperating attorneys, dated May, 1968.

[39] Civil Rights Cases, 109 U.S. 3, 19, 3 S. Ct. 18, 27 (1883).

[40] This list is intended to be illustrative rather than exhaustive: New York, N.Y., Administrative Code No. 55, 1955, 1961, 1966; Nashville, Tenn., Ordinance 65-697; Wisconsin, ch. 439 of Act of 1965; Los Angeles, Cal., Ordinance 131, 700; Providence, R.I., Ordinance ch. 1570 (1963); New Jersey Ch. 17, Acts of 1966; Sacramento, Cal. Ordinance 918; Charlotte, N.C. Ordinance (1968); Greensboro, N.C., Ordinance (1967); Raleigh, N.C., Ordinance.

Act. The author knows of no southern state which has enacted a state-wide statute creating a State Human Relations Commission to implement a state-wide anti-discrimination statute. North Carolina, however, has created in the Office of the Governor an advisory agency known as the North Carolina Good Neighbor Council. This council consists of a chairman, vice chairman, and eighteen members. It employs a staff of six. According to its chairman,[41] the council works in an advisory capacity in connection with complaints under Title II of the Civil Rights Act of 1964. The complaints it receives are investigated and reported to the proper authorities of the United States Commission on Civil Rights. The chairman noted that the council has received very few complaints relating to Title II violations.[42]

The lack of state-wide anti-discrimination statutes has increased the demand for local ordinances. In some communities these demands have met with two avenues of resistance: (1) state law does not give the municipality the power to create a local commission, and (2) federal law has pre-empted the field. Neither argument is persuasive.

Most, if not all, of the charters of the cities where the lack of power argument has been raised give the city the power to enact ordinances to promote the peace, good government and welfare of the city, the morals and happiness of its citizens, and to perform all municipal functions. Municipalities have had little difficulty in finding, under this broad grant, the power to pass ordinances similar to the "Weenie Shop ordinance,"[43] or to enact curfew ordinances—as so many of them did immediately following the assassination of Dr. Martin Luther King.[44] Yet it is insisted that these broad grants of power do not enable municipalities to enforce and protect what since 1875 has been assumed to be an essential right of the citizen.[45] It strains credibility to assert that the promotion of good local government—a government close to the people—does not encompass the protection of the essential rights of the people.[46]

The assertion that federal law has pre-empted the field is equally spurious. As pointed out in the beginning of this paper, the Federal Public Accommodations Act was passed pursuant to the commerce clause of the United States Constitution. There are a large variety of business enterprises whose effect on interstate commerce is either minimal or non-existent. It is in this area where state and local governments can properly operate, and many

[41] Letter from D. S. Coltrane, chairman, to author, March 29, 1968.

[42] The author has had some contact with the council. It is known that the council has exerted a great deal of influence in the creation of local community relations councils in several cities throughout the state. The conciliation work of these local councils may be responsible for so few complaints reaching the state level.

[43] *Supra* note 2.

[44] *See* The Washington Post, Apr. 9, 1968, at 1, col. 3.

[45] *Supra* note 39.

[46] *See Genesis* 27:22: "The voice is Jacob's voice, but the hands are the hands of Esau."

of them have.[47] It is well known that when Congress enacted the Wagner Act[48] and the Taft-Hartley Act[49] several industrial states enacted little Wagner and little Taft-Hartley Acts in an effort to promote industrial peace in those industries not covered by the Federal Acts. None of these acts, operating on a purely local basis, have been declared invalid on the ground of pre-emption. A local anti-discrimination act enforceable by a local human relations commission, operating in the areas not affecting interstate commerce, is as lawful and desirable as the state's local labor relations acts.

The reinforcement by state and local agencies of the ideal born in Title II of the 1964 Civil Rights Act remains the great unfinished task of local government officials at this historical junction. Local statesmen must rise above the minutiae of daily life and the nostalgia for things that cannot again be, and face the present-day reality that discrimination against any individual or group because of race, religion, national origin or cultural background promotes tensions and conflicts; that such prejudice, discrimination, tensions and conflict are a menace to peace, public welfare, and security; and that the elimination of such prejudice and intolerance promotes public health, morals, and welfare. This is in the highest tradition of good government.

The most effective way to accomplish these goals appears to be by way of local community relations commissions or councils, composed of representatives from a cross section of the community which they are to serve.[50] The commissions should have the power to receive complaints, investigate them, subpoena records and witnesses, engage in conciliation and mediation of complaints, propose and recommend solutions, make reports to the local governing body and the people, and recommend further legislation to the local legislative authority. If the success of our jury system can be taken as an example, then it is certain that the people of a community will respond more favorably to the efforts of a local community relations commission composed of their peers than they will to a commission far removed from the scene.

The effective implementation of Title II by state and local governments is in the historical tradition of a government of a free society. Free access to the marketplace, either as producer or consumer, should be unencumbered by monopolistic tendencies on the one hand or racially discriminatory exclusion on the other. If the zeal, vigor, energy and skill which public officials have employed in the past to establish and perpetuate an American brand of

---

[47] *See* Brown v. Draper, Pa. Human Rel. Comm. Doc. No. P376, Nov. 3, 1965; In Matter of Babbert's Club, Ohio Civil Rights Comm. No. 17, Aug. 24, 1964 and Nov. 10, 1964.

[48] National Labor Relations Act, 49 Stat. 449, 29 U.S.C. § 151 et seq. (1935).

[49] Labor-Management Relations Act, 1947, 29 U.S.C. § 141 et seq. (1964).

[50] The underlying principle of our jury system is that it is representative of the community where the crime was committed. The jury system is deeply cherished in our jurisprudence because it is close to the people.

apartheid will be employed by these officials—federal, state, and local—to implement, nourish and develop the ideals underlying Title II, the dawn of the 21st century will find us one nation—immigrants all, Americans all. True, since 1776, such a state of affairs in this country has never been. But if America is to accomplish its historical mission and keep faith with its ideals and its posterity—why not?

THE NEWPORT NEWS AGREEMENT— ONE BRIEF SHINING MOMENT IN THE ENFORCEMENT OF EQUAL EMPLOYMENT OPPORTUNITY

BY ALFRED W. BLUMROSEN*

I. Introduction

IN MARCH OF 1966, the United States Government conducted negotiations with the Newport News Shipbuilding and Drydock Company to remedy the pattern of racial discrimination against the Negro workers at the shipyard. During these negotiations the government utilized its total power, including the Equal Employment Opportunity Commission, the Departments of Justice, Labor, Defense and Navy, to combat employment discrimination. The result was a detailed written agreement providing for substantive revisions in the industrial relations structure at the shipyard and establishing procedures for its administration.[1] The initial administration of the agreement took approximately one year. During that year, more than 3,000 of the 5,000 Negro employees at the yard were promoted, and 100 became or were designated to become supervisors.[2] Our estimate was that the agreement added approximately one million dollars a year in income to the Negro community in the Newport News area.[3] Later, this agreement came under sharp criticism from Senator Fanin of Arizona and *Barron's* business magazine.[4]

* ALFRED W. BLUMROSEN. A.B. 1950, J.D. 1953, University of Michigan; Professor of Law, Rutgers University School of Law. Professor Blumrosen was Chief of Conciliations for the U.S. Equal Employment Opportunity Commission, 1965–67, and serves as a consultant to the EEOC.

Editor's Note: Professor Blumrosen served in 1968 as special Attorney for the Civil Rights Division, Department of Justice, dealing with employment discrimination matters. He served as a consultant to the New Jersey Civil Rights Commission and to Rutgers University with respect to construction employment problems. He is a member of the Labor Arbitration panels of the American Arbitration Association, the Federal Mediation and Conciliation Service, and the New Jersey Mediation Board.

The views expressed in this article are those of Professor Blumrosen and do not necessarily reflect the opinions of the EEOC, the Justice Department or the New Jersey Division on Civil Rights.

[1] The full text of the Agreement appears as app. I p. 299 *infra*.

[2] The figures are conservative. In my analysis for the Equal Employment Opportunity Commission entitled "The Impact and Significance of the Newport News Shipbuilding Agreement," I reported that the shipyard has confirmed that 3890 promotion actions had taken place with respect to the Negro employees at the shipyard. Some of these involved multiple promotions for the same individual. See app. III p. 310 *infra*.

[3] Precise figures showing the increase in wages to Negro employees are not available at this time.

[4] Barron's initial criticism (*see* app. II p. 307 *infra*) was later inserted in the Congressional Record by Senator Fanin. On August 22, 1967, Senator Javitts published in

97

As this article is written in the fall of 1968, the Newport News agreement stands alone. The various government agencies have not combined their resources to repeat the type of performance demonstrated there. For those involved in the struggle to end employment discrimination through law this fact represents the greatest frustration. The government has the power, and it has the machinery and the experience, to end discrimination in major concerns across the country without relying on the long drawn out administrative and judicial process. Newport News points the way to an efficient, thorough and fair method of eliminating discrimination in industrial relations systems. But it has not been duplicated or seized upon as an example. Rather, we seem bent either on judicializing these problems through formal judicial and administrative hearings or on holding high level general conferences.[5]

One of the reasons for writing this article is to prevent the lesson of Newport News from being lost in the rapid personnel changes among those who administer equal employment opportunity laws. Already many of the people involved in the original agreement have left the government, either voluntarily or otherwise.[6] Once the agreement came under senatorial attack,

the Congressional Record a reply to the charges of Barron's Magazine which called the criticisms of the EEOC "unjustified." This reply (see app. III p. 310 infra) included my analysis of "The Impact and Significance of the Newport News Agreement." On September 18, 1967, Senator Fanin responded with further criticism (see app. IV p. 313 infra) and continued his attack on the EEOC in "Does Washington Force Racial Bias?", NATION'S BUSINESS, Mar. 1968, p. 77, and in his minority report to S. 1111, 90th Cong., 2d Sess., 1968, opposing a bill to give the Commission cease and desist powers.

[5] The Office of Federal Contract Compliance in the Department of Labor, which administers the anti-discrimination clause in government contracts, made an effort at a systemwide settlement in connection with the Crown Zellerbach Corporation. See the aftermath in Crown Zellerbach Corp. v. Wirtz, 281 F. Supp. 337 (D.D.C. 1968) and in United States v. Local 189, United Papermakers and Paperworkers, 282 F. Supp. 39 (E.D. La. 1968). Since then, it has moved in the direction of formality by calling hearings with respect to the issue of compliance with the executive order involving five companies. At present writing, September 1968, two of the hearings are underway.

The Civil Rights Division of the Department of Justice, acting under Section 707 of the Civil Rights Act of 1964 has instituted more than 30 suits and is concentrating on this activity. The EEOC has held a public hearing on the Textile Industry in the Carolinas and on White Collar Discrimination in New York (see EEOC, HEARINGS ON DISCRIMINATION IN WHITE COLLAR EMPLOYMENT (1968)) and has conducted interagency confrontations with employers in cooperation with such other federal agencies as the Food and Drug Administration.

[6] The following is a partial list of the positions whose occupants have been replaced since the negotiation of the Newport News Agreement in March, 1966, in the departments of government concerned with it.

A. *Justice Department:* Assistant Attorney General for Civil Rights; First Assistant A.G., several trial attorneys.

B. *Equal Employment Opportunity Commission:* Only one of the five Commissioners in office at the time of the agreement remain as of this writing. He is Dr. Luther Holcolm. Commissioners Graham's and Jackson's terms were not renewed, and Chairman Roosevelt and Commissioner Hernandez resigned before their terms expired. The Executive Director of the Commission, Mr. Herman Edelsberg, was succeeded by Staff Director Gordon Chase. Deputy Executive Director Walter Davis resigned, Special Assistant to the Executive Director Winn Newman resigned. The Director of Compliance, George Holland, re-most administrators hesitated to duplicate the performance lest senatorial ire be directed at them. The effect of Senator Fanin's attack has been to force administrators to balance gains and losses carefully before undertaking another such effort. In this administrative calculus the path of least resistance is to lose sight of the gains made at Newport News and to reach the conclusion that the agreement was not a model, but an aberration which brought down senatorial wrath without compensating advantages. It is even simpler to "forget" this approach altogether and never face the question of whether the gains are worth the risks. To stem a tide which I sense is beginning to run in this direction, this paper is devoted to a study of the Newport News Agreement, and the context in which it was reached and administered. It is important to the enforcement of anti-discrimination laws to retain in an industrial relations system the concept of a massive change directed toward ending discrimination and reached through careful negotiation in a context in which the government exercises all of its existing powers.

The elimination of employment discrimination is one of the most important tasks of this decade. Newport News demonstrated that it can be done quickly, fairly and efficiently through tough-minded negotiation and sensitive administration. If we use this as a model for changing industrial relations systems, we can move quickly throughout the land to end employment discrimination. If we judicialize the entire process, and thus assure the business and labor community that we will do nothing until the courts have acted on a case by case basis, we are perpetuating the problem of discrimination and the tensions and difficulties which it generates. Yet this seems to be the course we are taking. Both the Labor and Justice Departments are moving toward more formal hearing activity and away from any concept of massive negotiated system change. I consider this a fundamental error of government strategy in dealing with employment discrimination.

II. BACKGROUND

Newport News, Virginia, sits across Hampton Roads from Norfolk. Downtown Newport News is shabby and unimpressive. It is crowded in on the west by the shipyard, which seems to run for miles along the main

signed; General Counsel and Deputy Counsel resigned; Directors of Congressional Liaison and Public Affairs resigned. I was succeeded as Chief of Conciliations by Kenneth Holbert, who assisted in the negotiation and administration of the agreement as my deputy.

C. *Department of Defense:* Contract compliance programs have been completely reorganized and personnel have been scattered. Mr. Girard Clark, Department of the Navy, who was instrumental in laying the groundwork for the Agreement was "reorganized out of existence" and has left the government. An account of the episode involving Mr. Clark's departure was inserted in the Congressional Record by Congressman Ryan (*see* app. VI p. 325 *infra*).

D. *Department of Labor:* Edward Sylvester, Director of the Office of Federal Contract Compliance, resigned to become Assistant Secretary of HEW. Several attorneys in the Solicitor of Labor's office, including Jack Caro and Henry Rose who were active in connection with the Agreement, have either left or have assignments out of the civil rights field.

highway into town. The yard, reputedly the largest in the free world, produces major naval vessels, such as the carriers Enterprise and Kennedy, and an important part of the nuclear submarine fleet. It also produces heavy equipment for industry. It employs 22,000 workers, including some 5,000 Negroes. It is the largest single employer in Virginia.

The Newport News Shipbuilding and Drydock Company had not been the typical southern employer. Its employment practices differed in three important respects from, for example, those of the steel industry around Birmingham, Alabama. First, the company had not followed the traditional southern pattern of confining its Negro employees to lower paying, lower skilled jobs. In 1965 there were at least 400 Negro employees who were in the top group of job classifications called mechanic. This meant that there was a reservoir of trained skilled manpower from which supervisory employees could be identified. In most southern plants three years ago it would have been impossible to find a substantial number of Negroes who had been promoted to first class mechanic status.

The second major difference between Newport News and the typical southern plant was the lack of any seniority system for promotions and only a minimum system of seniority in operation for purposes of layoff. The broad range of company discretion with respect to promotions in this situation made it possible to reach solutions at the yard without facing difficult questions of seniority rights as between incumbent Negro and white employees. These questions have prevented settlement of racial discrimination cases in many plants throughout the South. The workers at the shipyard were represented by the Peninsular Shipbuilders Association, an independent union. The collective bargaining agreement in effect at the yard in 1966 was brief. To one familiar with industrial relations practices in the manufacturing industry, the brief coverage of issues in the contract suggested a broad range of managerial discretion.

Third, the company was at least 75 percent dependent on government contracts and therefore had to be especially sensitive to its relations with the government.

I know little of the efforts of the government to deal with problems of discrimination at the shipyard before 1965. As a major government contractor, the shipyard had been subject to Executive orders prohibiting discrimination in employment since those orders were first promulgated.[7] There was no significant effort at enforcement of these orders until the adopting of the so-called Kennedy Order, E.O. 10925, in 1961. This order created the President's Committee on Equal Employment Opportunity (PCEEO) which was supposed to secure compliance with both the "no discrimination" and the "affirmative action" provisions of the order by supervising the work of

[7] See M. SOVERN, LEGAL RESTRAINTS ON RACIAL DISCRIMINATION IN EMPLOYMENT, ch. 5 (1966), for a description of the operation of the Executive orders dealing with discrimination by government contractors.

the specific contracting agencies. The theory of the order was that the primary responsibility for assuring compliance rested with that agency which was the dominant contractor with the particular company. That agency was called the "Predominant Interest Agency" (PIA) for that employer. Each government contractor was thus assigned to one of the agencies for compliance purposes. Each agency was supposed to establish its own office of contract compliance, and to supervise the actions of the employers under its jurisdictions by answering complaints and by conducting periodic compliance reviews. In addition each agency was to report its findings and recommendations to the PCEEO for approval and for review. This awkward system was devised because Congress refused to establish and fund a single agency for this purpose. The above system functioned within the appropriations to each of the specific agencies. The PCEEO itself functioned within the administrative framework of the Department of Labor. The system as described still remains largely intact, although the PCEEO has been abolished and replaced by an OFCC (Office of Federal Contract Compliance) in the Labor Department.

There may have been a compliance review of Newport News in 1961 by the Navy Department, which was the PIA for the shipyard, but there was little activity thereafter until 1965. Rumor had it that discriminatory practices at the government owned and operated shipyard in Norfolk were so bad that it would have been embarrassing for the Navy to have pressed Newport News before cleaning its own house. At any rate, the new era dawned in 1965 when two events of significance took place.

First, Title VII of the Civil Rights Act of 1964 became effective on July 2, 1965.[8] This gave individuals and groups aggrieved by discrimination a new forum, the Equal Employment Opportunity Commission. The EEOC was to investigate, decide whether reasonable cause existed to believe that the title had been violated, and then make an informal effort to settle the matter through conciliation. If this failed, the aggrieved party could litigate the question of discrimination in the federal district court.[9] In addition, the Attorney General could institute suits, either on his own motion or on referral from the EEOC, if he had reason to believe there existed a pattern or practice of resistance to the full enjoyment of Title VII rights.[10]

The NAACP and the Legal Defense Fund both organized group efforts to make use of the provisions of Title VII. In Newport News the local NAACP chapter was headed by Reverend Fauntleroy, who was a minister and also an employee of the shipyard. Shortly after Title VII went into effect, Reverend Fauntleroy and some 40 other Negro employees filed charges of discrimination under Title VII.

---

8 Pub. L. No. 88-352, § 716(a), 78 Stat. 253, 42 U.S.C. § 2000e (1964). Hereinafter, sections of Title VII will be cited by official section number only.

9 See § 706.

10 See § 707.

The second relevant event of 1965 at the yard was the launching of the George Washington Carver, a large nuclear submarine. The yard decided to make an important public affair of the launching of a vessel named after a distinguished Negro. All high federal officials concerned with equal employment opportunity were invited, including Secretary of Labor Wirtz and the five newly appointed members of the Equal Employment Opportunity Commission.[11] Rumors of discontent among the Negroes at the shipyard seeped back to the office of the Secretary of Defense so the Equal Employment Opportunity Office of the Navy was directed to make a quick check at the yard, primarily to assure that there would be no embarrassment to Cabinet level personnel attending the launching from any manifestations of Negro discontent. The Navy Office, under the direction of Girard Clark, conducted a compliance review and found the yard to be in noncompliance with the Executive order. However, the review also established that it would be "safe" for government personnel to participate in the launching ceremonies. These ceremonies went off without a hitch.

As a result of the activities of the summer, therefore, two government agencies, EEOC and the Navy Department, were for the first time actively concerned with the problems of discrimination at the shipyard. At the conclusion of its investigation, the EEOC made a finding as to whether there was reasonable cause to believe that Title VII had been violated. EEOC findings were and are made after an informal administrative investigation in which a field representative interviews the charging parties and the respondent and also examines the premises and company records. The investigator makes a written report called a Field Investigation Report. This report was, at that time, assigned to the offices of one of the Commissioners where an administrative assistant prepared a draft decision on the question of whether there was reasonable cause to believe that the statute had been violated. The draft was then reviewed and approved by the Commissioner and circulated for Commission approval. At one period, including the time of the finding concerning the shipyard, the individual Commissioner signed the decision on behalf of the Commission. In the case of Newport News, Commissioner Hernandez signed the decision.

After 1965, various functions described here tended to change hands. First they were delegated to the staff in Washington, and then, gradually, to the field offices. Thus, as I write today, the draft decisions are no longer prepared in the Commissioner's offices but are a staff function in Washington. I predict it will not be long before decisions are drafted in the field offices. Individual Commissioners no longer sign the Commission decisions, rather the secretary to the Commission does so. But the essential high level consideration of the question of "reasonable cause" expressed in the written decisions does remain the hallmark of the Commission.

The use of written decisions on the reasonable cause issue has the twin

[11] The Commission originally consisted of Chairman Franklin D. Roosevelt, Jr., Vice Chairman Holcom, Commissioners Hernandez, Jackson, and Graham.

effect of forcing development of rules of law concerning discrimination and of laying the foundation for meaningful conciliation efforts. As the first Chief of Conciliations for the Commission, I was adamant in insisting that we should never undertake conciliation without a written decision on reasonable cause, because without that we had no basis on which to insist on relief or on changes in industrial relations system. The history of soft settlements in the field, plus my own study of the failures of the New Jersey anti-discrimination agency, had convinced me that only with the foundation of a written, official Commission decision could meaningful settlement agreements be achieved.[12] Without this foundation employers would deny discrimination and then agree to a nuisance settlement to get rid of the conciliator. The conciliator and the complainants would be hard put to resist this technique. With the written decision the concilator could assume the existence of discrimination and move on to discuss settlement. Furthermore, the decision became a basis for our insistance that the rights involved were individual rights and for refusing to accept any settlement which was not signed by the charging party. The written decision became part of a process by which the Commission administratively determined that it would honor the concept of individual rights and would not follow the path of predecessor agencies of informally settling claims of discrimination regardless of the wishes of the victim of discrimination. We rejected the paternalistic theory of administrative action in favor of a theory which tried to reinforce the individual right to be free of discrimination—a right which had, we thought, been written into Title VII.[13]

The written Commission decision in the Newport News case was developed within the framework I have just described. The Commission found reasonable cause to believe that:

(1) Wages of Negro employees doing the same work as white employees were lower than white employees;

(2) Negro employees were promoted at a slower rate than white employees;

(3) Negro employees were not promoted to supervisory status under the same circumstances as white employees;

(4) Negro employees were restricted in their access to the apprenticeship program, and

(5) Locker and shower facilities were segregated.[14]

---

[12] See M. SOVERN, supra note 7, Ch. 3; Blumrosen, Anti-Discrimination Laws in Action in New Jersey: A Law-Sociology Study, 19 RUTGERS L. REV. 189 (1965); Hill, Twenty Years of State Fair Employment Practice Commissions: A Critical Analysis with Recommendations, 14 BUFFALO L. REV. 22 (1964).

[13] The process of conciliation is more fully described in Blumrosen, The Individual Right to Eliminate Employment Discrimination by Litigation, Proc. 19th Ann. Winter Meeting, Indus. Relations Research Ass'n. 88 (1966). This view of the rights of individuals with respect to conciliation efforts has been confirmed in Cox v. United States Gypsum Co., 284 F. Supp. 74 (N.D. Ind. 1968).

[14] See app. III p. 310 infra.

Once this decision had been rendered, it was sent to my office. At that time I had only two persons to assist me: Kenneth Holbert, who had come from a Dallas law practice with a Negro firm to the Labor Department in 1961, and who transferred to the Commission in September of 1965; and Herbert Belkin, who had been one of my students at Rutgers and who came down to Washington after graduating in 1965. To cope with the mass of cases for conciliation, we drafted persons from other parts of the Commission. The Newport News file was given to Delano Lewis, a young Negro attorney with little prior experience. He and I discussed the remedies he was to seek and he went down to Newport News.

His visit was treated lightly. The Company representative, an elderly vice president in charge of labor relations, denied the discrimination, and the Union also declined to conciliate. After several trips, Lewis gave up.

I reviewed the file, recommended that it be referred to the Attorney General for possible suit under Section 707 of the Act, dispatched "notice letters" to the complainants indicating that the conciliation efforts had failed and that they had 30 days in which to file suit under Title VII, and sent the file to the office of the General Counsel. That was November 1965. I heard no more of the case until the following March.

III. The Foundation for Negotiation

In the interim the processes of government ground on. The Department of Defense continued the investigation which had begun before the launching of the Carver and reached the conclusion that action should be taken. The PCEEO was abolished, and its functions transferred to a new institution, the Office of Federal Contract Compliance (OFCC). Its new energetic director, Edward Sylvester, Jr., sitting on top of substantially the same staff and organization as the PCEEO, was prepared to exercise the contract suspension power which had been rarely used in the past.

At the same time, the EEOC file on Newport News was referred by the Commission to the Department of Justice. Attorneys from the Civil Rights Division went down to Newport News and conducted extensive interviews. By March 1966 the Department was prepared to institute litigation against the shipyard. In the meantime the Negro employees who had complained to the EEOC filed suit on behalf of themselves and similarly situated employees in the federal district court. Their local attorney was affiliated with the Legal Defense and Education Fund of the NAACP.

Through unofficial channels, the Company learned of the impending suit by the Justice Department and attempted to head it off. Mr. Holden, who had met Commissioner Hernandez at the launching of the Carver, came to her office. She indicated to him that she was aware that the shipyard was in difficulty and referred him to me.

Our posture was that, as far as we were concerned, conciliation had failed, but we would always be glad to discuss the problems of discrimination with him if that was appropriate. He indicated he wanted to negotiate a solution. I called Herman Edelsberg, then Executive Director of the Commission, and learned that the Department of Justice was within days of filing suit. I so advised Mr. Holden, and told him that we would be prepared to work with him to reach an agreement if it was appropriate, but that we could do nothing at that time.

The activities of the Company precipitated an interdepartmental meeting in the office of John Doar, then Assistant Attorney General for Civil Rights. Present were representatives from the OFCC (including Ed Sylvester), the Department of Defense (Mr. Moskowitz), the Navy Department (Mr. Clark), and the EEOC (Mr. Edelsberg, Mr. Berg and myself). In all there were about 20 people sitting in a semi-circle around Mr. Doar's desk. For an hour we discussed the pros and cons of whether to file suit and then negotiate, or whether to accept the current offer of the company to negotiate first. EEOC's view was that Justice should file suit and that we would negotiate afterwards. Our theory was that when a company turned down the Commision's offer to conciliate, they should not be given another opportunity before the Justice Department filed suit. To give this opportunity would weaken the incentive to negotiate with the EEOC.

After an hour, Doar announced his decision. He would not file suit, but would allow opportunity for negotiation. During these discussions, Sylvester pressed the Department of Defense officials for a memorandum which would enable the Department of Labor to suspend further contracting with the shipyard, and DOD and Navy officials agreed to supply a memorandum of non-compliance with the Executive order dealing with government contractors. When Doar announced his decision, Herman Edelsberg stood up and said, "Very well, EEOC will conduct the negotiations." This was agreed to by everyone in the room, and we promised to be in touch with the various agencies as we moved toward the negotiations.

Edelsberg had grabbed the ball, figuratively speaking, from the other agencies, and thereby stamped the entire effort as an EEOC venture. It became my responsibility to develop proposals to remedy discrimination at the shipyard, and to shepherd these proposals through the bureaucratic maze of the Commission and of three other government agencies before we could begin to negotiate.

This responsibility was significant. Unlike the manner in which a collective bargaining agreement details the operation of a plant, there was here no satisfactory history for the preparation of binding agreements which detailed the responsibility of employers to make massive changes in industrial relations systems to eliminate discrimination. Most employer statements made at the request of the government up to that time had consisted of generalities concerning equal opportunity.[15]

I sat down with Delano Lewis and prepared a first draft of a proposal

---

[15] Blumrosen, *supra* note 12. For a followup study, see Frakt, *Administrative Enforcement of Equal Opportunity Legislation in New Jersey*, 21 RUTGERS L. REV. 442 (1967).

based on our analysis of the file and his discussions with the charging parties. We sent it to the General Counsel's office where additions were made. We were then ready for a meeting with Executive Director Edelsberg and his staff and others in the Commission concerning the proposals. One of our proposals had been to establish a preferential promotion list for Negro employees who were the victims of discrimination. We heard that this was to be opposed by some on the Executive Director's staff on the theory that the agreement should provide for equal treatment in the future without remedying the past discrimination. On this key issue Ken Holbert suggested that we needed allies so our final preparation for the meeting consisted of outlining to Commissioner Hernandez our proposals and the difficulties we expected to face. She agreed with our approach and indicated that, if we had trouble in the office of the Executive Director, we could come back to her and she would, if necessary, take the matter up with the Commission.

To the uninitiated our action seemed a breach of the bureaucratic tradition. We had deviated from channels by going around the Executive Director to one of the Commissioners. At that time in the history of the Commission, there was a serious dispute as to the role of the Commissioners vis-à-vis the Chairman concerning who "ran the Commission" and as to the relation between the Commissioners and the staff. The Chairman and the Executive Director felt that they ran the staff and that the Commissioners should be advisors to the Chairman, while the Commissioners thought that they were entitled to participate in important day-to-day decisions. The resulting confusion allowed staff people to seek the most favorable forum for various positions they wanted to take; this was our reason for going to Commissioner Hernandez. Such a maneuver would be unlikely today. The Commissioners are now much further removed from the day-to-day operation of the Commission, which is largely centralized under the Staff Director, who reports to the Chairman. The flexible days of the first year of the Commission are no more.

At any rate, armed with the support of Commissioner Hernandez, Holbert and I went to the staff meeting and won our point concerning the scope of the remedy sufficiently so that we did not feel it necessary to seek the Commissioner's assistance in the formulation of the proposals. The proposals were broad, and included remedies for past discrimination as well as system changes for the future. They dealt extensively with all of the problems of the shipyard which we had identified and ran some 20 pages doubled-spaced. Over the weekend we had them duplicated and called an interagency meeting for early the following week. Meanwhile, we advised the shipyard that our negotiating sessions would take place in Washington rather than Newport News because of the numbers of government personnel who would be involved.

On the Sunday before the negotiations several of us flew to Newport News to meet with the leaders of the charging parties to make sure that our proposals for solution to the problems of discrimination made sense to them. Discussion of proposals with charging parties prior to submission to respondents was and is part of the Commission's procedure. This assures that the interests of complainants will not be ignored and makes it more likely that an agreement based on such proposals will later be acceptable to the charging parties.

We met the charging parties in the office of their attorney, Phillip Walker. They ran the gamut from Reverend Fauntleroy, a grizzled veteran of civil rights efforts, and Thomas Mann, the first Negro graduate of the apprenticeship school of the yard and who had not been promoted as had his white colleagues, to Arthur Ford and James Lassiter, long time employees at the yard who had seen their white contemporaries promoted past them. We discussed the tentative proposals and returned to Washington that night after driving past the shipyard.

Early the following week, we held an interagency meeting and distributed our proposals. Present were representatives from Labor, Defense, Justice, OFCC and Navy. We discussed the proposals for nearly two hours, and secured informal acquiescence in them from the other agencies involved. For the first and the only time thus far in the history of federal efforts to end employment discrimination, we had a firm position from which to negotiate, agreed to by *all* of the government agencies involved and the aggrieved parties. The concept of a single government position in the field of employment discrimination usually is a myth. There is not one government; there are several agencies, each with its institutional viewpoint and each reflecting the viewpoints of dominant personnel. It is a most difficult feat to secure a "government position" in this field. But this one time it was obtained.

IV. THE NEGOTIATIONS

The negotiations began on a Wednesday. Mr. Edelsberg opened them with a short statement and then turned the session over to me. Sitting next to me was Ken Holbert, my deputy. Around the end of the table was Girard Clark, the aggressive Navy contracts compliance chief. To my left was a representative of the Justice Department, either Stephen Pollock, then First Assistant and now Assistant Attorney General for Civil Rights, or Gerald Choppin, Executive Assistant to the Assistant Attorney General for Civil Rights. The entire federal governmental structure dealing with employment discrimination was thus represented at the government end of the bargaining table. At the other end were the president of the company, Mr. Holden, the company's counsel, Mr. Pat Gibson, and various company officials.

I made a short opening statement indicating that our proposals had been carefully worked out and were seriously presented, but that we were prepared to discuss the details of each of them in terms of their practicality in light of the conditions at the shipyard. We distributed copies of the proposals and then recessed to allow the company time to consider them. At this point, the statute draws a curtain over our initial proposals and the discussions which followed.[16] Nothing "said or done during and as a part of" conciliation efforts may be made public without the written consent of the parties. My files reflect four separate and distinct drafts of the conciliation proposals which emerged during our discussions which took more than a week. The point I wish to make is that in fact these were genuine negotiations, and there were many changes made in the initial government proposals before the agreement was finalized. The government, despite its array of "power," did not purport to have a monopoly on wisdom or on the most practical method of effectuating equal opportunity at the shipyard. No "take it or leave it" attitude was expressed by the government during the negotiations. Someday it may be practical to compare the initial government proposal with the agreement as signed to make clear that negotiations did take account of issues raised by the shipyard. It was this factor which contributed, I believe, to the decision by the company to implement the agreement in good faith. For the moment, however, the reader will have to take my word that the negotiations were genuine.

On the day after the negotiations opened the Secretary of Labor issued his order suspending further contracting by any government agency with the Newport News Shipyard. The suspension order interrupted contracting for several naval vessels, of which the Navy Department was aware, as well as a Maritime Commission contract, of which the Labor and Defense Department officials were unaware. At the last minute there was hesitancy in the government channels as to whether to suspend contracting—after all, the officials of the yard had come up to negotiate and were thus demonstrating "good faith." My opinion was sought on this question and I was strongly of the view that the contracting should be suspended. I was doing the negotiating, and I was fully aware that all that had happened up to this point was that the company had received our proposals. Their past performance and the manner in which they had brushed off prior proposals did not suggest to me that there was any great willingness to take all steps necessary to end the discriminatory system at the shipyard. I wanted to negotiate from strength, and the strongest position was one in which the shipyard was under great pressure to settle. Thus the suspension was, in my view, crucial to the outcome of the negotiations. Without the suspension I do not believe we would have achieved the full scale solution to the system of discrimination at the shipyard. With the suspension we were able to

16 *See* § 706a. *See also* § III(6) of the Agreement, app. I p. 299 *infra*.

negotiate from strength. This view prevailed, and the suspension order was issued.

There is another feature of our system which made these negotiations genuine even though the contracts were suspended. The company had the option at all times to seek judicial intervention against the disruption of contracting. They thus had a "choice" even though the contracts were suspended. This presence of judicial control is a healthy limitation on any risks of administrative excess.[17]

One must always be careful not to confuse bargaining power with wisdom. The fact is that there was considerable give and take on various issues after the order had been issued. The negotiations took at least a week, the discussions were genuine, and extensive changes were made in the government proposal. Finally, agreement was reached. This agreement was reviewed by the Navy, Defense and Labor Departments and was considered a comprehensive plan justifying the lifting of the contracting bar. Justice decided, on the strength of the agreement, not to institute suit. The agreement led to the settlement of the private litigation. In short, the agreement was approved by the various government agencies as well as by the company and the charging parties and the Legal Defense Fund, the civil rights organization backing the litigation. Since Reverend Fauntleroy was the NAACP official in Newport News, it is fair to say that the agreement received the endorsement of the concerned civil rights community. Finally, the agreement was approved by the Commission and made public.

V. Correcting an Error of Omission

In all of this flurry of activity which took place within a two week period, the Peninsular Shipbuilders Associations was not consulted by the government. We had been rebuffed once by the PSA and we were inclined to accept the view that the proposed changes could be made within the framework of the existing labor agreement as a matter of management's discretion. This was a feasible position in light of the facts that the collective bargaining agreement left so many matters to the discretion of management, and that it contained no provision dealing with seniority for promotions and only limited protection for long service men in cases of layoff. In retrospect, it is clear that we erred in not consulting with the PSA prior to the signing of the agreement with the company.[18]

We paid an appropiate penalty for this omission. The AFL-CIO became worried that we might not consult its affiliates before signing with companies in cases where there were substantial issues at stake, and we reformed our conciliation procedure to make sure this would not happen again. The PSA officials were highly insulted and upset, and threatened to take

---

[17] See Crown Zellerbach Corp. v. Wirtz, 281 F. Supp. 337 (D.D.C. 1968).
[18] See NLRB v. Katz, 369 U.S. 736, 82 S. Ct. 1107 (1962).

the company to the NLRB for making unilateral changes in working conditions without negotiating. I marked on my private calendar the point in time six months from the signing of the agreement as the period within which the PSA could file with the NLRB and thus cast a cloud over all of our work.[19] We then began a protracted course of negotiations with the PSA itself. Ultimately these negotiations paid off. PSA and the company signed a supplemental agreement shortly before the six months period expired. In it the PSA recognized the conciliation agreement. PSA then began to process grievances under the agreement. This not only constituted a waiver of any objections to procedure the PSA might have had, but also brought the union in as an agency to enforce the agreement, an agency closer at hand than the EEOC offices in Washington.

What prompted the union to give up a claim which might have shattered the agreement and left the whole concept of a major negotiated system change in jeopardy? I believe it was the self-interest of the union and of the employees in the yard for the agreement gave to all of the employees in the yard, not just the Negro employees, two important benefits which they had never had before. First was the posting of notices of vacancies so that men could seek to improve their own position in the yard. This posting of vacancies increased intraplant mobility for all of the employees, white and black. Secondly, the agreement provided that vacancies were to be filled on the basis of length of service where "skill, ability and efficiency are fairly equal."[20] This provision benefited all except those who preferred the principle of supervisory favoritism as a basis for promotions.

And so this one fumble in the processing of the Newport News Agreement was recovered. Strangely, in a subsequent proceeding the Labor Department did not involve the Papermakers Union in negotiations to change the seniority system at Crown Zellerbach and was, on that account as well as others, enjoined from suspending government contracts with Crown.[21] The lessons from that experience were two: first, be sure to involve the union even where the agreement seems to fall within the ambit of management prerogatives; and second, many mistakes by government can be corrected by patient and careful action.

VI. The Administration of the Agreement

The signing of the agreement was hailed by EEOC Chairman Roosevelt as a milestone and as a model for others. But the signing was only the beginning of a year of administration which taxed the feeble resources of

[19] The National Labor Relations Act requires that a charge be filed within six weeks of an unfair Labor Practice. See Sec. 10(b) of the National Labor Relations Act as amended, 61 Stat. 136, 29 U.S.C. 141 (1964).

[20] See § II(3)(a) of the Agreement, app. I p. 299 infra.

[21] Crown Zellerbach Corp. v. Wirtz, 281 F. Supp. 337 (D.D.C. 1968).

the EEOC to the limit. In discussing the administration of the agreement, it is necessary to sketch the procedural posture of the agreement, and the strengths and weaknesses of the administering agencies.

The agreement provided that its general administration would be in the hands of the EEOC. This meant, for practical purposes, that it was administered through the office of conciliations. However, the agreement provided that the provisions relating to promotions of Negroes to supervisors (called quartermen) would be handled by the Department of Defense. Further, it provided that a number of crucial questions relating to promotion of Negroes in non-supervisory positions would be determined by an expert, to be retained at company expense, who would be acceptable to the Commission. Thus the administration of the agreement involved a substantial number of parties: the charging parties and the NAACP, the union, the company, the expert, the Defense Department and the Commission. To manage all of these relationships my office had expanded somewhat. Jules Gordon and Andrew Muse, both attorneys, joined the office during the administration of the agreement and participated in it. Holbert and Belkin also spent time at Newport News. Newport News administration thus consumed an important part of the time of the entire office of conciliation during the 1966-1967 year. Toward the end of the period, when the Defense Department dropped out of the picture, I spent nearly full time with five DOD staff persons to conclude the administration of the agreement. To say that we were spread thin in the administration of the agreement is to put it mildly. But government usually functions this way. Much government service involves routine and dull activity requiring no great talent or energy. This is suddenly displaced by extraordinary demands requiring all concerned to function far above their expected capacity.

In addition to having to cope with all of the groups involved, our office was faced with a shifting superstructure above us. Chairman Roosevelt resigned shortly after the agreement was negotiated to run, unsuccessfully, for Governor of New York. Vice Chairman Holcolm took over for several months, to be replaced by Chairman Steven Shulman. Shulman's administration replaced Mr. Edelsberg as Executive Director with Mr. Chase. The Director of Compliance at the beginning of the agreement, Mr. Holland, left the Commission, and was succeeded by my deputy, Ken Holbert, in an acting capacity.

I emphasize all these difficulties to attempt to place the administrative process in its human context. Government is not an impersonal mindless bureaucracy, at least at the level in which I encountered it. On the contrary, it is an intensely personal process. This of course reinforces the necessity for fully documented written agreements. Only in this way is there some likelihood that matters will be carried forward in some relation to the original intention of the negotiating parties. This applies to the government side as well as to the position of the charging parties and respondents.

PROBLEM	SOLUTION	RESULTS
1. Negro employees were underpaid for doing the same work as white employees and were promoted at a slower rate than white employees.	Retention of an experts, (Case and Co.) approved by the Commission to prepare job descriptions to determine the rate and conditions for promotions of white employees, and to determine which Negro employees were underpaid and had been promoted at a slower rate than white employees.	Case and Company conducted an intensive study of each of the more than 30 departments at the shipyard. It then issued a report on each department to the company and Commission indicating which Negro employees should have been promoted and the positions they would have reached if their rate of progress had equaled that of the white employees. The company promoted these employees or placed them on a list for future promotion. While promoting these employees, the company continued its normal promotional practice with respect to white employees. Actually, nearly half of the Negro employees whom Case & Company found entitled to promotion had already been advanced by the Company before the study was completed. This indicated the company's cooperative attitude. This provision of the agreement accounts for the nearly 39 hundred promotion actions on behalf of Negro employees during the year after the agreement was executed.
2. Negro employees restricted to certain departments, not permitted to transfer to higher paying jobs in previously all white departments.	Company to post notices of job vacancies so that employees can bid for them and allow Negro employees to transfer to previously all white departments.	Company posted vacancies for the first time in its history and employees, both white and Negro, began to take advantage of the transfer provisions.
3. Negro employees alleged they were passed over for promotion.	Establishment of proposal that promotions are henceforth to be given by seniority and ability.	Application of this proposal on behalf of both Negro and white employees.
4. Negro employees were restricted in promotion to supervisor. At the time of the agreement, only 32 of the nearly 2 thousand officers and managers were Negro although 25% of the labor force was Negro.	DOD and company developed a profile of the qualifications of the last 100 white employees promoted to supervisors. Selected Negro employees to be measured against this profile and those who matched or exceeded it, to be promoted prior to promotion of others. Company could request exceptions in special circumstances. Disputes between company and DOD to be submitted to Case & Co.	This provision requires substantial interpretation in light of problems which arose after the agreement was executed. Rather than the last 100 white employees, it was agreed to use the last 5 whites promoted in each department as the basis for the profile because of variation in standards. EEOC assumed responsibility for administration. Company promoted more than 20 Negroes to supervision during the administration of the agreement, and at the end of the period agreed to promotions of an additional 75.

PROBLEM	SOLUTION	RESULTS
		Negroes who had been certified by their own supervisors as qualified to become supervisors. Exceptions were granted in two instances by the Commission, one of which involved a white employee who was the lead foreman handling scaffolding on the Carrier Kennedy, and the other man with special technical skills. The extensive promotions to supervisors were possible because the Company had, over the years, permitted some Negro employees to advance to mechanical status and thus had a reservoir of high skilled men who were available for promotion. All promotions were worked out by agreement between the Commission and the company and it was not necessary to submit any disputes to Case & Company.
5. Restriction of Negro applicants to apprentice schools, segregation of apprentice school staff and selection of committee. Only 6 of the 500 students were Negro. The apprentice school is a 4 year advanced technical school.	Negotiation of staff and committee, recruitment efforts among Negro schools, elimination of restrictions on married students, those with prior college education, and raise maximum entry age to 25 years, with notification to present Negro employees who might qualify under these standards, of their new opportunities.	Nearly 50 Negroes admitted to the school during the first year after the agreement; prompt integration of staff and selection committee; identification of employees who might qualify, and as part of the closing administrative phase of the agreement, notification to them by the Commission of their opportunities under the agreement. The company engaged in recruiting contacts with the various NAACP branches in the labor market area.
6. Segregated locker, shower, and toilet facilities.	Reconstruction of toilet facilities in accordance with a diagram attached to the agreement to eliminate their segregated character. Reassignment of locker and shower facilities on an alphabetical basis.	This was accomplished by company action within 30 days of the signing of the agreement. No serious difficulties were reported.
7. The specific complaints of the 4 individual charging parties regarding restriction on their promotional opportunities because of race.	Agreement to promote 3 of the 4 individuals to supervisor and to promote the 4 to a higher paying job class.	This provision was implemented the week after the signing of the agreement. The private law suit was dismissed with payment of cost and attorney fees by the company.
8. Resolution of the other 37 complaints which involved rate of pay and promotional opportunities problems.	Agreement on an expedited procedure to resolve these problems.	Charges were satisfactorily adjusted within 3 months of the agreement.

VII. The Results Summarized

Shortly after I returned to Rutgers Law School in the summer of 1967, I was asked to prepare a discussion of the impact of the Newport News agreement for EEOC staff members. This analysis was later placed in the Congressional Record by Senator Javits, and it is reproduced as appendix III, below. I insert a part of that document here to give substance to what has gone before and to the remainder of this account. One of the great difficulties in evaluation of governmental action is that frequently there is no followup or feedback, and thus it is impossible to determine the effectiveness at any level of a given program. To deal with this problem of evaluation of the Newport News Agreement, I prepared this three column chart which was included in the Congressional Record[22] under the following introduction:

> "There follows a table indicating the nature of the problem of discrimination at the shipyard, the solution reached in the conciliation agreement and the results of the application of the act."

The chart is reproduced on pages 284–85.

VIII. The Company Takes the Initiative

Some phases of the administration of the agreement were over quickly. The company desegregated the toilet facilities and reassigned locker space in accordance with the agreement. There was some grumbling from the union, but this was promptly done. The policy statement of the president was distributed in pay checks; group meetings were held to explain the agreement to all employees; bulletin boards for posting job vacancy notices were erected and put into operation.

In the most meaningful sense of the word, that is in their actions, the company demonstrated "good faith" in the initial administration of the agreement. Those things which they could do at once they did. They established procedures to anticipate the formal enforcement of the agreement and executed them. Where there were serious difficulties, they did not hesitate to say so and to negotiate firmly with us to the end that their own interest in flexibility was maintained as much as possible, while complying with the agreement.

In anticipation of the enforcement of the specific provisions of the agreement, the company made a major undertaking of its own. First, it promoted a great many Negroes. I believe the figure was between 1,200 and 1,500. Secondly, it scoured the yard for Negroes who were already mechanics to determine how many it could promote to supervisory status. It then promoted some 20 Negroes to supervisory positions without awaiting the enforcement of the agreement. This reflected both good faith and good sense on the part of the company. By acting in anticipation of the administration of the agreement, the company was able to exercise more of its discretion in selection of per-

---

[22] *See* app. III p. 310 *infra*.

sonnel, and thus retain the sense of control over the operation of the yard, and at the same time demonstrate to the government that it was carrying out the spirit of the agreement. Later, however, others used the fact that the company had gone ahead as minimizing the role of the government with respect to all of these promotions.[23] It is clear, however, that but for the major governmental effort which culminated in the agreement, this mass of promotions of black employees would not have taken place. Within this framework it may be useful now to describe in such detail as the statute permits the administration of two phases of the agreement, relating to promotions of Negroes to non-supervisory status and promotions to supervisory status.

A. Promotions to Non-Supervisory Positions—Enter the Experts

The Commission had found cause to believe that Negroes were promoted at a slower rate than were whites. This finding was not based on an examination of the rate of promotion of all blacks in the yard compared to whites. Rather it was based on a number of specific situations. In order to determine which Negroes had in fact been promoted at a slower rate than whites, the conciliation agreement provided for the selection of an expert, who could either be an individual, a management consultant or an operations research institution. The expert was to be knowledgeable in race relations and acceptable to the Commission. The expert was given various roles under the agreement and was central to its successful administration.[24] Thus, the identification of the expert became a matter of great concern to both the company and the government. During the negotiations we did not agree either on a mutually acceptable expert or to agree on a formula for selection of such an expert. Thus, it was left that both the company and the government could nominate experts, the company could select, and the Commission could veto. If the process did not produce an expert within 45 days, the parties would reconvene for the limited purpose of solving the problem.

The government nominated a group of individuals, and the company, after reviewing proposals from several management consultant firms, nominated Case and Company. One senior official of Case had been president of the Urban League of New Jersey some years previously. Case retained a Negro adviser to assist it in carrying out the assignment. With these considerations Case and Company was deemed acceptable. Again, this demonstrates the advantage which the company gained by taking the initiative in the selection of the expert. If it had engaged in foot dragging, the entire arrangement could have come unstuck and they might have been saddled

---

[23] Thus Barron's magazine suggestion that only a few Negroes were promoted under the agreement (see app. II p. 307 *infra*, note 4) is explainable only if all the other promotion actions of the company are treated as unrelated to governmental action.

[24] *See* § § II(i)(4), III(5)(c) of the Agreement, app. I p. 299 *infra*, for provisions relating to the expert.

with an outsider not of their choosing. As it was, Case and Company has performed generally useful work for the shipyard. Case assigned Mr. Montgomery with a staff to undertake the preparation of job descriptions and the analysis of the rate of promotion of Negro and white employees, and to carry out the other tasks under the agreement. The company provided working space near its records and cooperation through its knowledgeable personnel.

The task of preparing the various analyses took nearly a year. One phase of the task was the receipt of complaints from Negro employees of slow promotion or under-payment compared to whites. The analysis of the rate of promotion of Negro versus white employees had the effect of resolving most of the questions of depressed rates of pay. This was because of the wage structure at the shipyard. Employees were divided into four major job groupings, called classifications. These were in descending order: mechanic, handiman, helper and laborer. Within each of these groups were three levels, first, second and third class, each carrying a corresponding rate of pay. Thus there were in effect 12 rates, and a promotion ladder up these rates from laborer to first class mechanic. The company had retained considerable flexibility with respect to assignments to specific tasks so that it was possible that a first class mechanic and a third class helper could be working together on the same job. If the third class helper was a Negro whose rate of promotion up the ladder had been discriminatorily retarded, as compared to the white mechanic, a correction of his rate of pay would automatically correct the "inequity" of Negroes doing the same work as whites but at lower rates. None of us had realized this fact until the concluding phase of the administration of the agreement. This made it considerably easier to conclude the administration than it would otherwise have been.

The task of Case and Company was of considerable magnitude. There were basically two problems arising from the agreement, and they gave both the government and the company substantial difficulty. The theory of section II(4) of the agreement was that the expert would develop a profile of the "rate and conditions" of promotion of white employees in selected departments in cooperation with the Defense Department. The history of progression and promotion of Negro employees would then be compared with this profile; if the Negro had not been promoted in accordance with the rate and conditions for promotion of whites, he would forthwith be placed in the first grade in his present job classification (e.g., if he was a third class handiman, he would be made first class) and would be put on a preferential promotion list to move into the higher classification if that was indicated by the expert.

The agreement provided a mechanism by which the company could demonstrate that the employee had not been promoted "for reasons of physical handicap, improper attendance or other conduct on the premises." The company had the burden of proof on this issue. Then the agreement provided that "considerations of skill and ability are not germane to this section."[25] The theory of this section was that the expert would adduce a standardized rate of promotion of whites, based largely on length of service, and that this movement up the wage ladder should be considered as automatic within each group of jobs. In the administration of this provision it was argued that since the profile of the white employees included "rate and conditions" for promotion, some questions of skill and ability were properly included in the calculus as to whether employees were promotable. We finally decided not to resolve this question of interpretation. I think the considerations leading to this conclusion were as follows: first, we found variations in the criteria used for promotions in the various departments in the yard; and second, the argument on the language was not wholly without merit, although the specific language of section 4(f) would seem to be more persuasive than the generality of the term "rate and conditions." At any rate for the purposes of administration, we did not press the issue. The effect of this was that some Negro employees were not promoted. But the number rejected on grounds of lack of ability was, I believe, far smaller than would have been the case if the "skill and ability" language had not been included in the agreement.

I think this was sound administration. It would have been awkward to litigate this question. Our posture would have smacked too much of the views attributed to EEO programs by their opponents—of attempting to secure promotion of incompetents. Our argument, that the rate of promotion was really an automatic wage increase and that we were simply correcting past inequities, might well be lost in the resulting furor. At any rate, we made the judgment to back away from literal application of the clause during the administration of the agreement, leaving the issue to be raised, perhaps, another day.

The other issue with respect to the administration of the agreement dealt with the measurement of rate of promotion. The argument was as follows. If, for example, the sample disclosed that the average time in grade of white employees before promotion from third to second class handiman in a given department was 11 months, I took the view that all Negroes who had been in the third class more than 11 months were entitled to promotion insofar as the time element was concerned. This was a literal reading of the agreement.[26] The contrary view was that the number of Negroes considered for promotion should be such that the overall average time in grade for both Negro and whites equalled 11 months.

These two competing interpretations of section 4(f) were discussed. Finally, I asked Case and Company to identify the individuals whose promotions were at stake depending on which view prevailed. Once this was

25 See § II(4)(f) of the Agreement, app. I p. 299 infra.
26 See § II(4)(f) of the Agreement, app. I p. 299 infra.

done, we found we were talking about relatively few employees. As a part of the wrap-up of the administration of the agreement, the company acquiesced in my view on this issue, and the promotions were made.

I hope these two illustrations suggest the degree of informality and practicality involved in the administration of the agreement and dispel the concept that it was administered on a wooden "take it or leave it" basis. I do not suggest that we were soft or easy in our approach, but we did take realistic account of genuine issues and considerations. At the same time, since we were dealing with group claims, we always ran the risk of doing less than full justice to the individual claims involved. I will discuss this aspect of administration later.[27]

The result of the course of action described above was a total of 3980 promotion actions for Negro employees during the first year of the agreement.

B. Promotions to Supervisor

The problem with respect to promotions to "quarterman"—the term for foreman in the yard—was that there were 25 percent Negro employees but only 1½ percent of the persons listed as officers and managers were Negro. The Commission had found that Negroes were not promoted to supervisor under the same circumstances as whites. This finding was based on a few cases, not on an exhaustive investigation of all situations. Three of the four principal charging parties, Fauntleroy, Mann, and Lassiter, were promoted to quartermen as part of the settlement agreement.[28] But more importantly, procedures were established under sections II(2)(a)-(e) of the agreement to review all of the skilled Negro employees in the yard and provide for their promotion to quartermen if they met the criterion applied to the promotion of the last 100 whites who had been made quartermen. The implementation of this agreement was to be done by the Department of Defense and the company jointly.[29]

Promptly after the agreement was signed, the company examined its Negro employees for those who had supervisory capability, and proceeded to promote some 20 of them to quartermen, in addition to the three appointments of the charging parties. The Department of Defense was slow in implementing this phase of the agreement, and shortly the company found itself in need of additional quartermen.

The company believed it had promoted all the qualified Negroes to quartermen, and therefore the provision of section II(2)(d) for the appointment of Negroes to vacancies as quartermen was no longer applicable.[30]

[27] See § IX of this article.
[28] See § II(7)(c) of the Agreement, app. I p. 299 infra.
[29] § II(2)(b) of the Agreement, app. I p. 299 infra.
[30] In the Agreement there is a provision under which the company would promote qualified Negroes in the interim period. We had not provided for the contingency

Faced with the need to make additional quartermen, the company took two important steps. First, it pressed persistently in Washington, both with DOD and with the EEOC, for the government to come down and administer this phase of the agreement, and second, it began to promote whites to temporary quartermen positions.

During late 1966, DOD made a beginning at solving the quarterman problem by sending some men down to the yard, but it soon developed that the provisions of the agreement were simply unworkable. Since criteria for promotion to quarterman varied from department to department, the use of the last 100 whites promoted as the basis for establishing criteria did not work. Thus DOD and the company agreed, with EEOC approval, to substitute a profile based on the last five appointments in each department prior to July 2, 1965, as the basis for determining qualifications. Having gotten this far, DOD then bogged down.

As 1967 opened, the company pressure mounted to finish this aspect of the agreement. Many employees had been temporary quartermen for months, and they were restive in their position. I believed the company was rapidly moving into a position where, with justice, they could say that the government had defaulted on its obligations to administer the agreement; that they had promoted all the qualified Negroes they could find, and that they would consider this phase of the agreement at an end. They then might have made their temporary promotions permanent. This would have created additional problems and would have publicly discredited the agreement and the efforts of the government. We began to pressure the DOD to complete the inventory. Suddenly, we found that an internal struggle over the EEO program in the Department of Defense had crippled DOD's ability to administer the agreement. At one point in this struggle (which resulted ultimately in the elimination of Mr. Girard Clark, the aggressive Navy EEO Chief who had pressed so insistently for the action against the shipyard[31]) we were notified that DOD personnel would not go back into the yard. This caused a major crisis in the office of conciliation. The entire concept of a system-wide change through a master agreement was again jeopardized. The government effort would be discredited if we could not deliver on our promises made in the agreement. Chairman Shulman agreed with our estimate of the seriousness of the situation, and contacted high officials in the office of the Secretary of Defense. The upshot of his conversations was a typical bureaucratic solution. DOD would not go back to the yard, but it would detail five men to work for EEOC for one month to conclude the administration of the agreement.

Thus it was that in March 1967 I began shuttling between Newport News and Washington to complete the administrative phase of the agree-

of slow government action and an arguable case that there were no more qualified Negroes available.

[31] See note 6 C, *supra*.

ment. The problem which had stalled the DOD personnel was this: once it had been agreed to utilize the last five whites promoted prior to July 2, 1965 as the basis for the development of a profile of those made supervisors in each department, it was necessary to determine the elements of that profile, and then to apply it to each of the Negro mechanics in the department. The enormity of this task virtually stopped the DOD personnel cold. They spent weeks in a single department interviewing employees and supervisors, but did not simplify the mass of data so that they could apply specific criteria to the Negro mechanics. When I arrived and met the DOD men, most of whom had been in the yard before, I concluded that their prior work had not required sharp decisions; it merely urged better corporate action in general terms.

I organized a procedure to resolve the supervisor question. First, we took the formal criteria of performance ratings of the whites who had been promoted to supervisor and applied these criteria to the Negro mechanics. I resolved doubtful questions in favor of including Negro employees in the list of those eligible for promotion. When this was done, we reduced the group of Negro mechanics for consideration to somewhere between two and three hundred. I then instructed the DOD men to ask supervisors of these men whether in their opinion, these Negro employees had the qualities to become quartermen. The decision to proceed this way was a calculatd risk on my part. It was realistic because, when whites were promoted to quartermen, it was on recommendation of their supervisors in addition to certain formal standards of performance, but there was the danger that racism would infect the judgments of the supervisors and that in proceeding as I did, I was allowing the racially discriminatory pattern to be perpetuated. In effect, I was allowing a decision which should have been made by government to be heavily influenced by the supervisors. In lieu of any other practical approach, I was prepared to gamble on the integrity of the foremen, and their making an honest appraisal of the Negro employees. At least, I thought, we should try this approach. I left Newport News for Washington one day, leaving the five DOD personnel, who were highly skeptical of this procedure, under the immediate supervision of one of my staff, Jules Gordon. (This phase of the administration of the agreement tied up both Gordon and myself during the entire month of March, and thus immobilized one third of the conciliation staff of the EEOC from other activity.)

I returned two days later, and was met at the airport by a group of the DOD personnel who had a surprising story to tell me. They had expected the supervisors to report that none of the Negroes were qualified to be supervisors. This was not an unrealistic expectation for the reasons mentioned above and also because the company had asked the supervisors about promoting Negroes to quartermen when they made their first round of promotions. The report, however contradicted the expectations. The supervisors were reporting that between 30 and 50 per cent of the Negroes who met the formal criteria were qualified to be quartermen. The DOD personnel were literally stunned by the response. I was greatly heartened. The gamble had paid off. We carefully documented these answers, and I directed that we carry out this procedure in all 31 departments in the yard. When we were done, we had a list of around 100 Negroes who met the formal requirements and had been "certified" as capable to be quartermen by their supervisors. As the information came in, I began feeding it to the company on forms which we had prepared for the occasion. The company cooperated fully in making personnel available for interviews, in making records available and in providing secretarial and duplicating services. When the information was all in, the company indicated its willingness to promote some 70 of those whose names we had submitted but not the entire list. The time had come to decide whether to settle.

But there was one preliminary hurdle. The company was unwilling to demote white employees who had been promoted to temporary quartermen and who had been serving in that capacity for some time, due to the slowness of the government in resolving this issue. We were then faced with a serious problem of potential conflict between those Negroes who qualified by our standards and those whites who had been serving as quartermen. Once again, it appeared that the entire agreement was in jeopardy, and that, rather than assisting in solving the problems of discrimination, we were about to generate a new problem of great difficulty. We turned to the facts and were again happily surprised. In only three or four instances were there conflicts of the type we had anticipated. Otherwise, the Negroes whom we wished to see promoted were not in conflict with whites. The reason then became apparent —the bulk of the Negroes who were qualified for quartermen were in primarily Negro departments. The company had not placed white temporary quartermen in those departments, hence there was little conflict between white and Negro for quarterman positions.

What conflict there was could be resolved as a part of the wrap-up of the agreement. We gave two exemptions to the company for whites with specialized skills (one of whom was in charge of the scaffolding on the Carrier Kennedy) allowing them to remain as quartermen ahead of Negroes who were qualified. In another conflict situation the company agreed to promote the Negroes in such a way that it would not be necessary to demote the whites.

We were then down to the final issue: would we settle for the 70 additional Negro quartermen which the company was prepared to make or at least to place on a preferential promotion list, or would we insist on all of the 100 or so names that we had submitted.[32] In submitting these names, and in the development of these lists, I had instructed the DOD personnel when in

---

[32] In theory we could have submitted disputes to Case & Company under § II(2)(e) of the Agreement and then reviewed their decision under § III(5)(c), but I had no reason to expect that Case would have overruled the Company on this issue.

doubt to make decisions, as to whether the Negro employees met the criteria and in interpreting the comments of the foremen as to their qualifications, in favor of the Negro employees. I was thus satisfied that we had rejected few qualified applicants through the administrative process, and that we were probably pressing for promotion of a few men whose credentials were marginal.

As we pressed toward a narrowing of the list of promotable Negroes, I began to sense unrest among the DOD personnel. It was an integrated team, two Negroes, three whites, and they were becoming increasingly unhappy with me as we narrowed the list. My diagnosis of their unhappiness was as follows: they had not been in a decisional situation before. They had not had to make judgments securing promotions for some and not for others. Their prior activities had not produced these kinds of results, and they were not accustomed to the hard role of decision making. Thus they resented the decisions which would strike men from the preferential promotion list, even though those decisions were necessary if others were to get on such a list.

The morning of decision I got up early and went for a walk in the late March sunshine of Newport News. I had a sense that this was the day in which we would conclude the agreement's administration except for certain problems. I hoped that the conclusion would be one which could be viewed as a success by the government, the civil rights interests, and the shipyard. Yet I needed to be sure that my own desire to make the agreement work was not overcoming my judgment. I went back to the motel and sat down at a large table, waiting for the others to come down for breakfast. I posed two questions, individually, to the DOD personnel. (1) If we refused to settle, and the company then declined to promote the men we wanted promoted, did they think that DOD would cut off contracts with the company? The answer was uniformly "no." (2) If we refused to settle, and those men who were not promoted sued, could they win a case of discrimination or of violation of the conciliation agreement? Again the answer was uniformly "no."

I was convinced. They individually had given the same answer to each question. When they were all assembled, I interpreted their conclusions as dictating that we settle the promotion issue on the most favorable terms we could get, and explained to them that their answers to my questions meant that we had no more bargaining leverage on these issues. Somewhat unhappy at being made parties to the decision to settle, they reluctantly agreed that settlement was necessary.

Jules Gordon and I then went to the personnel office and sat down with William Myers, the director of industrial relations, to work out the details of the settlement. Some 75 of the men on our list were placed on preferential promotion lists to become quartermen. The basic phase of the administration of the Newport News agreement was finished. The following week I resigned as Chief of Conciliations and began a process of withdrawal from the activities of the Commission which brought me back into law teaching at Rutgers in September 1967.

IX. EPILOGUE

In the months following our leaving Newport News, a strike occurred for the first time in the history of the yard. *Barron's* a conservative weekly, attributed this to the involvement of the EEOC in an article which was, I thought, unfair to the Commission. The article found its way into the Congressional Record, and Senator Javitts, in rebuttal, inserted other material in the Record, making it clear that the strike was not over racial questions and including an analysis of the agreement which I had prepared for the EEOC.[33] While the strike was not directly related to Commission activities at the shipyard, it is clear that our proceedings did cause a review and reconsideration of many aspects of labor relations at the yard which had been accepted in the period before the agreement. In this sense, once the agreement had been executed and administered, industrial relations at the yard were on a new footing and new tensions could be expected to develop.

Senator Fanin and *Barron's* magazine have waged a sporadic attack on the operation of the EEOC in connection with the Newport News Agreement since that time. While these attacks have been without merit, they have not been without effect. I think they have been one factor which has discouraged the government from operating since that time as they did in Newport News. There has been no such concerted effort with any company since the agreement was negotiated. Thus that week in March 1966 stands as the "one brief shining moment" when the government did marshall its resources and produce significant results with a major firm in ending a pattern of discrimination. There are other reasons why this pattern of joint action (called "ganging up" by its detractors, as if employers had a vested interest in having the government act in an *uncoordinated* manner) has not been repeated. One reason has been bureaucratic jealousy; EEOC did get most of the public credit for the agreement. I think this was probably deserved, but surely there was enough to go around for Justice, DOD, Navy and Labor. Also, general bureaucratic caution set in. Officials, particularly in DOD, pulled back from the concept of massive system changes to eliminate discrimination. They decentralized the contract compliance function and, within a year, eliminated Mr. Clark from any role in the program.[34] In short, the collective will of the government agencies which had joined for that brief moment could not be crystallized again during the time that I remained in Government after the agreement. I have kept up my connections with the federal programs since leaving the EEOC staff and am in a position to say that the joint effort mounted at Newport News has not been repeated as of September 1968.

[33] *Supra* note 4.
[34] *See* app. VI p. 325 *infra.*

Instead, each agency is going its own way, and the effect of the dis-jointed action of the federal government is to judicialize the administration of the anti-discrimination law and make it unlikely that many companies will be faced with the major system changes which confronted Newport News. The OFCC is now holding several hearings to decide whether to suspend contracting. The Department of Justice has filed a number of law suits under Title VII. Meanwhile, the contractors who are sued keep their contracts, and the contractors subject to hearings deny discrimination and will have a trial and appeal on particular issues. Enormous amounts of government manpower go into each of these proceedings, leaving little government energy for other activities. The net effect of these proceedings will, of course, be healthy. There will be definitions of discriminatory conduct, and out-lining of required remedies. Both of these are badly needed in the field.[35] And yet, this course of events means that very few companies will be subjected to systematic review and revision of their industrial relations systems such as was accomplished at Newport News with minimal invest-ment of manpower, compared to that of the filing, preparation and trial of a proceeding before OFCC or the Federal Court. And the range of solutions achieved in negotiation, as demonstrated at Newport News, is likely to be far broader than that which will issue from a judicial or administrative pro-ceeding. Thus I think there remains today an important place in any sound program of administration of anti-discrimination laws for the Newport News type of joint governmental action, and I think it part of our national tragedy that the government has not followed the pattern established in that case.

The Newport News approach, however, did have it limitations. The ad-ministrative process settles large issues, and, of necessity, must sometimes ignore individuals. Perhaps some of those Negroes who were not placed on the list for promotion to quartermen are entitled to sue under the agreement as third party beneficiaries. It is one of the consequences of a negotiated solu-tion that some possible beneficiaries will not receive the assistance that individ-ualized attention to their situation would dictate. For this reason I am sharply in favor of the retention of the individual right to sue against employment dis-crimination, regardless of whether administrative agencies are given more power in the area, and I oppose amendments to Title VII which would restrict the individual right to sue.[36] The individual right is important for two reasons; first, it will "prop up" the administrator so that he is more likely to assist the individual than settle to get rid of his case, and second, it enables the individual who believes himself injured by a settlement agree-ment to secure de novo a judicial review of his rights. If administration has done a good job, the judicial review will uphold the settlement; if the

---

[35] The first formal decision of the Secretary of Labor interpreting the requirements of the Executive order was rendered in January 1969 in Matter of Allen-Bradley Co., see CCH Employment Practices Guide, New Developments, Para. 8070,8065 (1969).

[36] See Blumrosen, *supra* note 13.

administration has not done a good job, then the settlement should not be upheld. I do not fear that the individual right to sue will interrupt the settlement process; it will only deter the entering of meaningless settlements which should be discouraged anyway. If the settlement is a decent one, then it will be so recognized by all concerned parties. But my own experience as an administrator, disposing of bulk claims over a conference table as in the Newport News situation, has confirmed my belief in the importance of the individual right to sue with respect to these matters.

Finally, I would not leave the impression that the administration of the agreement brought repose to the shipyard. Problems of discrimination persist. Certain issues were never resolved. Promotion of some and the opening of opportunities have generated new ambitions and aspirations on the part of those who may not have had them before. The internal problems of the union have become complicated.

But repose is not an object of modern industrial relations. These relations are recognized by all as dynamic, as involving constant readjustments of positions and situations in light of the myriad of changes in circumstances which bear on any given system. The development of new methods of ship-building and the take over of the shipyard by one of the conglomerates simply illustrate new factors which continually change and challenge the industrial relations situation at the shipyard. This is typical of modern industry. Men knowledgable in industrial relations know this and are not ashamed of a temporary solution or of an adjustment for a limited period of time. A willingness to live with change is an essential ingredient in our ability to participate in the affairs of our time. What the Newport News Agreement did, as it was administered, was to shatter the old system, shake up the patterns of wage rates, and provide a new basis, not tainted with discrimination, on which the business of the shipyard could be conducted. The affairs at the shipyard are not tranquil, but they are operating on a more civilized basis. Most major systematic discriminations built into the industrial relations systems over time have been shaken out by the agreement and its administration. Future problems will look more and more like individual grievances under a collective bargaining agreement which can be resolved within the industrial relations framework, or as "ordinary" matters before the EEOC.

X. The Negotiated Settlement

This article has been concerned with the nexus between law and life in the new industrial state—with the points of contact between law, the administrative processes of government, and the intricate pluralism of union, management, civil rights groups and individuals involved in any serious effort to untangle the web of racial discrimination and set employment matters off on a new non-discriminatory footing. Coping with the myriad of personalities and interests, conceiving and developing substantive solutions which work, and seeing these solutions through the negotiation and administration of the Newport News agreement has provided a perspective on the negotiated settlement in the field of employment discrimination. I believe the objective of all such processes should be to force all parties to reach an agreement which will root out discrimination and its consequences. Whether this is done through administrative sanctions, such as the threat of suit or the suspension of government contracting as was the case in Newport News, or through a judicial decision that the law has been violated and that the parties should submit a proposed order, is a matter of highly important detail.

In the last analysis, system changes such as those achieved in Newport News are intricate and complex; they require careful negotiation to be workable. I believe that government should adopt a full enforcement approach in the field of employment discrimination by utilizing all of its power. Once this power has been applied, in most cases sensible negotiations will work an end to discrimination. But an enforcement policy without the negotiated solution as its objective may prove to be as sterile as the "soft" policies which government has historically followed in this field. A litigation program alone will not achieve the end of employment discrimination.

Except for the suggestion in *Crown Zellerbach Corp. v. Wirtz*[37] there is no right to a government contract; and it does not necessarily follow that a government contractor is entitled to a trial-type hearing on the question of whether he has discriminated before he loses the opportunity for future contracts. There are occasions on which the government can act without a trial-type hearing. I submit that in the field of employment discrimination a trial-type hearing *prior* to suspension of government contracts is inappropriate. Suspension of contracting, on a temporary basis after informal administrative investigations which includes a full opportunity for respondent to present evidence and argument, can set the stage for major system changes such as those achieved at Newport News. After entering into a negotiated agreement for the kind of changes which the discrimination requires, the employer may comply with the agreement or seek judicial relief from its consequences. In the vast bulk of cases, the agreements reached will be honored, and discriminatory practice set aright. Where this is not a practical course, it is better to let the large institutions, the companies and the unions, seek judicial relief against overreaching by government rather than to leave the victims of discrimination with their burden pending judicial decisions. This structuring of the situation will facilitate negotiated solutions which can bring an end to employment discrimination. A trial-type hearing is not neces-

<hr>

[37] 281 F. Supp. 337 (D.D.C. 1968). § 208(b) of Executive Order 11246 requires a "hearing" prior to the issuance of a notice under § 209(a)(6) prohibiting further contracting unless and until the Secretary of Labor is satisfied that the contractor will carry out the policies of the order. However, as § 208(a) makes clear, the "hearing" contemplated under the order need not be a trial-type adversary proceeding. The order may mean no more than a requirement that contractors be afforded a full opportunity to present evidence and argument.

sarily the most sensitive process for achieving the elimination of employment discrimination. I hope that the conference table will once again be utilized for that purpose by a government utilizing all of its powers to assure that the resulting bargain does in fact carry out the national purpose of establishing equal employment opportunity.

APPENDIX I

Conciliation Agreement Between Equal Employment Opportunity Commission et al. Newport News Shipbuilding and Drydock Company

Equal Employment Opportunity Commission, Washington, D.C.: Case No. 5–7–235, 5–7–237, 5–7–520 and 5–7–521, in the Matter of the Conciliation Between Equal Employment Opportunity Commission; Thomas Mann; James Lassiter; Arthur Ford; Reverend J. C. Fauntleroy, et al; Complainants and Newport News Shipbuilding and Drydock Company, Respondent

Charges having been filed under Title VII of the Civil Rights Act of 1964 by the Charging Parties, the Commission having found reasonable cause to believe the charges to be true and the matter having been conciliated, the parties hereby agree to and do settle the above matter in the following extent and manner:

I. STATEMENT OF PRINCIPLES

1. All hiring, promotion practices, and other terms and conditions of employment shall be maintained and conducted in a manner which does not discriminate on the basis of race, color, religion or national origin in violation of Title VII of the Civil Rights Act of 1964. All present and future employees will be classified and assigned without discrimination on the basis of race, color, religion or national origin. All job classifications shall be open to all employees without discrimination as to race, color, religion or national origin.

2. The Company agrees that all facilities owned, operated or managed by or on behalf of the Company shall be available for the use of any employee without regard to race, color, religion or national origin; that there shall be no discrimination against any employee on said grounds with respect to the use of said facilities, and that the notice required to be posted by Title VII of the Civil Rights Act of 1964 will be posted.

3. The Company agrees that there shall be no discrimination or retaliation of any kind against any person because of opposition to any practice declared unlawful under Title VII of the Civil Rights Act of 1964; or because of the filing of a charge; giving of testimony or assistance; or participation in any manner in any investigation, proceeding or hearing under or with respect to matters covered by Title VII of the Civil Rights Act of 1964, Executive Orders 10925 or 11246, and Regulations issued thereunder, or this Agreement.

II. GENERAL REMEDIAL ACTION

1. Evaluation of jobs

a. The Company and the Commission shall forthwith undertake a general review to determine if Negro employees are improperly classified with respect to the job they are performing and the rates they are paid relative to white employees doing the same or substantially equivalent work. With respect to several job categories in which, predominantly, Negroes are employed and there is no direct basis for comparison with rates of pay of white employees, a review will be made of such categories to determine whether the rate of pay is discriminatorily depressed on the basis of race.

b. To conduct this review, the Company shall as soon as possible but not later than 45 days from the date of this Agreement, retain at its expense an expert in job evaluation and statements of work content, knowledgeable in race relations, who is acceptable to the Commission, to make this determination. In the event an expert acceptable to the Commission is not designated within 45 days, the parties shall forthwith reconvene for the sole purpose of designating the expert. The expert shall report his findings to the Company and the Commission. The company shall implement the decision of the expert by re-classifying such employees and/or adjusting the rate of pay accordingly within a period of 30 days from the date of determination. The Company shall supply said expert with adequate staff and facilities and shall make available all records and other information necessary to perform this function. Such review shall be concluded within 120 days of the appointment of the expert, unless the expert requests and the Commission agrees to a reasonable extension of time for this purpose.

c. The scope of the review is to be general, and shall not be limited by or to the complaint of individual employees. However, this review will encompass the rate and classification of any Negro employee who requests such a review. If, as a result of this review, the Commission believes that an employee's job is improperly classified relative to jobs held by white employees or that a rate is lower than that paid white employees performing the same or substantially equivalent work, the Commission shall so notify the Company which will take appropriate action to correct the situation. As a part of this review procedure, there shall be developed written statements of the work content for all jobs involved, which reflect the work actually performed.

d. The expert described above may be an individual, management consultant or operations research organization. Both the Commission and the Company may nominate persons or organizations to be retained as the expert. It shall be the expert's responsibility to conduct the review set forth in the first paragraph of this section.

2. Promotion to supervisor and other positions, upgrading, and vacancies

a. As the Company's last report to the Government showed that only 32 of 1997 persons employed by the Company as "Officials and Managers" were Negroes, the Company agrees that, to comply affirmatively with Title VII of the Civil Rights Act of 1964, the Executive Order of the President and the Regulations of Departments and Agencies of the Federal Government, it will afford affirmative opportunities for promotion to and within supervisory levels, including staff supervisors, junior and senior quartermen, foremen and assistant foremen, assistant superintendent and superintendent, to qualified Negroes employed by the Company. Accordingly, the Company agrees to revise its promotion policies and practices with a view to improving opportunities for qualified Negro personnel for promotion to and within supervisory levels, as follows:

b. An inventory of the skilled Negro employees, indicating their seniority (defined as continuous service with the shipyard) and qualifications, and an inventory of the seniority and qualifications of the last 100 persons promoted to quarterman positions to July 2, 1965, will be conducted jointly by the Company and by Industrial Employment Policy Specialists of the Department of Defense as an interested party, and in the interests of contract compliance, commencing within 30 days of the date of this Agreement. Within 60 days of the conclusion of the inventory, a list of those Negro employees whose seniority and qualifications exceed those of white employees among the 100 persons described above will be developed jointly by the Company and by the Industrial Employment Policy Specialist and will constitute the order of placement, as supervisory positions open, for which the employee's qualifications are relevant, until the list is exhausted. Refusals of Negro employees to accept offers of promotions to supervision must be documented in each case.

c. Provided however that where the Company desires to fill a vacancy with an employee with greater seniority of qualifications than Negro employees on the list, the company may present has [sic] qualifications in writing to the Commission, along with a demonstration of special circumstances and unusual need for which it wishes to promote said employee. If the Commission is satisfied that the request is free of discrimination on the basis of race, color, religion or national origin, it shall grant the request. All appointments to supervisory posts shall be made without regard to the race of the employees who will be subject to such supervision.

d. Prior to the completion of the list described above and its use as a basis for selection of supervisors, supervisory vacancies may develop. Said vacancies will be filled by qualified Negro employees. Where the Company has special reasons for desiring to fill any such vacancy with a white employee, it shall first notify the Commission in writing, stating its reasons. If the Commission is satisfied that the request is free of discrimination, it shall grant the request.

c. Any disagreement between the Company and the Industrial Employment Policy Specialists, with respect to matters described in the first paragraph of this section, shall be resolved by the expert mentioned above, if appointed and available, and otherwise by the Commission.

3. Promotion and transfer to nonsupervisory positions

a. The Company agrees to post at the Employment Office, Yard Personnel Office, and at all normal access gates into the yard, notices of the existence of all job vacancies. Applications to fill such vacancies will be considered and qualified applicants for such jobs shall be selected on the basis of their length of service where their skill, ability, and efficiency are fairly equal.

b. The Company shall permit employees from predominately Negro job classifications to transfer to vacancies in other departments for which they are qualified. If, within two weeks, the employee is unable to perform in the new job, he may return to his old job. If the vacancy to which he transfers is a lower rate step in his classification, he will be transferred at his rate before the transfer.

c. Employees in predominantly Negro departments shall be given the first opportunity for training in programs in which they are qualified to enter.

d. The Company will apply a liberal policy in the application of this section to advance the basic purpose of this Agreement.

e. To comply affirmatively with Title VII and Executive Orders in the matter of promotion and training, the Company agrees to undertake an intensive re-evaluation of the skills of its Negro employees, to institute training programs to develop and improve the skill levels of such employees, and to promote and adjust compensation on the basis of such re-evaluation and/or training. Opportunities to acquire skills necessary for upgrading shall be afforded Negro employees on a non-discriminatory basis so that they acquire a rounded work experience.

f. The qualifications of all Negro applicants for employment will be reviewed and measured against minimum qualifications for all job classifications.

Such applicants will be given full consideration for filling vacancies in all such job classifications for which they may qualify. Review of applicant qualifications shall be concluded within 60 days after the date of this Agreement.

4. Adjustment of rate: Promotional opportunities

In order to adjust the pay rate and classification of Negro employees who may have been discriminatorily denied or delayed in their advancement through the wage and job structure of the Company, the following is agreed to:

a. To determine Company practices with respect to the rate and conditions of promotions of white employees both within steps of job classifications and from one job classification to another, control groups will be picked by a random sample method from the Fitters Department (X–11), the Painters Department (X–33), and Storekeepers (O–53).

b. The sample selected from each department shall be sufficient to trace the pattern of employment history of white employees in the department from the time of their original hiring.

c. From this sample there will be derived a profile of the rate and conditions for promotion of white employees.

d. This profile shall be developed jointly by the expert described in section 1 and the Industrial Employment Policy Specialists, Department of Defense.

e. Thereafter, the expert would compare the history of progression and promotion of individual Negro employees in said departments with the profile.

f. Upon establishment that a Negro employee has not moved up through the grades within the classification in which he is presently employed as rapidly as the norm or standard derived from the sample for white employees, he shall forthwith be assigned the first grade in his job classification, or such other grade as he would have achieved had his history followed the normal progression indicated in the study unless the Company demonstrates from such records as it keeps which are themselves not the product or result of discrimination, that the employee was not promoted for reason of physical handicap, improper attendance or other conduct on the premises. Considerations of the employee's skill and ability are not germane to this section. The burden of demonstrating that from Company records that the employee should not be upgraded is on the Company.

g. Where the expert finds that the Negro employee would have been promoted beyond his classification had the white rate of progress been followed, the Company may assert that the employee is not and cannot become qualified for promotion to the higher classification, using the same standard for promotion between classes heretofore used for white employees as derived from the sample.

h. If the evaluator finds that the Negro employee has such qualifications for promotion, or can achieve them through reasonable training, he shall be placed on a preferential promotion list and given at an appropriate time such training as may be reasonably necessary to equip him for promotion. Such promotion shall be given when need arises for additional members of the next higher class.

i. The sample and its results will apply to other departments to which reasonably applicable. Thereupon the expert shall apply the same standards of comparison of Negro employment records against the promotion and upgrading profile of white employees and the same actions will be taken as a result of that comparison as described in paragraphs 6 and 7.

j. If a further sample is needed, the department or departments from which it is to be drawn shall be discussed with the Commission. The expert will apply the results of any such further sample alone or in conjunction with the previous sample in such departments as are agreed upon in the manner described in paragraphs 6 and 7.

k. The entire Negro labor force will be reviewed in the manner set out above.

l. The Company may as a part of this process, and in its discretion, seek to determine if white employees have been unfairly treated in respect to ingrade progressions or promotions, and to attempt, in the event such unfairness is found, to correct it.

5. Apprenticeship programs

As the Company's last report to the Government (Form 40) showed that only 6 of the 506 apprentices enrolled in the apprenticeship program were Negroes, the Company agrees that, to provide affirmatively for equal employment opportunity, apprenticeship classes shall henceforth be filled as follows:

a. The Company shall, within 30 days of this Agreement, estimate the number of vacancies in the program for the coming year. Similar estimates shall be made each succeeding 12 months.

b. The Company agrees that qualified employees now on the payroll shall have first opportunity to fill apprenticeship classes during the next two years. For these employees, the Company agrees to accept a high school diploma or academic equivalent for admission, to accept employees up to the age of 25 years as entering apprentices, to accept married students as apprentices, to keep such as apprentices should they marry during the course of apprenticeship, and not to debar any employee from the apprenticeship program because of previous attendance at college or other institution of higher education.

c. A list of Negro employees eligible for the apprenticeship program under these provisions shall be compiled and shall be available to the Commission. Rejections of this opportunity by employees on the list shall be obtained in writing, with a copy to the Commission.

d. In filling vacancies in the apprenticeship classes, the Company agrees to exercise its utmost efforts to see that substantial numbers of Negroes are included in such classes. To this end the Company agrees, (1) to include in its recruitment efforts the predominantly Negro schools in the labor market areas; and (2) to notify civil rights organizations in said area of this Agreement and to solicit such organizations to send qualified applicants for such programs. The Commission shall, upon request, supply a list of such organizations. Copies of such notices and solicitations shall be furnished by the Company to the Commission. The parties to this Agreement recognize as a natural result of this recruitment effort that the ratio of Negro to white apprentices in any given year should approach the ratio of Negro to white employees and the ratio of Negro to whites in the labor market area but this provision shall not be construed to require or permit the rejection of any qualified applicant on the basis of his race or color.

e. When the Company has filled one-third of the estimated vacancies in any apprenticeship class for each year through the foregoing procedures, it shall notify the Commission of the proportion of Negro employees enrolled in the class, and the Company shall not fill more than half the remaining vacancies until the Commission has responded. The commission's response can be expected within two weeks. If it appears to the Commission that adequate numbers of Negro employees will not be enrolled in the class, the Commission may propose additional reasonable recruiting steps which the Company shall undertake to assure the fulfillment of its obligations under this section.

f. The Company shall integrate the apprenticeship faculty by October 1, 1966, and the apprenticeship Selection Committee forthwith.

g. Apprenticeship requirements shall be reviewed by the Company and the Commission within the next 60 days to determine whether increased numbers of Negroes can be appointed consistent with the maintenance of the requirements for qualified apprentices. After this review, the Commission may propose other reasonable steps to increase the number of Negro apprentices, and the Company shall take such steps.

h. All other training programs, formal and informal, including crash training, patternmaking and tack welding programs, shall be open to employees without regard to race or color.

The Company shall post in conspicuous places and otherwise publicize information to all its employees concerning the availability of these programs, and shall actively encourage Negro participation in these programs.

6. Facilities

In view of the desire of the Company to afford equal employment opportunity and to comply fully with the letter and spirit of the aforesaid Civil Rights Act of 1964 and the various Executive Orders and Regulations applicable to its activities, the Company agrees to take the following steps:

a. In addition to the elimination of a segregated facility in the Foundry, the Company agrees to alter the portable toilet facilities in the drawings attached hereto as Appendix II, and made a part hereof, in the manner indicated in such drawings. Such alterations shall be commenced within 30 days from the date of this settlement Agreement, and shall be completed not later than 75 days after work on such alterations has concerned.

b. Also, the Company agrees that all locker room facilities on the premises shall be available for the use of employees in that department without regard to race, color, religion, or national origin and there shall be no discrimination against any employee on such grounds with respect to the use of said facilities. All locker room space shall be reassigned in each department not later than the time specified in paragraph 1, on the following basis:

(1) Lockers in buildings devoted to locker rooms shall be reassigned to all employees on the basis of alphabetical order for all employees assigned to such buildings. Assignment to buildings shall be without regard to race.

(2) Locker rooms in other buildings shall be assigned alphabetically to employees using such facilities, in such a manner as to eliminate segregated use of locker rooms and related facilities.

(3) Henceforth:

(a) Lockers are to be assigned on the basis of needs and in the order of their vacancy regardless of race.

(b) An up-to-date record will be kept of lockers in all locker rooms with particular attention given to the following:

(i) Number and location of vacant lockers
(ii) Date of vacancy
(iii) Date of assignment
(iv) To whom assigned.

(c) During such alterations and locker reassignments specified in paragraphs 1 and 2 and for a reasonable time thereafter, the Company will post on all Newport News Shipbuilding departmental bulletin boards a notice which, in substance, states that all employees have equal rights to use all such facilities. Any employee who interferes with or intimidates employees in the exercise of their rights hereunder and/or takes any other action which is intended to maintain segregated facilities shall result in disciplinary action including, where appropriate, discharge.

7. Other affirmative actions

Take the following affirmative action to effectuate the policies of Title VII of the Civil Rights Act of 1964:

a. Upgrade and advance qualified Negro employees to positions as first-class mechanics.

b. Full-time operators of cranes in the Foundry of 20 tons or above shall be paid first-class mechanics' rates, when they are qualified to operate such cranes in a proficient and safe manner.

c. The Company agrees to promote Thomas C. Mann, Reverend J. C. Fauntleroy and James E. Lassiter to the position of quarterman in their respective departments, effective the first Monday after the signing of this Agreement. The Company further agrees to promote Arthur Ford to the position of materialman, and advance him to mechanic, third class, effective the first Monday after the signing of this Agreement. The Company will review with Mr. Ford his experience and understanding of its operations to determine the most effective use which can be made of his capabilities.

d. Cooperate with the Equal Employment Opportunity Commission with regard to the investigation, conciliation, and processing of the charges of 38 other charging parties without regard to the time limitations of Section 706 of Title VII.

e. With regard to certain charging parties, waive the statutory period within which the charging parties may institute a civil action in the event conciliation is not achieved.

f. In addition, to cooperate with the Commission with regard to the investigation and conciliation of any charges which may hereinafter be filed.

g. Persons aggrieved, whose cases are subject to the job evaluation review under section 1 hereof, but who are not among those listed above, shall not be entitled to retroactive back pay in the event the expert determines that they have been improperly classified or paid.

h. Any person against whom a new act of discrimination is committed after the date of this Agreement shall be entitled to his full remedy under Title VII of the Civil Rights Act of 1964.

III. GENERAL PROVISIONS

1. Policy statement

The Company agrees that its policy statement in support of the principle of equal employment opportunity, which was worked out with the Commission, and is attached to this Conciliation Agreement and marked Appendix III, is incorporated by reference herein as though fully set out. This statement emphasizes the Company's pledge of nondiscrimination with respect to recruitment, hiring, wages, hours, promotions, training, apprenticeships and all others terms and conditions of employment. This policy statement shall be published in full by the company within 30 days of the date of this Agreement by attaching said statement, signed by the President of the Company, to the pay check of each full-time employee of the Company. Copies thereof shall be displayed prominently on bulletin boards available to all employees.

2. Supervisory employees

The Company shall within 30 days assemble all supervisory employees. It shall read the policy statement set forth herein, advise the supervisors of the contents of this Agreement, including the Company's policy of encouraging equal employment opportunities and a fully integrated work force. In addition, supervisors shall be instructed that they shall encourage the use of facilities on an integrated basis, and that terms of address used in the plant shall be the same for whites and Negroes. Further, supervisors shall be instructed that a violation of the policy set forth in this Agreement shall result in disciplinary action including, where appropriate, discharge.

The Company shall also call departmental or other group meetings for all employees for the same purpose. Meetings of supervisors and all employees shall be completed within 30 days from the date of this Agreement. The Commission shall be advised 5 days in advance of the date of meetings to be held in three representative departments. A representative of the Commission may attend any or all meetings held for this purpose.

3. Implementing procedures

The Company shall establish implementing procedures which will include the assignment of responsibility within the Company for implementation of each and every provision of this Agreement, and a formalized feedback system to keep management apprised of the progress of the program by channeling to top management the substance of all decisions taken hereunder by officers, agents and employees of the company.

4. Reports

a. The Company shall prepare and furnish to the Commission not later than 90 days from the date of this Agreement a detailed report of the actions to comply with this Agreement. For 2 years thereafter the Company shall report at quarterly intervals its progress in complying with this Agreement. The initial and subsequent reports shall include the following statistical data broken down into the categories white and Negro:

(1) Applications for employment, by name, job applied for.

(2) New hires, by job title, department, name of employee and date of employment.

(3) Changes in rate or job classification, by name of employee, date and department.

(4) Promotions to non-supervisory positions within each department and to supervisor by name of employee.

(5) Entrants into apprenticeship and formalized training and educational programs, by program, by name of employee.

b. The reports required by this paragraph are in addition to other reports required by this Agreement. All reports required to be furnished to the Commission under this Agreement should be addressed to the Chief of Conciliation, Equal Employment Opportunity Commission, Washington, D.C. 20506.

c. After the first 90 days the Commission shall consider simplifying these requirements by accepting in summary form the information contained therein.

5. Review of compliance

a. The Company agrees that the Commission, on the request of any charging party named herein or in its own motion, may review compliance with this Agreement.

b. As a part of such review, the Commission may require written reports in addition to those otherwise provided for which are reasonably necessary to the audit of this Agreement, may inspect the premises, examine witnesses, and examine and copy records and documents.

c. The Commission shall determine whether the Company has complied with this Agreement, may review any finding or decision of the expert referred to in this Agreement, and may revise same where the Commission finds the revision necessary to prevent discrimination.

6. Publication of agreement

The Company agrees that the terms of this Agreement and the proceedings before the Commission, but not including the content of conciliation discussions between the Commission and the Company, shall be made public by the Commission.

7. Federal district court proceeding

The signing of this Agreement shall not prejudice the right of the plaintiffs in the Federal District Court action embracing the same subject matter from seeking an award of costs, expenses and reasonable attorney fees in said action.

> NEWPORT NEWS SHIPBUILDING AND DRYDOCK COMPANY
> THOMAS C. MANN
> REV. J. C. FAUNTLEROY
> ARTHUR FORD
> JAMES LASSITER

Date: I recommended approval of this Agreement; Alfred W. Blumrosen, Chief, Conciliations.

EQUAL OPPORTUNITY POLICY

I wish to emphasize the Company's fundamental policy of providing equal opportunity in all areas of employment practice, and in assuring that there shall be no discrimination against any person on the grounds of race, color, religion or national origin.

This policy extends to hiring, working conditions, employee treatment, training programs, promotions, use of company facilities and all other terms and conditions of employment. The Company encourages all employees to exercise their rights under this policy.

The importance of fulfilling this policy cannot be overemphasized. Any violation of the letter or spirit of this policy by any employee of this Company shall result in disciplinary action including, where appropriate, discharge. Specific instructions for affirmative action to implement ths policy wll be issued.

> D. A. HOLDEN,
> *President, Newport News Shipbuilding and Drydock Co.*

APPENDIX II

Barron's National Business and Financial Weekly, July 17, 1967 at 1, Official Bias: A Note on the Equal Employment Opportunity Commission. (Reprinted by courtesy of Barron's.)

As bureaucrats go these days, the Equal Employment Opportunity Commission has not gone very far. Created in mid-1965 to weed out discrimination in employment based on either race or sex, the agency boasts a budget of only $5.2

million and a staff of 314, smaller respectively than those of the Office of Coal Research and the Federal Crop Insurance Program. Personnel-wise, EEOC has been something of a revolving door: its first chairman, Franklin D. Roosevelt, Jr., quickly resigned to run for Governor; his successor, Stephen N. Shulman, quit after nine months to go into private practice. While the Commission reportedly has received over 15,000 complaints, it has cleared up only a few hundred. "We're out to kill an elephant," Mr. Shulman recently was quoted as saying, "with a fly gun."

*   *   *

In the wrong hands, however, even fly guns can be dangerous. Last Monday Newport News Shipbuilding & Dry Dock Co., the nation's leading builder of naval vessels, suffered the first strike in 81 years of doing business. On the following midnight, a riot, which injured over a score of people and was termed by local police the "worst disorder" in the placid history of Newport News, Va., broke out at the company's main gate. Newspaper accounts of the affair, which interrupted the construction of the world's largest aircraft carrier and led to the personal intervention of the Governor, were scanty at best. The walkout apparently began in protest over relatively minor grievances. However, union officials hinted that "other problems" lurk in the background. A Washington paper reported cryptically that "the issues go deeper."

Somehow nobody has chosen to identify the principal villain of the piece, which is none other than the fly gun-totin' Equal Employment Opportunity Commission. Backed by the firepower of the U.S. Department of Labor, which threatened the shipyard's government contracts, the Commission 18 months ago moved in on management. In particular, the agency coerced Newport News Ship into signing a so-called Conciliation Agreement, which, by pointedly favoring Negroes for future apprentice training and on-the-job promotion, made a new kind of discrimination official policy. "Shipyard in South Induced to Make Up for Past Bias," read the headline. Since then, in the words of an old hand at the yard, EEOC has done its worst to "set black against white, labor against management and disconcert everybody." In the alien world of bureaucracy, size is no measure of virulence.

Labor-management relations at Newport News Ship began to suffer in mid-1965, shortly after the Equal Employment Opportunity Commission set up shop. The company, which does roughly half a billion dollars worth of work per year, largely for the Navy or the subsidized merchant marine, was a logical target. It's also located in the South. The Commission swiftly set about building a case. According to our man in Washington (actually a charming lady named Shirley Scheibla, who was born and raised in Newport News), EEOC that summer began knocking on doors in Negro neighborhoods soliciting complaints of job discrimination. It managed to get 41, which, for one reason or another, ultimately narrowed down to four. Thus armed, EEOC began to negotiate with the company. After months of fruitless discussion, Washington got tough. Pleading a "pattern of discrimination," EEOC took the dispute to the Justice Department. At the same time, Labor Secretary W. Willard Wirtz ordered the newly organized Office of Federal Contract Compliance to crack down on the yard. A week later the company caved in and signed the notorious Conciliation Agreement, which some have called a "landmark in fair employment practices."

That's one way to describe a document which, in barring discrimination, moved to substitute favoritism. Thus, Newport News Shipbuilding agreed to hire an outside "expert in job evaluation . . . who is acceptable to the Commission" to determine whether Negro employes are improperly classified or working at rates set arbitrarily low. To arrive at his findings, the "expert" took a "random sample" of white employment histories, and, if a Negro worker's status lagged behind the resulting profile, he was deemed a victim of discrimination. Presumably to compensate for past sins, the company had to draw up a preferred promotion list consisting solely of Negroes (exceptions had to be cleared with the Commission). As to apprentice training, a company-run school, once the community's pride, was compelled to drastically change its admission practices. Though the number of applicants traditionally has far outstripped the available openings, Newport News Ship undertook to seek recruits in Negro schools and through civil rights groups. It also accepted a quota system under which "the ratio of Negro to white apprentices in any given year should approach the ratio of . . . Negro to white in the labor area."

The first outraged reaction came from the unaffiliated Peninsula Shipbuilders Association, which, though the recognized bargaining agent for most of the 22,000-man work force, was not consulted. Though subsequently made a party to the pact, the union has never overcome its resentment. Two months ago P.S.A., denouncing a Labor Department release on the company's promotion practices as self-serving and false, threatened legal action to set the record straight. The white community—Newport News Ship is far and away the leading local industry —has been equally aggrieved. One graduate of the Apprentice School wrote the local newspaper to protest against the lowering of admission standards to which, he argued, a quota system inevitably would lead. Another reader, the Rev. Richard B. Sisson of Hampton Roads, put the issue squarely in the moral realm. "I am for equal opportunity for all citizens in school, jobs, housing and all other matters. That is why I find the terms dictated by the government to the shipyard odious. The quota system is just as iniquitous as the exclusion of Negroes some have charged the Yard with practicing previously. . . It will result in very definite de facto discrimination against whites, Indians, Asiatics and all other non-Negroes. Two wrongs do not make a right."

Even the Negroes, in whose behalf the whole exercise presumably was launched, have wound up frustrated and angry. Like all demagogues, the Equal Employment Opportunity Commission promised far more than it has been able to deliver. "You need a militancy in this community," Samuel C. Jackson, former NAACP bigwig and current EEOC Commissioner, told an audience in Hampton Roads. Thanks to official action, he added, 5,000 of the company's 5,800 Negro workers would get "substantial raises." Instead, according to the union, such rewards have gone to precisely 155. While trying to mind somebody else's business, moreover, the Commission has failed to attend to its own; some 78 cases of alleged discrimination brought by the union have dragged on far beyond the statutory 60 days. Linwood Harris, Negro co-manager of the Peninsula Shipbuilders Association, represents the voice of the people: "The good the EEOC has done," he told Barron's prior to the strike, "is minute and not worth it because of the bad they've done."

* * *

Newport News is a relatively small place (though the company happens to be the sole remaining builder of U.S. capital ships). Yet what has happened there is a matter of national concern. Emboldened by its "success," EEOC is moving aggressively against other leading corporations. President Johnson has asked Congress to grant the agency power to issue cease-and-desist orders. Instead, to judge by the dismal record, we urge the lawmakers to hand down a stop order of their own.

APPENDIX III

Congressional Record (daily edition) Aug. 22, 1967, S12001.

UNJUSTIFIED CRITICISM OF THE ROLE OF THE EEOC IN THE RECENT NEWPORT NEWS SHIPBUILDING & DRY DOCK CO. LABOR DISPUTE

Mr. JAVITS. Mr. President, last week an article which appeared on the first page of Barron's, of July 17, 1967, was inserted into the RECORD. The article was very critical of the EEOC, and directly implied that the Commission's action in persuading the Newport News Shipbuilding & Dry Dock Co. to enter into a conciliation agreement which rectified longstanding racial discrimination against Negroes employed by the company was responsible for a recent labor dispute involving some violent episodes. The article suggested that the ostensible reason for the strike—the company's overtime policy—was not the real issue and that the strike was really attributable to resentment among white employees over the treatment of Negro employees pursuant to the conciliation agreement.

Mr. President, the article reading it carefully, does not actually state, in so many words, that the labor dispute involved the conciliation agreement, but it implies that this was the case.

Mr. President, the function of the EEOC is so critical to our overall fight against racial discrimination that I think the record should be set straight. The fact it seems to me demonstrates that racial discrimination and the conciliation agreement negotiated by the EEOC really had nothing to do with the recent dispute. I call the Senate's attention to a letter dated August 11, 1967, from Mr. Willoughby Abner, Special Assistant to the Director of the Federal Mediation and Conciliation Service, to Mr. Chris Roggerson, a conciliator of the EEOC regarding the dispute. Federal mediators were involved in the negotiations which led to the settlement of the dispute. Hence, they are in the best possible position to know what were the actual issues. The letter specifically states that at no time during either the joint negotiating sessions of the parties at which Federal mediators were present, or at separate sessions between the mediators with the union and the company was racial discrimination or racial unrest even referred to. The letter also states that:

At no time during the course of the mediation of this dispute did the Federal mediators involved sense or detect racial unrest or racial discrimination as a factor in the dispute.

Finally, the letter states that the only reason it could even be written, in view of the confidentiality of the mediation process, is that the subject of racial discrimination "simply was not dealt with at the bargaining table or in separate meetings conducted by Federal mediators."

Mr. President, attached to the letter is a copy of a settlement agreement executed by the parties which seems to me to confirm the statements in the letter. The agreement covers the concerted refusal to work overtime, disciplinary action against employees who participated in the strike, a study of the "incentive problem" and a study of "rate ceilings." None of these matters has any real connection with racial discrimination.

Mr. President, I ask unanimous consent that the letter from Mr. Abner, the settlement agreement attached to the letter as well as a letter from Commissioner Holcomb to the editor of Barron's concerning the article be printed in the RECORD. I also ask unanimous consent that the original conciliation agreement, and an analysis of it by Prof. Alfred Blumrosen be printed in the RECORD.

Mr. President, it has been suggested, on the basis of the Barron's article, that the powers of the EEOC should be curbed rather than expanded. As the cosponsor of S. 1308 and S. 1667, the two bills now being considered by the Committee on Labor and Public Welfare which would give the EEOC cease and desist order power, I am particularly concerned to set the record straight on this article. It would indeed be a travesty of justice if this story had any real influence on the important legislation regarding the EEOC.

There being no objection, the material was ordered to be printed in the RECORD, as follows:

*   *   *

THE IMPACT AND SIGNIFICANCE OF THE NEWPORT NEWS SHIPBUILDING AGREEMENT

(By Alfred W. Blumrosen, professor of law, Rutgers Law School, Newark, N.J., former Chief of Conciliations, EEOC.)

A major reason for the passage by the Congress of Title VII of the Civil Rights Act of 1964, and the establishment of the Equal Employment Opportunity Commission was that previous governmental activities had not provided full and adequate remedies for employment discrimination. The Conciliation Agreement signed March 30, 1966, by the Newport News Shipbuilding Company provided concrete and practical remedies tailored to meet the specific conditions and problems of racial discrimination in the ship yard. Under the agreement, more than 3,000 promotions of different kinds were received by the 5,000 Negro employees and 100 more are now supervisors or are in line to become supervisors. These figures are from Company records. In addition, the apprentice school has accepted nearly 50 Negro applicants, and the faculty of the school has been integrated. Lockers, shower rooms and toilet facilities have been desegregated. A seniority system providing for future promotions on the basis of length of service and activity, has been instituted.

No previous effort by the government approached this result. In achieving this result, the interest and concern of all parties—the company, union, civil rights organizations, employees, and the government—were fully taken into account. The cooperation of all of these interests, while carrying out the mandate of Title VII, was the greatest achievement at Newport News.

I. BACKGROUND

The Newport News Shipyard is the largest privately-owned shipyard in the free world. It employs 22,000 men, including some 5,000 Negro employees. It builds military ships, including nuclear aircraft carriers and submarines; repairs military and commercial ships and manufactures heavy machinery.

Charges of discrimination at the shipyard were filed in the late summer of 1965 with the Commission by 41 Negro complainants who work with the local chapter of the NAACP. The investigation of these complaints took place in the fall of 1965. On the basis of the investigation, the Commission found reasonable cause to believe that discrimination existed at the shipyard in the following respect:

(1) Wages of Negro employees doing the same work as white employees were lower than white employees;

(2) Negro employees were promoted at a slower rate than white employees;

(3) Negro employees were not allowed to become supervisors under like circumstances as white employees;

(4) Negro employees were restricted in their access in the company's apprentice program; and

(5) Locker rooms, shower rooms and toilet facilities were segregated.

In November 1965, a conciliation effort was made by the Commission. It was rejected by the company and union. The Commission referred the case to the Attorney General with a recommendation that a "pattern or practice" suit be instituted under Section 707 of the Act, and notified the charging parties of their rights to sue. They instituted a section 706 suit in the Federal District Court in Norfolk, Virginia, with the involvement of the Legal Defense Fund, Inc.

In March 1966, the Company learned that the Attorney General planned to institute suit and that the Department of Labor was considering suspending future government contracts. The company then sought to negotiate with the government. Assistant Attorney General John Doar decided to allow the opportunity for negotiation before filing suit. It was decided that EEOC would lead the negotiation with the participation of Justice, the Department of Defense, and the Department of Labor.

Initial conciliation proposals were developed by Alfred Blumrosen and Kenneth Holbert and refined by the EEOC staff. These proposals were then submitted to the other government agencies and accepted without substantial changes. The Department of Labor issued a letter suspending further government contracts as the negotiations began. The negotiations themselves consumed most of the last part of March. They were headed by Alfred Blumrosen who was then Chief of Conciliation. They concluded on March 30 with the signing of the agreement. The Labor and Defense Departments accepted the agreement as a comprehensive plan to eliminate discrimination which justified the withdrawal of the suspension from government contracts. On the basis of the agreement, the Justice Department concluded that it would not institute suit. The agreement paved the way for the dismissal of the civil suit brought by the charging parties.

The signing of the agreement paved the way for its administration. First steps were quickly taken. Facilities were integrated and the parties moved toward the selection of the expert who had been assigned several tasks under the agreement. Case and Company, a management-consultant firm recommended by the shipyard, was selected and began to work. During the summer and fall of 1966, many problems arose which were hammered out in negotiation sessions between the Commission and the company. These sessions took place frequently.

The Peninsula Shipbuilding Association (PSA) which represented the employees, attacked the agreement at first. After several conferences with the Commission and the company, PSA, in late summer, signed an agreement with the company which recognized the conciliation agreement. Since then, the union has processed more than one hundred grievances relating to the conciliation agreement. By signing the agreement, the union relinquished whatever legal objections it might have asserted in connection with the conciliation.

In the winter of 1966, the administration of the agreement lagged with respect to the identification of Negro employees who were to become supervisors. This project was the responsibility of the Department of Defense under the agreement. Due to the pending reorganization, DOD could not devote adequate manpower to this project. EEOC Chairman Shulman and Mr. Moskowitz of DOD agreed that five DOD personnel would be detailed to the Commission for one month to conduct the administration of this phase of the agreement. Mr. Blumrosen assumed personal direction of this effort and at the end of March 1967, secured agreement of the company to promote seventy-five Negro employees to supervisors, in addition to the twenty-five already promoted. The Commission then indicated that, except for certain problems, the administrative phase of the agreement was concluded.

The administration of the agreement was hampered by lack of adequate manpower. But all parties were understanding of the limitations of the Commission. The Negro employees and the NAACP understood that the Commission could devote but limited personnel to the administration of the agreement, and were patient with the Commission. The union came to understand that the Commission did not wish to supplant it as the representative of the employees, but rather was interested in seeing PSA act effectively on behalf of all employees. The company became aware that the Commission was sensitive to its basic needs and was prepared, in the administration of the agreement, to make adjustments to meet those needs as long as the basic thrust of the agreement was not blunted.

II.   PROBLEMS, SOLUTION, RESULTS

There follows a table indicating the nature of the problems of discrimination at the shipyard, the solution reached in the conciliation agreement, and the results of the application of the act:

(The table is reproduced in the text, *supra* at pp. 284-85. The article concludes:)

III.   SIGNIFICANCE OF THE AGREEMENT

The working out of the agreement has significance in several respects. First, it suggests that problems of employment discrimination can be solved through coordinated governmental activities, given the firm and courageous administration of Title VII. Secondly, it suggests that this can be done without serious harm to the interest of employers. Third, it suggests that in such actions, white employees may benefit as well as Negro employees The addition of a system of seniority promotion and the posting of job vacancies is inured to the benefit of both Negro and white employees at the shipyard. Fourth, the agreement demonstrates that it is possible to design and execute practical remedies to eliminate the present effects of discrimination. Fifth, it suggests that employers need not await Commission action before adopting a management program to improve their employment practices.

Many employers have been greatly impressed by the detailed and technical approach in the conciliation agreement. This has facilitated acceleration of their own programs to eliminate discrimination, and in this sense is now a model for elimination of discrimination in employment. Other government agencies, Justice and OFCC, are using the agreement as a model as is the Commission. The agreement will continue to have these far-reaching implications in eliminating employment discrimination for years to come.

The agreement represented true government action. It was the only time during my stay in government when Justice, DOD, OFCC and EEOC worked together with such harmony and unity. The result of this cooperation was truly striking. The moral is clear. The interlocking and mutually reenforcing joint action of these agencies can produce under present laws, clear, complete, and meaningful remedies which will eliminate employment discrimination.

APPENDIX IV

Congressional Record (daily edition) Sept. 18, 1967, S13106.

OFFICIAL BIAS

Mr. FANNIN. Mr. President, on August 8, 1967, I placed in the RECORD an article entitled "Official Bias," published in Barron's National Business and Financial Weekly. The article reported that the Equal Employment Opportunity Commission had coerced the Newport News Shipbuilding & Dry Dock Co., into signing an agreement which called for favoring Negroes in its hiring policies and with respect to its apprenticeship school—thus instituting a policy of discrimination in reverse. According to the report, this so-called agreement, in large measure, precipitated the first work stoppage in the company's 81 years of existence.

Subsequently on August 22, a statement by way of reply to this article was placed in the RECORD. Among material inserted to attempt to buttress this reply were the text of the conciliation agreement and an analysis of the background of the signing of the agreement written by professor Alfred Blumrosen, apparently the chief architect of the terms.

I had not seen either of these two documents before, and I am glad that they have been printed. They are shocking. To me the situation is worse than I originally thought. In fact it seems to me that the article in Barron's, told only about half the story for a careful reading of this material, leads inevitably to certain conclusions, which I ask unanimous consent to have printed in the RECORD.

There being no objection, the items were ordered to be printed in the RECORD, as follows:

(1) That the Equal Employment Opportunity Commission in negotiating this so-called "agreement" has in many respects completely exceeded any authority granted it under Title VII of the Civil Rights Act of 1964.

(2) That this so-called "agreement" was brought about by the most flagrant governmental coercion that has ever come to my attention. Had it been brought into being through the actions of any one other than a government agency, it could have been characterized as "blackmail" and probably subject to nullification by court action.

(3) That this "agreement" implemented in accordance with its terms would result in what might be termed "reverse discrimination" to the disadvantage of all personnel except non-whites singled out for preferential treatment.

(4) That since it is proposed that this so-called agreement be utilized as a model for elimination of discrimination in employment by not only the Commission but other government agencies such as the Department of Justice and the Office of Contract Compliance, a full and complete examination of the administration of Title VII of the Civil Rights Act of 1964 is in order to determine whether or not the administration of this Title by the EEOC is consistent with the authority granted it by the Congress and with the principles of fair play and due process of law.

Mr. FANNIN. Mr. President, a brief reference to the contents of the aforementioned documents will demonstrate the validity of the conclusions I have outlined above.

It seems clear from Professor Blumrosen's analysis that the complaints in this case were in some measure simulated since he notes that "charges of discrimination at the shipyard were filed in the late summer of 1965 with the Commission by 41 Negro complainants who work with the local chapter of the NAACP." There followed an investigation by the Commission and in November 1965 a conciliation effort was made by the Commission which was rejected by the company and the union. Professor Blumrosen further states that in March 1966 the company learned that the Attorney General planned to institute suit "and that the Department of Labor was considering suspending future Government contracts." The company then sought to negotiate with the Government and Assistant Attorney General John Doar "decided to allow the opportunity for negotiation before filing suit," and it was then decided that the EEOC would lead the negotiation "with the participation of Justice, Department of Defense, and the Department of Labor."

Subsequently, the Department of Labor did, in fact, issue a letter suspending further Government contracts with this company as the negotiations began.

Given this kind of governmental pressure on a company almost totally involved in Government contract work, it is not surprising that an agreement was reached. Following the conclusion of the agreement, the Department of Labor came to the conclusion that this would justify the withdrawal of the suspension from Government contracts and, further, on the basis of the agreement the Justice Department concluded that it would not institute suit. In addition, it is stated by Professor Blumrosen that "by signing the agreement, the union relinquished whatever legal objections it might have asserted in connection with the conciliation."

Without question, this is governmental coercion of the highest order and I am completely at a loss to find anywhere in title VII of the Civil Rights Act of 1964 any such coercive authority granted to the EEOC.

Of equal importance, however, are some of the terms and conditions which apparently were insisted upon by the EEOC for inclusion in the so-called conciliation agreement.

For example, the company is required within 45 days of the date of the agreement to "retain at its expense an expert in job evaluation and statements of work content, knowledgeable in race relations who is acceptable to the Commission" to make a review of the company's personnel practices to determine whether non-whites are in any fashion being discriminated against. I am not aware of any statutory language in title VIII which would authorize the Commission to require employment of an outside "expert" to examine a company's practices.

The company would then be required to implement the decision of the expert "by reclassifying such employees and/or adjusting the rate of pay accordingly within a period of 30 days from the date of determination." The company is further required to supply this said expert with adequate staff and facilities and to make available all records and other information necessary to the performance of this function.

This "expert", incidentally, must be acceptable to the Commission and the profile of employment practices is to be developed jointly by this expert and the Industrial Employment Policy Specialists, Department of Defense, presumably without regard to company participation. In other words, the company would in effect be required to turn over to one outside expert and a group of individuals from the Defense Department the authority to analyze and change in any way they saw fit the personnel and employment practices of a company which has functioned for over 80 years without ever having had a strike.

Again, I am unable to find any such statutory authority in title VII of the Civil Rights Act.

It should be noted that approval by the Commission is required at almost every step in this agreement which means, of course, a veto power over any actions which may be taken by the company. Continuing surveillance and participation by the Commission in company personnel actions is clearly provided for during the life of this agreement.

It is impossible to read this "agreement" without coming to the conclusion that it amounts to what might be called discrimination in reverse. Without question, this agreement makes other than nonwhite employees of this company the more or less "forgotten" man insofar as any protection he may seek pursuant to this agreement.

Notwithstanding statutory provisions designed to prevent the granting of "preferential treatment" to any individual or to any group because of his race, color, religion, sex, or national origin, this very preferential treatment is provided for in many sections of the agreement. As just one instance, in section 3(c) it is provided that "employees in predominantly Negro departments shall be given the first opportunity for training in programs in which they are qualified to enter." If I understand this correctly, this means that other than non-whites need not apply, which to me is discrimination in reverse.

One of the most flagrant examples of abuse of authority by the Agency is found in section 4 of the Conciliation Agreement dealing with Adjustment of Rates and Promotional Opportunities.

Under this section, the so-called expert and the "Industrial Employment Policy Specialist" establish a profile of the rate and conditions for promotions for white employees, a so-called norm. Thereafter, a Negro employee who has not moved up through the grades as rapidly as the "norm" for white employees would be assigned "the first grade in the job classification or such other grade as he would have achieved had his history followed" the norm. Section 4(f) states "conditions of the employee's skill and ability are not germane to this section. The burden of demonstrating that from company records that the employee should not be upgraded is on the company."

As a further example, in section 4(h):

If the evaluator finds that the Negro employee has such qualifications for promotion or can achieve them through reasonable training, he shall be placed on a preferential promotion list and given at an appropriate time such training as may be reasonably necessary to equip him for promotion. Such promotion shall be given when need arises for additional members of the next higher class.

As is well known, the Congress in title VII specifically provided that comparisons with, or quotas related to, the percentages of various races in the available work force in any community, State, section, or other area could not be required. Notwithstanding this, the Commission in section 5(d) of this "agreement" included a section which in practical operation would have no other effect. The section is as follows:

The parties to this agreement recognize as a natural result of this recruitment effort that the ratio of Negro to white apprentices in any given year should approach the ratio of Negro to white employees and the ratio of Negro to whites in the labor market area but this provision should not be construed to require or permit the rejection of any qualified applicant on the basis of his race or color.

Obviously, the disclaimer in the last few lines is designed to try and bring this provision within the language of the statute. I submit, however, that this comes in the "fine print" category and would be of questionable effect in forestalling the basic purpose outlined in the earlier part of this provision.

The company is further required to waive some of its statutory rights provided in title VII as set forth in section 7 (d) and (e) of the agreement which states as follows:

d. Cooperate with the Equal Employment Opportunity Commission with regard to the investigation, conciliation, and processing of the charges of 38 other charging parties without regard to the time limitations of Section 706 of Title VII.

e. With regard to certain charging parties, waive the statutory period within which the charging parties may institute a civil action in the event conciliation is not achieved.

This statutory period was inserted by the Congress with a definite design and purpose to eliminate stale claims and, in effect, fix a statute of limitations within which complaints must be filed. Notwithstanding, the Commission arrogates onto itself by the device of this so-called agreement to nullify the statutory protection provided by the Congress.

The foregoing is only a brief and quite incomplete indication of the lengths to which the EEOC has gone in bringing about this coercive agreement without statutory authority and in many cases in complete disregard of the language the Congress enacted. To me, the conclusion is inescapable that before the authority of this Commission is in anywise broadened a close examination of this Commission's activities is required in order to determine whether and to what extent the Commission is circumventing and ignoring the intent of Congress when it enacted title VII of the Civil Rights Act of 1964.

Mr. President, finally I ask unanimous consent that there be printed in the RECORD Barron's reply to the charge that the EEOC was unjustifiably criticized. This is an excellent reply and points up a frightening situation:

BARRON'S REPLY TO THE CHARGE OF UNJUSTIFIED CRITICISM OF THE ROLE OF THE EQUAL EMPLOYMENT OPPORTUNITY COMMISSION AT THE NEWPORT NEWS SHIP-BUILDING & DRY DOCK CO.

Barron's remains convinced that the Equal Employment Opportunity Commission (EEOC) was the principal villain in the first strike in the 81-year history of the Newport News Shipbuilding & Dry Dock Co. The record proves beyond doubt that the EEOC seriously damaged labor-management relations which heretofore had been noted as a model of harmony. It also created racial unrest and caused employee morale to sink so low that it resulted in a substantial drop in productivity. Under such conditions, it is not surprising that grievance procedures, which always had worked in the past, were inadequate to avert a strike.

Significantly, the dispute which led to the walk-out began in the company's transportation department which has a work force comprised 80% of Negroes. In addition, the union meeting which passed the strike vote was attended 85% by Negroes, and we have pictures to prove it.

Under the threat of withholding federal contracts, which make up most of the business of Newport News Ship, EEOC ordered it unilaterally to take certain so-called anti-discriminatory actions. The Commission moved without even consulting the Peninsula Shipbuilders' Association (PSA), the independent union which represents most of the 22,000 workers at the yard.

This was in violation of the National Labor Relations Act, which says a company must not change working conditions or pay without bargaining with the certified representative of the workers. Too, the Commission violated an order of the National Labor Relations Board certifying the PSA as the sole collective bargaining agent of the employees of Newport News Ship.

Thus the company had conflicting orders from two federal agencies, with one saying the firm should change working conditions only after bargaining with the PSA and the other saying it would put it out of business unless it changed them immediately.

When our editorial was written, Luther Holcomb was acting chairman of the EEOC. Barron's asked him how he could expect a firm to follow conflicting orders from two federal agencies. He emphasized that PSA was an independent union. "If the AFL-CIO had been involved, we probably would have had the head of the AFL-CIO Civil Rights Division, in," he declared. He abruptly terminated the interview when asked why he didn't perform the same courtesy for an independent union.

(According to Don Slayman, Director of Civil Rights for the AFL-CIO, his organization had threatened to handle the matter through litigation unless the EEOC carried out its obligation to discuss discrimination with both a company and a union.)

The EEOC publicly humiliated the PSA and got it in bad with the Negroes who make up 35% of its membership, to say nothing of the rest of the members who saw the union contract ignored. At the outset, the Commission gave the impression that it would take care of the Negroes where the PSA had failed. Understandably, this split the union between blacks and whites. However, both soon learned of the perfidy of the EEOC.

After the agreement was completed with Newport News Ship, the Commission belatedly acknowledged its error in ignoring the union by making it a party to it. But when the PSA tried to take an active part in handling cases of alleged discrimination, it was balked by the EEOC. The former filed 83 complaints with the Commission over six months ago and has yet to hear anything on a single complaint.

Linwood Harris, the Negro co-manager of PSA, told Barron's, "We're left as the fall guy because the EEOC doesn't act."

Kenneth F. Holbert, EEOC Acting General Council, says the agency just hasn't had time to get around to handling the complaints but admits there is a legal limitation of 60 days for it to do so.

Understandably, PSA officials do not share Mr. Holcomb's enthusiasm over the benefits of EEOC's activities at Newport News Ship. Mr. Harris declares, "The good the EEOC has done is minute and not worth it because of the bad they've done."

PSA President Leonard Gauley says, "They've stirred up a hornet's nest that was completely unnecessary."

PSA Co-Manager Robert M. Bryant says, "the EEOC is a complete farce" and that it has brought about the end of an era for both the company and its employees.

One employee after another told us they'd never seen anything like it—that EEOC upset everyone.

Under such circumstances, it is not difficult to see why a union might concentrate on grievances involving a department made up largely of Negroes. And with workers in a state of turmoil incited by the EEOC, it is not hard to understand why a strike ensued.

We notice that the EEOC does not deny that Commissioner Samuel C. Jackson called for militancy in the community; we don't see how it can, since it was a speech at a public NAACP meeting. We also notice that EEOC does not deny that it sent representatives to knock on doors in Negro neighborhoods in Newport News to solicit complaints of job discrimination.

Commissioner Jackson also stirred up trouble by making false charges. In the aforementioned speech, he declared, "I have investigated discrimination complaints all over the nation, and never have I seen such massive discrimination in my life as at Newport News Shipbuilding & Dry Dock." This hardly tallies with a later EEOC conclusion that Newport News Ship was not guilty in a single instance of failing to give equal pay for equal work.

Heaping coals on the fire, exaggerations and false claims followed the false charges. Commissioner Jackson said the company's Apprentice School did not have a single Negro teacher out of nearly 500 instructors. The union subsequently pointed out, "At last count, we didn't have 500 students in the Apprentice School."

Mr. Jackson claimed that at least 5,000 Negroes (the total number of Negroes employed by the yard) would receive substantial raises as the result of the Commission's work.

On May 1, 1967, Secretary of Labor W. Willard Wirtz and Stephen N. Shulman, then EEOC Chairman, announced that 3,890 Negroes had been promoted at Newport News Ship because of federal action to insure equal employment practices. Both union and management say this figure is false, and they have told the government so. As noted in our editorial, the union threatened legal action to set the record straight.

According to both labor and management, the 3,000 merit increases were regular ones and at a volume established long before the existence of EEOC. A grand total of 155 employees received raises as a result of the agreement. In addition 250 Negroes were put on preferential lists for promotions when openings occur.

PSA Co-Manager Bryant told Barron's that any time the Secretary of Labor will claim 3,890 promotions under an agreement which actually produced 155, "I've got a lot of reservations about whether he should be the Secretary of Labor."

In the face of criticism from both management and labor, we note that Mr. Holcomb now claims the agreement produced 3,000 promotions rather than the 3,890 claimed by Messrs. Wirtz and Shulman and the 5,000 promised by Mr. Jackson.

EEOC also brought about a further deterioration of labor relations at Newport News Ship by forcing discrimination in favor of Negroes. No white employee may be promoted until the preferred promotion list of Negroes is exhausted unless the EEOC gives express permission. Moreover, during the year it took to draw up that list, EEOC did not allow the yard to make any permanent promotions. Many employees told Barron's that this alone seriously damaged employee morale.

The agreement further promotes reverse discrimination by stating that Negroes shall have the first opportunity to participate in training programs provided by the company. It assigns legal status for the selection of apprentices to civil rights organizations listed by the EEOC. In authorizing them to send "qualified applicants" to the Apprentice School, the EEOC, in effect, has established privileged groups of private employment agencies for Negroes.

The agreement also says that Negroes shall be promoted as rapidly as whites as shown by a sample of white promotions and that "consideration of the (Negro) employee's skill and ability are not germane to this section."

In view of the documentation presented here, it is almost incredible that Mr. Holcomb would say, "The Newport News agreement indicated significantly how sound governmental action taken in cooperation with interested parties can solve problems of employment discrimination and can do so without serious harm to the interest of employers and that in addition, benefits can result for white employees as well as for Negroes."

As noted, the EEOC action was not taken in cooperation with all interested parties—if one considers the union an interested party. According to PSA Co-Manager Bryant, the first word the union had of the completed agreement was in a national announcement on April 2, 1966. The PSA did not receive a copy of the agreement until two days after the announcement.

Mr. Holcomb's claim that there was no serious harm to the employer also is without substance. Donald A. Holden, President and Chairman of the Board of Newport News Ship, told Barron's that productivity went down as a result of the EEOC because people were upset. "I think it cost us in seven-figure kind of money in a year," he declared.

We fail to see how Mr. Holcomb finds benefits for white employees since, as noted, the EEOC is discriminating against them.

In conclusion we would like to call attention to an article in our issue of October 17, 1966. We mentioned that anti-poverty and civil rights workers were campaigning to take over management of Greenbelt Consumer Services, Inc. One of the candidates of the insurgents for the board of Greenbelt was Timothy L. Jenkins. According to literature distributed by his sponsors, he was a Deputy to the EEOC and also "has held responsible positions in such groups . . . as the Federal Programs Section of the Student Non-Violent Coordinating Committee." While Mr. Jenkins no longer is with the EEOC, the records of its personnel office indicate he was serving as consultant to the chairman when the Commission was working on the Newport News case.

APPENDIX V

Reflections on the Newport News Agreement by Alfred W. Blumrosen

Senator Fannin has raised some important questions concerning the agreement between the Equal Employment Opportunity Commission and the Newport News Shipbuilding and Drydock Co. in the Congressional Record of Sept. 18, 1967, S. 13160-0- (daily ed.). This agreement, along with an explanation of its impact and significance was inserted in the Congressional Record by Senator Javitz on Aug. 22, 1967, pp. S. 12001-07 (daily ed.) The agreement, which was negotiated by EEOC with the cooperation of the Departments of Justice, Labor and Defense, resulted in major changes in the industrial relations system at the shipyard, eliminating the remnants of discriminatory patterns, and lead to the promotion of some 3,000 Negro employees.

Senator Fannin suggests that the agreement is defective in three respects; (1) it was brought about by governmental "coercion," (2) the EEOC exceeded its authority under the Civil Rights Act of 1964 in negotiating certain provisions and (3) it would result in "reverse discrimination" by giving preferential treatment to Negroes. These are serious matters which deserve full consideration because of the important principle involved in the Newport News agreement.

This principle is that all concerned Federal agencies may join in negotiating with an employer or other respondent who is subject to federal law, an effective and comprehensive plan for the elimination of patterns and practices of discrimination; and may administer that plan and review compliance with it to assure that the promise of the laws against discrimination are carried out in the day to day life of the work place. This is what happened at Newport News. The importance of this principle cannot be underestimated. It is basic to the assumption that problems of discrimination can be solved through lawful processes. That assumption in turn is fundamental to the insistence on the maintenance of law and order.

The necessity for broad remedial programs such as that at Newport News is clear. If the government is confined to the remedying of individual cases of discrimination, the antidiscrimination laws will not work. Newport News is the symbol for governmental action to correct discriminatory employment practices throughout an entire establishment. The broad principle that the EEOC will seek to change entire systems, and not restrict itself to individual complainants cases, underlies the Newport News Agreement.

This principle is both explicit and implicit in title VII of the Civil Rights Act of 1964. Congress made the following points very clear in that statute:

(1) The Congress is concerned with the elimination of employment discrimination in individual situations (Sec. 706)

(2) Congress was concerned with the elimination of patterns and practices of discrimination (Sec. 707, 706(e))

(3) The Congress desired appropriate coordination between various agencies of government involved in the elimination of discrimination. (Sec. 706 (b)-(d) [state agencies], Sec. 709 (d), 703 (b) [Federal agencies], Sec. 705 (g) (1), 705 (i), and 716 (c) [all public and private agencies])

(4) Congress wished the details of the solution to the problems of discrimination to be worked out through negotiation and conciliation, if possible, rather than by litigation. (Sec. 706 (a) provides that if the Commission determines there is reasonable cause to believe a respondent has committed an unlawful employment practice, "the Commission shall endeavor to eliminate any such unlawful employment practice by informal methods of conference, conciliation and persuasion.")

(5) In reaching solutions to problems of discrimination, Congress envisioned that employers and other respondents would take "affirmative action" (Sec. 706 (g) to effectuate the policies of the act)

It is therefore appropriate to deal with each of the issues raised by Senator Fannin.

1. *The "coercion" issue.* Senator Fannin suggests that the government "coerced" the agreement.

The Commission lacks coercive powers. EEOC cannot "order" anyone to do anything. It has no sanctions at its disposal. The Labor Department—Defense Department decision to suspend contracting with Newport News was neither disputed nor litigated. The power has been in existence for a number of years and has been recognized by the Congress. (See Sec. 709 (d) which refers to the President's Committee on Equal Employment Opportunity, which had this power. The existence of the PCEEO or its successor is assumed in the cited section.) The private law suit which had been filed against Newport News had not come to trial. Each federal agency involved was carrying out its appointed function.

The Newport News Shipbuilding Co. is the largest single employer facility in the state of Virginia. It is headed by highly competent management, and has been entrusted with the task of building a major part of the naval forces of the United States. Its counsel is an outstanding and distinguished attorney. The Company was not without resources to protect its interests against "overreaching" by the federal government. The Company demonstrated industrial statesmanship of the highest order, when it chose to solve its problems, rather than litigate concerning them.

The Peninsular Shipbuilders Association (not affiliated with the AFL-CIO) is represented by able and aggressive officers and counsel. Fully aware of the channels of recourse open to it, the Union chose to adopt the agreement rather than challenge it. It made this decision months after the agreement was executed. This too was industrial statesmanship.

Thus the suggestion of coercion appears to be without foundation. The doors of the Federal Courts were at all times open to both Company and Union to prevent overreaching by the government. Where competent and resourceful parties who are fully capable of exercising their rights preferred to settle the matter rather than litigate, there seems little room for the suggestion of coercion.

This disposes of the "coercion" issue, except for the suggestion that the agencies, EEOC, OFCC, DOD and Justice, "ganged up" on the Shipyard. It is true that the activities of these agencies were coordinated; but this should be applauded, rather than condemned. There are serious problems of duplication of effort, of overlapping activity by various agencies in the Equal Opportunity field. These activities may have the effect of burdening respondents with repeated investigations by different agencies, and may lead to the uneconomical allocation of government resources. Coordination of various agency activities is desirable. In fact, had there not been coordination, it is quite possible that the agencies would be criticized for duplication of activity, wasting scarce government resources and imposing unnecessary burdens on employers and other respondents.

2. *The "excess of authority" issue.* This breaks down into a review of four aspects of the agreement: (a) the provision for the retention of an expert, (b) the provision for promotion of Negro employees who had been promoted at a slower rate than whites (c) the provision for recruitment of apprentices and (d) the waiver of the statute of limitations with respect to certain claims.

a. *The retention of an expert.* The agreement to retain an expert to review the rate and conditions of promotion of Negro employees was a major innovation in the field of Race Relations. Did the negotiation of a provision for such an expert, which provided that the parties would, within limits, be bound by his decisions exceed the authority of the Commission under title VII?

First, under section 705 (g) (1) and (3), there is authority in the commission to utilize private agencies and individuals, which would include the "expert." Secondly, and far more important, Congress clearly intended that the difficult and complex problems of discrimination be resolved through conciliation. Conciliation presupposes the adoption of practical measures to solve problems of discrimination. The retention of the expert was such a practical solution. The alternatives to this solution were not inviting. They were either a time consuming case by case investigation of thousands of employment records by government personnel or the conduct of such an investigation through the judicial processes of discovery and trial. Both of these alternatives would have plunged the employer, the government and the charging parties, into interminable proceedings which would have been costly, would have engendered hostility, would have taken extensive time of overcrowded Federal Courts. Such proceedings might well have exacerbated the dispute rather than resolved it.

The agreement followed many precedents in the field of labor-management relations in that the parties submitted their dispute to an outside expert acceptable to both. The expert selected, Case and Company, is a nationally known management consulting firm which was suggested by the Company and found acceptable by the Commission. Case and Co. brought a technical expertise to bear on their enormous problems at the shipyard. While it is unlikely that either the government or the Company agreed with all of the conclusions of Case and Co., both believed that their overall interests would be served by acquiescing in the conclusions reached by the expert.

Senator Fannin expresses concern that the Commission reserved the right to review the decisions of the expert. This reservation was essential. The Commission has been charged with the duty of enforcing title VII prior to litigation and may not delegate that authority to a party not of its own choosing. Congress would have been critical, and properly so, of any such delegation. In fact, in most of the issues which arose during the administration of the agreement, the government and the Company accepted the conclusions of Case and Co. Where this was not possible, they negotiated a settlement of the issues. In retrospect, the use of the expert was one of the most satisfactory aspects of the agreement.

The language of the statute, the intention of Congress, the concept of conciliation, the experience in other areas of labor relations and the practicalities of the situation all combine to sustain the conclusion that the agreement to retain the expert to evaluate employment practices was appropriate under title VII.

B. *The provision for promotion of Negro employees.* The Senator expresses concern with paragraph 4 of the agreement which provides a procedure for determination of whether Negro employees were promoted at a slower rate than white employees and remedies by way of promotion and preparation for promotion. The immensity of this undertaking is demonstrated by the fact that there are 5,000 Negro employees at the yard. To apply the Commission finding that Negroes were generally paid less than whites and promoted at a slower rate than whites to this many people was a monumental undertaking. If the procedure used had not been adopted, there might have been thousands of individual complaints each going through a formal procedure. The procedure avoided this piece-meal approach in favor of a general system-wide review.

Once it was determined that Negro employees had been promoted at a slower rate than whites, the provision for a remedy by way of either immediate or prospective promotion was obvious. There is clearly nothing "preferential" in this solution.

c. *The recruitment of apprentices.* The Shipyard conducts an apprentice school, which is a four year technical college. In its history, it had had six Negro students at the time of the negotiation of the agreement. The student body numbered nearly 500. The agreement provided for recruitment efforts to increase the proportion of Negro students. In an area where Negroes make up between twenty and twenty five percent of the population and the labor force, it was certainly appropriate for the shipyard to engage in "affirmative action" in recruiting (see Sec. 706(g)). Many employers which had engaged in "affirmative action" had, in the experience of the Commission, hired only a token few minority employees. It was important, therefore, to make clear that the recruiting effort was not to be token. Thus the language expressive of the long range goal, suggesting that the "natural result" of the recruitment effort would be that the ratio of Negro to white apprentices would approach that of Negroes and whites in the labor market area. In no sense is this a quota. No court called upon to interpret it would call it a quota. No one is entitled to an apprenticeship because of it. It is designed to make clear what Congress expressed in the phrase "affirmative action" in section 706(g). What is required is meaningful compliance with the statute, not tokenism. This compliance will be measured by the extent of the performance, not the language of the promise.

(d) *The waiver of the statute of limitations.* Senator Fannin was further concerned with the agreement of the shipyard to waive the statute of limitations with respect to some individual cases which were not resolved at the time of the Conciliation Agreement. This waiver provision was inserted for highly practical reasons. The basic agreement had been hammered out in several days of hard negotiation. It did not serve the interest of any of the parties to delay the execution of the agreement for the additional time it would take to resolve these remaining cases. The waiver of the statute makes it feasible for the parties to execute the agreement with the understanding that these other cases would be promptly disposed of. This is what in fact happened.

Statutes of limitation are often waived by the parties when it is in their interest to do so. In this case, the waiver facilitated the signing of the basic agreement without further delay. It enabled the respondent and the government to take such additional time as was necessary to work out settlements of these additional issues, without forcing the charging parties in those cases to file law suits to protect their rights under title VII.

Congress certainly did not intend that an employer who was cooperating fully with the government should be unable to enter into agreements which would extend the time for settlement of issues. If the respondent could not waive the statute of limitation, then charging party would be forced to file suit to protect his legal rights, even though it was clear that good faith negotiations were proceeding toward a settlement which was likely to be satisfactory. This unnecessary litigation was certainly not desired by a Congress which sought for solutions through concilation. The statute must be read so as to facilitate negotiation, not to encourage litigation. Since waivers provide additional time for negotiation, they should be favored, not discouraged. The provision in the Newport News agreement was aimed at supporting the Congressional policy in favor of a negotiated settlement in these cases.

3. *The "reverse discrimination" issue.* This is an important issue which must be understood in the terms set by Senator Fannin. His conclusion is:

> "That this 'agreement' implemented in accordance with its terms would result in what might be termed 'reverse discrimination' to the disadvantage of all personnel except non-whites singled out for preferential treatment."

This problem has several aspects.

a. *Remedying discrimination is not preferential treatment.* This is an obvious fact which can be easily illustrated in other fields of law. If A and B are both employees in a factory and the roof collapses, injuring A but not B, due to the employers negligence, everyone would understand that A could recover but B could not, because A was injured and B was not. No one would say that A got preferential treatment over B because A recovered either in tort or in Workmen's compensation payments. A was made whole for the injury which the employer had caused. B, not having been injured, received nothing. So too in the case of discrimination. The remedy runs in favor of the minority employee because he has been injured. The administration of an appropriate remedy for him does not constitute "preferential treatment" at all. If an employer has been paying Negro employees less than whites doing the same work, then he should raise the wages of the Negro employees. The fact that white employees do not get raises at the same time does not constitute "preferential treatment" of the Negroes. In fact, the argument that it does constitute preferential treatment is in effect, an argument that the white employees should continue to get more than Negroes for doing the same work. But the phrase "preferential treatment" cannot be used to support the claim of a white employee that he would be better off if the employer continued to discriminate against minority group employees. Title VII mandates the elimination of discriminatory treatment, and will not permit its continuation under some other label. Remedying discrimination does not constitute "preferential treatment."

During the period of administration of the agreement, there were constant promotions of both Negro and white employees. It was simply not the case that only Negro employees were recruited as apprentices, promoted to higher positions and to supervision. There was no "reverse discrimination."

b. *Sensitive administration required.* The parties faced many difficult practical problems during the year after the signing of the agreement. These problems were discussed extensively in both Washington and Newport News. From these meetings flowed adjustments and refinements which no one had anticipated during the negotiation of the agreement, which were necessary for its successful administration. It is possible that a rigid unthinking bureaucracy could have turned the agreement into an unworkable instrument. But this did take place.

The administration of the agreement was sensitive to the practical needs of the parties, as the settlement of the promotion to supervisor question indicates. The proof of this lies in the affirmative results of the agreement.

CONCLUSION

Senator Fannin suggests several additional points. If they are each discussed, the document becomes unduly extended. If they are not, it may be challenged as failing to meet the issues. While I am prepared to deal with these other issues, my analysis will follow that used above.

The critics of the agreement also face a dilemma. Either the government was too "coercive" and achieved "too much" preferential treatment or the government bungled and accomplished nothing. The critics simply cannot have it both ways. I submit that the truth does not lie in either of these positions. The simple fact is that the agreement was successfully negotiated and administered to carry out the Congressional purpose of eliminating employment discrimination, by agreement if possible, but by the force of law if necessary. The good faith of the Company was very important in the execution of the agreement and I hope these discussions do not embarrass it unduly.

The government learned many things through its experience with Newport News. It learned that cooperation among agencies was possible; that a written agreement requiring far reaching changes in an employer's industrial relations system was practical and would produce meaningful results. The Commission reexamined its procedures to assure that no question of inadequate consultation with labor organizations would arise in the future.

There is serious and deeply felt doubt in the land that the law is capable of coping with and resolving problems of discrimination. This doubt is expressed in the universities, the meeting halls, and, sometimes, on the streets. Newport News stands as the principle evidence that the law can solve these problems. The support for this proposition is worthy of our greatest effort.

APPENDIX VI.

Congressional Record (daily edition) Feb. 29, 1968, H 1536.

ENFORCEMENT OF CIVIL RIGHTS LEGISLATION

* * *

Mr. RYAN. Mr. Speaker, throughout America today public officials are echoing the call for law and order. But for all the talk about riots in the cities and crime in the streets, seldom is there a mention of a fundamental hypocrisy in law enforcement. Despite legal prohibitions against racial discrimination, discrimination persists without effective legal redress. America remains a white man's society where Negroes and Spanish-speaking Americans are short-changed. Until civil rights laws are vigorously enforced, black America can hardly be expected to have faith in white America.

In no area is this hypocrisy more apparent than in job discrimination. In no area is the right to equal treatment more clearly written into law and public policy. And in no area is the law less enforced.

In Newark, which exploded in riot last summer, construction projects will soon begin using Federal funds under the model cities program. The work force, constructing the buildings in full view of passersby, will be almost entirely white.

Unemployed Negro residents, many of whom were driven by despair to the point of rioting last summer, will witness an almost all-white work force in jobs paying $6 and $8 an hour in their own neighborhood, knowing that these jobs are barred to them. The irony of public officials who call for law and order, but fail to uphold laws guaranteeing equal treatment is not lost on the ghetto.

*   *   *

EXECUTIVE ORDER 11246

Executive Order 11246 was issued by President Johnson in September 1965. It is the latest in a series of orders dating back to 1941, which prohibit job discrimination by Federal contractors.

Unlike previous orders, 11246 covers not only employment directly related to the particular contract involved, but all employment in companies with U.S. Government contracts in excess of $10,000. In this way, the order is estimated to cover one job in three in the national economy, or between 20 and 25 million jobs out of 74.1 million jobs.

The language of Executive Order 11246 is unambiguous. It specifies that language shall be written into Federal contracts providing that:

The contractor will not discriminate against any employee or applicant for employment because of race, creed, color, or national origin. The contractor will take affirmative action to ensure that applicants are employed and that employees are treated during employment, without regard to their race, creed, color, or national origin.

The order also requires contractors to furnish the Government with a breakdown of racial employment data. Agency contract reviews are mandated, whether or not there have been specific complaints. And, unlike title VII of the Civil Rights Act of 1964, the order contains a potent enforcement sanction—the withholding or cancellation of lucrative Government contracts. It provides that the Secretary of Labor or the appropriate contracting agency may—

Cancel, terminate, suspend or cause to be cancelled, terminated, or suspended, any contract, or any portion or portions thereof, for failure of the contractor or subcontractor to comply with the nondiscrimination provisions of the contract.

If the administration took this order seriously, it could open new, formerly denied job opportunities to millions of Americans. Yet, the history of Executive Order 11246 is an inexcusable story of bureaucratic betrayal.

Since that order was issued in September 1965, not one contract has been canceled for noncompliance. Nor was a contract ever canceled under any of the predecessor orders.

Precious few contracts have ever been held up, even in cases of overt, documented discrimination. Companies, which have been cited for discrimination by the Equal Employment Opportunities Commission or State FEPCs or against whom the Department of Justice has brought action under title VII of the Civil Rights Act of 1964, continue to benefit from Federal contracts in flat contravention of the order.

This leniency tells other companies, in effect, that they have nothing to fear from the order, that it is not to be taken seriously. Despite the good intentions of many equal opportunity officials, the complaint bureaucracy subverts the purposes of the order.

Under a system established in 1965, the principal enforcement body is the Office of Federal Contract Compliance—OFCC—in the Department of Labor. However, in practice, OFCC is merely a loose supervisory body, with a staff of only 12. Actual compliance enforcement is delegated to an equal opportunity program in each major Federal agency which contracts with the private sector.

This system subordinates an agency's compliance staff to officials who place the smooth flow of contracts above the promotion of job equality. The result is a dismal picture of mass tokenism. If a company can demonstrate anything remotely resembling "progress," it is usually "let off the hook." In the absence of firm support from higher officials, compliance officers are discouraged from energetic action, for their efforts will only be undermined. Where individual compliance officers here and there do make vigorous efforts to monitor contractors, they often do so at the peril of their own careers.

What has emerged instead of effective enforcement is a totally ineffective pattern of tokenism and voluntary compliance.

The so-called plans for progress program emerged in 1961 to enlist voluntary support of major companies which would declare themselves "equal opportunity employers" and pledge to recruit minority workers. More than one equal opportunity official has said that it is common knowledge that joining plans for progress enables a contractor to avoid close supervision under Executive Order 11246. In fact, plans for progress was sold to many contractors on precisely these grounds.

I do not mean to impugn the sincerity of every plans for progress employer. Plans for progress includes some genuinely progressive organizations. But it also includes companies against which the Department of Justice is proceeding, and other companies whose policies on equal employment have been deplorable.

Recent Equal Employment Opportunity Commission hearings in New York City established that out of 100 major companies, which voluntarily submitted information, the 46 which were signatories of plans for progress had minority employment records much worse than the 54 which were not. The Equal Employment Opportunities Commission report dated January 18, 1968, states:

While non-members had 1.2% Negroes in positions as officials and managers, Plans for Progress members had only 0.3% in these jobs.

Voluntary compliance is no substitute for enforcement. It is an easy way out, which tells minority job seekers and employers alike that the government is not serious.

On February 15, 1968, more than 2 years after Executive Order 11246 was issued, regulations pursuant to that order were proposed by the Office of Federal Contract Compliance. The Office of Federal Contract Compliance has been operating under regulations which apply to the previous order, which exempted certain categories of contracts and related to the President's Committee on Equal Opportunity. This is a sad indication of how seriously the administration takes its own order.

In the 2 years and 5 months since September 1965, when President Johnson issued the Executive order, the racial crisis has tragically deepened in large part because Negroes continue to be denied job opportunities. Recently the President announced a job opportunities in the business sector program for the hard-core unemployed, relying once again on the voluntary cooperation of the private sector, in effect cajoling industry to take minority trainees. Certainly substantial progress could be made by simply enforcing an order already on the books.

THE DOD CASE

I have said that the bureaucratic system which delegates contract compliance authority militates against effective enforcement. Let me describe, chapter and verse, the undermining and eventual dismemberment of the most effective Federal compliance program—that of the Department of Defense.

Approximately 80 percent of the dollar volume of Government contracts comes through the Department of Defense. About 20 million jobs are with companies which in one form or another do business with the Department of Defense. All of these jobs could be available on an equal opportunity basis.

For a little over a year the Department of Defense had a contract compliance program which took seriously Executive Order 11246. Beginning in October 1965, following the issuance of the order, separate Army, Navy, and Air Force compliance programs were centralized under the direction of a dedicated official named Girard Clark, with 94 men under him. The Department of Defense compliance program began reviews of all Defense contractors industry by industry. Corporations in a particular industry were reviewed at random. Where there seemed to be a pattern of job bias, employment patterns of the entire company were reviewed in depth. The company's senior officials were then told what steps were necessary in order to continue receiving defense contracts. In this way, unprecedented strides were made and employment barriers broken. In case after case, when corporations were confronted with a credible risk of loss of contract, they proved cooperative.

The BVD Co., for example, whose only link to the Defense Department was through the sale of articles to PX's and ship stores was informed that it could no longer do business with the Government until it took steps to desegregate plant facilities in the South—Pascagoula, Miss. Only after the company agreed to take the necessary action, did the Defense Department learn that it had in this way effected the first industrial desegregation in the State of Mississippi.

A few companies refused to open employment opportunities to Negroes, and they were barred from receiving further contracts. During the year in which the program was operating effectively, there were 40 top-level confontations involving 35 companies. All but seven agreed to make the necessary changes in opening employment opportunities to Negroes.

The most spectacular and effective confrontation involved the Newport News Shipbuilding and Drydock Co.

The Newport News Shipyard, although a private company, depends almost exclusively upon Government contracts. In 1965, the NAACP filed complaints with EEOC, to the effect that Negro workers were barred from good jobs, paid lower wages for performing the same work, impeded from entering the company apprentice program, made to use segregated toilet and locker facilities, and other related complaints. The company initially refused conciliation. It was only after the Department of Defense and the Office of Federal Contract Compliance threatened to refuse the Newport News Co. bids on four submarines that the company agreed to integrate its facilities and open job opportunities to Negroes on an equal basis with whites. According to Alfred Blumrosen, then Chief of the Department of Labor Conciliation Service, the Newport News case was "the only time during my stay in Government when Justice, DOD, OFCC, and EEOC worked together"—CONGRESSIONAL RECORD, August 22, 1967, S12007.

The Newport News success clearly proves that the Government has the power to open up jobs to Negroes, if it only has the will to use it.

By August 1966, when the Newport News conciliation agreement was signed, the Department of Defense compliance program was already on the way out. The program had incurred the wrath of both industry and many senior procurement officials. For example, a panic was created at the Department of Defense when sanctions were recommended against U.S. Steel for overt discrimination at the

Fairfield works at Birmingham, Ala. Although the compliance program director found that the charges were accurate, and that in no case was U.S. Steel the sole source of supply, top officials in the Department overruled the director of the compliance program and declined to take action.

Every time compliance officials are overruled in this way, industry is again served notice that it does not have to take the equal opportunity requirement very seriously. Every time an agency's compliance staff can be circumvented, the force of the order is undermined.

In February 1967, the DOD compliance program was reorganized out of existence. Gone was the centralized compliance office; compliance was put under the Defense Contract Administration Service, where it could no longer be an embarrassment. Actual contract supervision is now accomplished through regional procurement offices. There no longer exists an independent office within DOD which sees its task as the promotion of job equality. Compliance officers are now subordinate to procurement officers, who are much more inclined to put a premium on the maintenance of cordial relations with contractors.

The company reviews, which were an effective means of opening up job opportunities in an entire company, have been abolished. In short, the former Department of Defense compliance program was dismembered for being too effective.

In September 1967, 5 months after the effective DOD program was dismembered, officials of the new DOD program explicitly refused to cooperate with the supervisory Office of Federal Contract Compliance—OFCC. Specifically, they refused to inform OFCC in advance of compliance reviews, to provide OFCC with review summaries, or to notify OFCC when a defense contract officer had requested a review. DOD representatives said they regarded it "as an interference with their management prerogatives for OFCC to have any role whatsoever in the establishment of priorities, and in DOD determinations of contractor compliance."

This is a sorry contrast with the successful result of DOD–OFCC cooperation in the Newport News case a year earlier.

As an outrageous example of the failure of current DOD compliance policy, I cite the example of the Timken Roller Bearing Co., of Canton, Ohio. No less than five Government agencies have acknowledged that there is job discrimination at Timken. More than 2 years ago, complaints were raised that Negroes at Timken are kept in dead-end jobs, regardless of their seniority.

In the summer of 1966, complaints were filed with the EEOC and the Ohio Civil Rights Commission, both of which have since acknowledged that extensive discrimination is practiced by Timken.

The OFCC has publically charged Timken with refusal to cooperate—Wall Street Journal, November 1, 1966, page 1. The National Labor Relations Board has documented that Negroes are kept out of "white-only" job progression lines.

To this day, nearly 2 years after documented proof of deliberate and massive discrimination, the Timken Roller Bearing Co. continues to get government contracts.

Since the undermining of the Department of Defense program more than a year ago, a Government mandate to open up millions of jobs has gone unused. A random examination of OFCC employment data on defense contractors shows hundreds of companies located in areas of Negro population concentrations, which have large payrolls and employ no Negroes whatsoever.

It should be stressed that a great many of these jobs involve skills which can be learned in apprenticeship training or on the job.

One company in New York employed over 1,000 workers throughout the State, and not one Negro. Another company in New York City employed 429 workers and no Negroes. A major airline had a payroll of 129 in New York, and no Negroes. Innumerable other companies employed Negroes, but only at unskilled or menial levels.

With many thousands of companies reporting employment data, it is inconceivable that the Department of Defense can even pretend it can fulfill its responsibility with a total compliance staff of 50. In the entire New England region there are only three DOD compliance reviewers.

HOW TO EARN FEES FOR REPRESENTING CLIENTS IN NEED OF HOUSING

BY ANN FAGAN GINGER*

I. LAWYERS AND HOUSING LAW

A. New Opportunities

ALTHOUGH MOST LAWYERS ARE accustomed to handling real estate transactions, only a handful have made themselves experts on housing law and funding opportunities. Of this handful most are retained by construction companies, developers and financial interests. However, the present need is for general practitioners who will become familiar with construction from the point of view of their urban neighbors, the tenants from rundown areas next to downtown office buildings who want new housing built in the same area or want existing housing remodeled and brought up to decent standards.

What has been holding back the average lawyer in an urban area from getting involved in housing law? Probably the fact that he does not think he can earn a fee for working on housing projects for low and middle income tenants. It is also likely that tenants have not come to him for advice, and perhaps he has failed to discuss housing construction possibilities with his institutional clients—trade unions, churches, cooperatives and pension funds.

There is a critical housing problem in the United States today. Part of the problem is the insufficient quantity of housing. Another part is the failure to enforce fair, nondiscriminatory housing practices. Both are aggravated by the economics of housing in this country which provides higher returns in periods of housing shortage and in areas where racial discrimination and slumlordism are practiced. Both are affected by continuation of the concept that housing is private property intended to produce a profit,[1] rather than seeing the housing industry as serving a public function by fulfilling the universal human need for housing. The third factor in the crisis is that low-cost housing cannot be built. All housing is high cost, even when the latest construction methods are used and all corners are cut within the limits of acceptable quality. What exists is the need to build high-cost housing for low-income tenants and home buyers.

At this moment there is a great opportunity to do something about providing an adequate number of fair housing units. This is due to the

*ANN FAGAN GINGER. B.A., 1945, LL.B., 1947, University of Michigan; LL.M., 1960, University of California (Boalt Hall). Editor, Civil Liberties Docket; President, Meiklejohn Civil Liberties Library.

[1] See, e.g., Butler, An Approach to Low and Moderate Income Home Ownership, 22 RUTGERS L. REV. 67 (1967). Throughout this article the footnotes are suggestive rather than definitive.

variety of programs approved in the 1968 Housing and Urban Development Act[2] and the possibility of federal funding for them, the passage of fair housing provisions[3] in the 1968 Civil Rights Act,[4] and decisions of the United States Supreme Court in *Mulkey v. Reitman*[5] and especially in *Jones v. Alfred H. Mayer Company*.[6]

In order to make full use of this opportunity, the talents of many lawyers are needed. Legislation passed by Congress does not automatically build housing units; a great deal of paper work is required. Housing legislation never provides for the funding of people in need of housing, or for experts in the construction of housing, but only for corporations prepared to construct housing. Tenants' and nonprofit organizations must be established to seek funding to meet all sorts of housing needs. Negotiations must be carried out with a multitude of public and private agencies.

B. Outline and Approach

This article therefore undertakes to do three quite separate things. First, it tries to describe broadly the nature of the economic and legal roots of the urban housing problem in the United States today, the functions of housing, the myth of private ownership and control of housing, and the reality of government servicing of housing units. This section concludes by asking whether housing is a public utility. If it raises significant questions, it will have fulfilled its function even if it provides no final answers. Secondly, the article reconsiders the proper rule of the general practitioner in representing tenants and home buyers, touching on the related problems of how to become a housing law expert, how to get retained and collect a fee for work in this field. This section includes a short list of the types of programs authorized in the 1968 Housing Act and the challenge the Act poses to the lawyer. And thirdly, the article presents a list of key government programs, pamphlets, statutes, articles and books a practicing lawyer should study in order to handle his first or second affirmative housing client.

In other words this is a bread-and-butter article, but don't hold your breath for practical tips—they won't emerge until some theoretical basis has been laid, because the general practitioner who waits in his office for a traditional client to come in seeking advice on how to fill out a form to apply for federal funding of a housing project will have a long wait. Some of the money available for building and converting housing units is earmarked for nonprofit organizations. Such groups will not come to a lawyer for advice until they somehow discover the provisions of the Housing Act of 1968 and decide they should consider going into the housing business, which they have

---

2 Pub. L. No. 90-448, 82 Stat. 476.

3 42 U.S.C. §§ 3601-3619, 3631 (1968) (penalty).

4 Civil Rights Act of 1968, tit. VIII, Pub. L. No. 90-284, 82 Stat. 73.

5 387 U.S. 369, 87 S. Ct. 1627 (1967).

6 392 U.S. 409, 88 S. Ct. 2186 (1968).

never thought about before. They probably won't go to a lawyer even then because they won't realize the need for legal advice at that early stage. They may not even know a lawyer they think would be interested in this kind of work. Left to their own ignorance of the operation of the laws and the government, few organizations will be prepared to take advantage of the law.

The lawyer who wants to get into housing law therefore may need to rethink what he knows about housing and property law to see whether it is still relevant. He may have to see himself, his institutional clients, and government aid to housing in a new light.

In discussing these questions, I have eschewed law review style. If analysis, citations, and statistics—or photographs, essays, and plays—could bring us fair and sufficient housing, surely the innumerable government hearings[7] and reports,[8] the special issues of legal periodicals,[9] the Margaret Bourke-White photographs[10] from the 1930s, the Civil Disorder Commission photographs[11] from 1967, Lorraine Hansberry's *Raisin in the Sun*[12] and Anne Braden's *The Wall Between*[13] would have brought this about by now. Perhaps at this time it will be more meaningful to others who practice law for me to cite my own experiences where they seem relevant and typical.

I do not pose as an authority on housing in general, or on the new legislation. As a citizen and constitutional lawyer,[14] I have been deeply interested in housing all my life and I have gained some knowledge in the time spent working in and on my house in the role of wife and mother. Like virtually all women I have put in much more such time than the average man, and believe that one of the many mistakes in the housing field has been the failure to include enough women in organizing, planning, and action.

The analysis in part one is based on reading and on my own experience. My housing as a child was, I think, fairly typical of white middle class

[7] See hearings listed in the Bibliography (Part 3), *infra*.

[8] REPORT OF THE NATIONAL ADVISORY COMMISSION ON CIVIL DISORDERS (1968) (hereinafter cited as the KERNER COMMISSION REPORT). *See also* reports listed in Bibliography (Part 3), *infra*.

[9] *See, e.g.*, 114 Chicago Daily L. Bull., Apr. 26, 1968; *Housing, Part I: Perspectives and Problems*, 22 LAW & CONTEMP. PROB. 187 (1967); *Housing, Part II: The Federal Role*, *Id.* at 371.

[10] M. BOURKE-WHITE & E. CALDWELL, YOU HAVE SEEN THEIR FACES (1937).

[11] KERNER COMMISSION REPORT.

[12] L. HANSBERRY, RAISIN IN THE SUN (1959).

[13] A. BRADEN, THE WALL BETWEEN (1958).

[14] My interest as a constitutional lawyer is in how to encourage and protect the exercise of civil liberties, to insure the use of due process, and to guarantee equal protection. At one point I wrote on "Litigation as a Form of Political Action," in KING & QUICK, LEGAL ASPECTS OF THE CIVIL RIGHTS MOVEMENT 195 (1965), believing litigation provides an effective approach to constitutional problems. This article could have been entitled "Representing Low-Income Tenants as a Form of Political Action," but that would have required an explanation of the broad meaning of "tenants" as all those in need of housing, and it would not have attracted practicing lawyers who need to combine morality with paying bills. *See* text following note 97, *supra*.

families at the time and quite unlike middle class families today. My parents married in 1918, lived in apartments in a city (Lansing, Michigan) until their oldest child was born, at which time, about 1920, they bought a new, boxlike house in a suburb (East Lansing). They made payments directly to the owner every month. When the house was partially paid for, my parents decided to put on an addition to accommodate the four children born between 1920 and 1930. We all knew the name of the owner of the house and I still remember it, probably because my parents discussed each request to him that we skip a monthly payment. During the depression, they also discussed the several times we borrowed money from him on his house. The oldest child left home in 1937, the youngest in 1946, and in that year my father died. My mother moved back to Detroit in 1947. The last payment on the house was made about 1949.[15] The house was rented for a few years and then sold.

Since 1941 I have lived in rented rooms, apartments, and houses in Ann Arbor, Chicago, Detroit, Cleveland, Washington, Boston, Brooklyn, and Berkeley. I lived in an integrated neighborhood in Detroit and each time I have moved it has been to another integrated neighborhood. Although I did not move out in order to move higher on the hill or out to a suburb, still my occupation permitted and my marital status required this lateral mobility, and I did leave. Each neighborhood I left is now called a black ghetto, and most of the streets on which I lived have been burned or looted in recent summers.

II. Conceptual Overview

A. The Nature of the Housing Problem

1. Housing Is a Necessity

Housing, like food and clothing, is a necessity of life. This means that every living person must be housed every day if he is to survive, whether he is employed or unemployed, well or ill, a criminal or a solid citizen, young, middle-aged, or old, and regardless of his economic condition or family status. Even the person who burns down his own house in a ghetto revolt or to collect on the insurance needs another house that very day.

Human beings need adequate housing to stay alive. A person cannot live forever in a strip cell[16] without losing his human qualities even if he is properly fed and clothed meanwhile. This indicates that there is a minimum level of housing essential for survival, although the type of housing required varies with climatic conditions.

In order to fulfill his highest creative potential, a human being needs much more than minimum housing. He needs a place for himself and a place

---

[15] Cf. A. Miller, Death of a Salesman (1949).

[16] See Brooks v. Florida, 389 U.S. 413, 88 S. Ct. 541 (1967), although in that instance the convict was not given proper food either. Consider the care given to housing the astronauts in confined quarters for short periods of time.

for his food, clothing, and possessions—a clean place with sufficient air, light, heat, plumbing, furniture, and privacy. Many people need a feeling of permanence; others feel trapped in permanent housing. Many, like their forebears, need a piece of ground however small to cultivate. Closets and storage space are essential in view of man's tendency to accumulate things.

Housing is not a commodity to be consumed. On the contrary, it provides innumerable opportunities for self-expression through the use of colors and arrangement of furniture. The need to decorate, remodel and repair is at least as old as civilized man. Transforming an impersonal housing unit into an attractive home involves the exercise of great creativity. People who have gone through this process take considerable pride in their accomplishment and are often prepared to join with other homemakers in activities to maintain and develop the community around their homes.

2. Housing Needs Change

It is not easy to provide adequate housing for each person all of his life. While each person needs housing each day, he needs different kinds of housing at different times. He is usually born in a publicly-financed house called a hospital. He moves to a private house or apartment to live with his parents and brothers and sisters. In a few years he may spend vacations in a tent in a summer camp publicly-financed through a community chest. In the usual case he leaves home in his late teens or twenties and either lives in an apartment or spends some time in institutional housing—in a college dorm, a hotel, an Army barracks, a live-in job, or, if his luck is bad, in a hospital or prison.

When he marries (probably in a public house of worship) and goes on his honeymoon to a new hotel (probably constructed with funds insured by the government), the cycle starts again. First he needs a small unit for two. As children are born, he needs more room for them and their things. He may even want to build a second, vacation, house. For culture and recreation he goes to institutional housing units containing zoos, galleries, movies, plays, or opera. When the children leave home, he doesn't need as much room. As he grows older, he prefers or needs a unit with little upkeep. At his death, he probably still wants a house in a casket buried in a plot of earth he purchased from a cemetery.

3. Needs and Income Unrelated

There is an inverse relationship between the amount of housing most men need at each stage of their lives and the amount of income they can earn at each stage. The young father is at a low income-producing stage in his occupation; the successful middle-aged worker watches his teen-age children move out of the larger home he can finally afford. The retired worker doesn't want to pay taxes on a 40-year-old house requiring major repairs, but if he moves into an apartment he will have to pay higher rent for the caretaker.

Similarly, the people who are most dependent on society for assistance sometimes need more expensive housing than those who are independent. That is, children need publicly-financed school houses by day as well as homes at night, although they are dependent and cannot help pay for either. People who are ill or handicapped or emotionally disturbed need hospital rooms or rehabilitation centers built with their special needs in mind.

4. Housing Related to Employment

Of the three necessities of life, housing is most closely related to source of income and employment. The decision on where to live is determined by employment: people live somewhere near their work. Clothing and food can be adjusted accordingly.

Despite this intimate relationship between housing and employment, the housing of workers is not now considered the responsibility of the person employing them. Ours is the first era in recorded history in which this has been true.

Under slavery the master provided housing for the workers on the land they worked as slaves or adjoining his home. Under feudalism the vassal lived in housing built on a piece of the land he worked for the lord. Much later, in the United States, tenant farmers lived on the landlord's property, miners and others lived in company towns, while self-employed farmers built their own farmhouses (often with the help of their neighbors). However, in urban areas, workers did not have employer-landlords; they had employers who paid them wages and landlords to whom they paid rent. Of course many employers also invested in real estate.

Slaveowners pointed out,[17] near the end of their era before the Civil War, that the heartless northern capitalist did nothing to house his employees when they were laid off for lack of work, while every slaveowner put a roof over the heads of his slaves, even when the crop failed. More accurately, one economic system relied on buying, breeding, selling, and using slave labor power the year around, and therefore had to house the workers. (One reason the slave system was not economically feasible in the north and west was the need for more expensive housing in those areas due to severe weather.) The other economic system relied, and continues to rely, on a mobile labor force that can be laid off, rehired, and moved about from time to time as economic conditions warrant, with society as a whole providing housing and food in slack times.

Jobs tied to housing in company towns and on tenant farms are few in number today, and declining. In industries with strong unions, companies may agree to pay part of the moving costs for union members when the company moves a plant, and every large company or university has a department

---

[17] See, e.g., the description of the viewpoint of John C. Calhoun in R. HOFSTADTER, THE AMERICAN POLITICAL TRADITION 67-91 (1949).

to assist its executives in finding suitable housing. But most workers are left to fend for themselves in finding, repairing, and paying for housing whether they are working, on strike, or between jobs. People new to the labor market—youth, women, hard-core unemployed—have no money to pay for housing and they have no idea where to settle or how much they can afford to pay until they find work.

5. Housing the Unemployed

Paying for housing creates problems that do not exist with food and clothing. While it is customary to receive wages only after the work is done, it is customary to pay for a week's or a month's lodging in advance. When payment is made by the day, the rate is greatly increased. The result is that the very people with the least money, and no jobs to provide steady income, are the ones who must pay for housing by the day while they seek work so they can save enough money to pay by the week or month. By the time they find work, they are in debt to a landlord.

When a place of employment is moved to another geographical area, or an employer changes his method of production, a worker with a house near his work suddenly becomes an unemployed person with a house located in limbo. He may not be able to sell his house as quickly as he lost his ability to make the payments on it. Similarly, a person with adequate housing convenient to his job may have his property condemned so that a road or other type of housing unit (public school or housing project) can replace it. The worker is required to move to another house that may be farther from his work or more expensive.

The National Committee Against Discrimination in Housing has documented an additional problem: the lack of nondiscriminatory housing in the suburban and rural areas where new factories are being built creating jobs for which large numbers of minority group works can qualify.[17a]

The separation of the responsibility for housing from employment has created economic and social problems which we have not faced up to. We have patched together a mixture of public and private housing located near public and private industries, with public and private charity to help fill economic gaps. This has not solved the problems of housing or employment, nor has it permitted the pursuit of liberty and happiness.[18]

B. The Function of Housing

At one point in American history, not so long ago, the house was the

---

[17a] THE IMPACT OF HOUSING PATTERNS ON JOB OPPORTUNITIES: AN INTERIM REPORT OF A STUDY ON WHERE PEOPLE LIVE AND WHERE THE JOBS ARE (1968).

[18] Constitutional lawyers who have recently read the Declaration of Independence, with its ringing call to revolution in order to establish a government that permits men to pursue happiness, may be in a better position to understand some of the goals of the hippies, Diggers and black power advocates who feel that the pursuit of happiness is a timely goal in this affluent society.

center of the economic activity that provided family income. The farmhouse was used for certain types of work and the farm wife was an essential worker who provided food and shelter for farm laborers. She also produced table foods from her garden. In the same era much industrial work was done in the steaming tenements of New York and other cities, and was paid for by the piece as home work. Many families lived behind or above the family carpentry or print shop, meat market, or other small business, with several family members working there. The divorce rate was low in this period; so was the standard of living.

Today housing is almost completely separated from the production of family income, except for some white collar workers who use part of the home for a second office (with tax benefits), or those who write or do paper work solely at home. It is not economically feasible to produce some kinds of goods in the small quantities possible in the home, and zoning provisions frequently prohibit other kinds of income-producing work that could still be done there successfully.

As a result, only three functions of interest to society as a whole are permitted to be performed in the home today: consuming, relaxing, and child rearing. Even the child-rearing function gets moved out of the home the moment the mother decides to become a wage earner. Since she can't earn money at home, she probably takes her children to a nursery school or alternative baby-sitting arrangement. (She is likely to take the laundry and other household tasks to be done in institutions at the same time, although this varies with community custom.)

Several factors suggest rethinking the limitation of functions permitted in the home. As industries become automated, they create more commodities and more unemployment. However, the commodities produced in this way frequently need to be modified or decorated in order to be used by a particular buyer, and many need to be serviced and repaired at intervals. These functions create some new jobs that may be able to be based in a home. The tremendous increase in the number of active, retired workers, and in the number of young families that break up suggests that it may be economically feasible and emotionally healthy to encourage some families to go into certain kinds of businesses in the home as one method of encouraging joint interests, common understanding, and mutual respect. Obviously, strict government regulation would be necessary to prevent a return to sweatshop conditions.

After a family has broken up, the wife's income may depend entirely on child-support payments from her former husband. She may not want to leave the home to find employment, preferring to raise the children herself. But she needs part-time employment both for income and for interest. Home work would suit her needs admirably for a certain period of time.

These questions relate to housing problems directly. Every break-up of a family means the creation of two housing units, one that is too large and expensive for its remaining tenants (wife and children), and one that is too small and expensive to suit its new tenant (husband). One of the major housing problems today in many urban ghettos is how to find housing adequate to the needs of one-parent families at a price the one-parent families can pay. If such families can not find their own answers, society must bear the burden through welfare payments or provision of low-cost public housing units.

Thinking about these human functions of housing, one tends to forget that housing also has a totally different function in this country. Legislation on housing problems comes through the House and Senate Committees on Banking and Currency rather than committees on housing and urban problems. The reason probably is that the housing and construction industry is a major factor in the national economy. Congress and the President can affect the operation of the economy by raising and lowering the amount of money available for loans for construction and remodeling of housing and for insuring such loans. To fulfill this function, it is not important whether the housing is for people, factories, or shopping centers. The question in this regard is not whether construction helps solve the social problem of housing those who are now homeless or ill-housed, but whether it will increase or decrease the amount of money available for loans and investments, thus hastening or slowing down inflation.

C. The Myth of Private Ownership and Control of Housing

1. Control of Private Housing

Professor Powell, after a lifetime of study of real property, felt moved to sum up the relationship between property rights and civil rights as Californians faced the proposal to nullify the state fair housing act.[19] He reviewed

"some twenty aspects of the law in which the absoluteness of property rights has been rejected because of the basic proposition that one cannot use what he owns in a fashion harmful to the community of which he is a part. The rule against perpetuities, unpermitted restraints on alienation, illegal uses of the bait of wealth to dominate the lives of other people, formalities prerequisite to an effective deed or will—all these define property rights with subtractions as to the power to dispose, stemming from the preservation of public welfare. When one turns to the area of permissible uses of property, easements by necessity, the law of nuisance, the division of the benefits of water, regulations as to sanitation and sewerage, building codes, the maintenance of at least a minimum of morality, soil conservation, over-grazing, timber control, zoning, planning, blight prevention, housing adequacy, and the protection of those short in bargaining power, such as renters and borrowers, are aspects of our legal background in which progressively property rights have been trimmed for the protection of society. In each of these twenty areas the criterion

[19] Powell, *The Relationship between Property Rights and Civil Rights*, 15 Hast. L.J. 135 (1963).

has been basically the same. Is the claimed exercise of property rights one which is consistent with the public welfare? If so the claim is given effect. If not the claim is found not to be a right at all."[20]

2. *The Public Sector*

Perhaps it is a sign that a government has been organized when the first jail is built to house law violators. In any event, it has long been accepted that governments will provide free housing for criminals. (Until recently, it has also been assumed that this free housing will be, at best, uncomfortable, unattractive, unlike home, and very expensive to guard and maintain.) The custom of housing soldiers is also ancient, with most governments showing the ability to construct hardy quarters for the troops and pleasant, even occasionally sumptuous, quarters for the officers. Governments also must house themselves and some of their leading officials. These government buildings have typically been of grand design, frequently in the latest style, and they have often been built with an eye to posterity (and the tourist trade). Governments have also built large public buildings for entertainment functions, giving considerable attention to the comfort of the patrons of the arts.

3. *Responsibility for Housing*

More recently, society has accepted the responsibility for housing people with problems they cannot solve individually—the ill in hospitals, the handicapped in special institutions containing school and work rooms, and those without families in homelike institutions. Housing for these people is often financed in part by government and in part by charity. In either case the money comes from those who are working, either through enforced payment of taxes or through more or less voluntary contributions to community chests (often collected, today, by employers).

In this era, society as a whole has been made responsible for housing people who are able to work to pay for their own housing but who are unable to find work. The depression of the 1930's led to large scale government construction of permanent housing projects administered by the government. This was the first time government had built housing for people who were not employed by the government, handicapped in some way, or being punished for wrongdoing. Perhaps for this reason a stigma has frequently been attached to living in government housing, a stigma fed by the failure of the architects, landscapers, and managers to construct and maintain attractive units in which a self-respecting person would be proud to raise his family. This may explain, also, why private practitioners have not hurried to learn about new housing legislation or to recommend that their clients seek government funding for construction of projects.

[20] *Id.* at 148-149.

4. *The Private Sector*

Frequently we continue to think in old terms while experiencing new realities. This has certainly been true of government housing. While the federal government was openly constructing public housing units in large projects in the cities, for which people were eligible due to low incomes, it was less directly building individual homes in the suburbs for which people were eligible if they had incomes high enough to make the down payments and regular monthly payments. Plans for individual suburban homes were checked carefully by government agencies because the housing was being built on government-insured money and sold with government-insured mortgages. These government-insured housing units, sometimes built singly and sometimes in developments, frequently took into account the needs, for privacy, utility, beauty, landscaping, tool rooms and closet space, forgotten in some low-cost urban projects. They seldom were built with consideration of land use, rapid transit or urban blight, and the developers were not required to show that they were part of a workable plan for development of the suburban area. Neither in the urban public housing units nor in the suburban tract housing developments were the needs, desires and suggestions of prospective tenants actively sought or followed in most cases.

Translating these facts into personal terms, of the many people I have known in the cities in which I have lived in the past twenty years only a few couples have finished paying for their homes, and most of these have retired. I do not know anyone who is buying a house entirely with his own money. Most people have loans from a government agency or from a private agency whose loans are insured by the government. I know only two families that built housing to their own specifications—one hired a contractor, the other, very slowly, did the work themselves. Everyone else I know has gone through about the same housing experience I have.

When I was young I rented an inexpensive, ugly, privately-owned, furnished apartment, and spackled and painted the walls, scrubbed the oven and put linoleum on the floors. When the rent was increased as a result, I moved to another apartment in the same city and repeated the process. Or I moved to another city and did the same. When my children were young and I sought permanence in their lives and my own, I had no money for a down payment on a house, although I was lucky enough to live in a rent-controlled apartment in Brooklyn. By the time we had saved enough for a down payment, my children were almost in their teens. Because my husband came under the veterans' housing law, the state veterans' agency inspected an old house we wanted and agreed to pay the seller's price if we paid the down payment. The agency insisted that certain repairs be made before the deal was closed. The house is certainly not our dream house, but the shrubbery softens its basically square design. We made some structural changes as soon as we moved in and the house is big enough for the children to grow in, although by the time we had started paying on the principal, one had left for college. If we do not have to move for some reason, and if we are able to make regular monthly payments for the next twenty years, we will own this house by the time my husband has retired, having paid what amounted to rent all these years.

Our house is not our castle.

In fact, people are no longer buying and selling private property, that is, homes that they own; they are exchanging housing units owned by a bank or other lending institution. In the case of new housing, the money to construct the unit was probably loaned or insured by the government. In the case of old housing, the mortgage was probably insured by the government.

In other words, most people who say they are buying their own homes are not doing that at all. The same is true of people selling their homes. The seller probably never owned the whole house. He made payments for a period of time (on principal, interest, insurance, taxes, repairs) and now he plans to leave the neighborhood. He doesn't care whether the new owner (tenant) pays anything other than the down payment because, in most cases, the house is financed through a bank which will collect monthly payments from the new "owner" until he also sells the house for which he hasn't finished paying. In a sense, the bank may not care whether the new owner keeps up the payments either because the government has probably insured payment of the mortgage if the buyer defaults.

In view of this reality, the argument that a private seller should be able to determine the race, religion, or required credit rating of a private buyer seems outdated as well as being unconstitutional.[21] It has been said that a seller may want to insure the continuation of the character of the neighborhood he is leaving in deference to his good friends who will remain there. This also rings false to many city dwellers. For one thing, it is impossible to define the "character" of a neighborhood in which each family is quite different from the others, however similar they may appear on the surface. And I remember the amazed look on the face of my Brooklyn neighbor when I tried to borrow a teaspoon of vanilla from her at a crucial moment in mixing cake batter. Even in Berkeley, my friends are not my immediate neighbors but adults living in other parts of the Bay Area. Only children tend to make friends of their next door neighbors in modern city living, and children often remain color blind and un-class conscious long after their parents have lost these democratic traits.

The effect of the changes in financing of so-called private housing is to abolish the concept of private housing. The government is in the housing business at every level of housing accommodations: large public buildings, large commercial and industrial buildings, large inexpensive housing projects,

[21] Jones v. A. H. Mayer Co., 392 U.S. 409, 88 S. Ct. 2186 (1968).

large expensive cooperative apartments, and expensive individual suburban homes. It also is in the business of destroying certain housing because it is decrepit and because it stands in the way of constructing other kinds of buildings.

At a recent conference on Housing: A Joint Venture for Public and Private Action conducted by the Department of Housing and Community Development of the State of California, Harold B. Brooks, Jr., of the Bay View-Hunters Point Joint Housing Committee of San Francisco, commented:

> "The majority of public servants and big companies suckle off the poor. Big companies receive payments from the government to develop projects, and then collect profits from the tenants or customers. But they treat recipients of government *welfare* payments differently. It seems to me it's either welfare or communism when everyone gets money from the government."

5. Disinheriting Housing

The housing in which we live will outlive us. It has a high initial cost of construction, a low cost of upkeep at first and a high cost of upkeep in later years. Each housing unit is used by several people at once and by several generations.

Nonetheless, I have no reason to believe that my children will want to live in the house we are buying after we die, any more than I even considered living in my parents' house when it was empty. Of all my friends and acquaintances, I do not know one adult who lives in the house in which he was born, or who lives in a house inherited from his parents or other relatives.[22] Many have inherited property, which they sold, using the income to make a down payment on a different house usually in a different city. As a result, it is difficult to see any advantage to our children from bequeathing our house to them. We could just as well bequeath them money we saved by not paying interest all these years.

D. The Reality of Government Servicing of Housing Units

Not only does the government control many aspects of housing, it also controls the servicing of homes. Parents usually ask about the quality of public schools in the vicinity of a house they are considering occupying. They know that the quality of educational services provided by the govern-

---

[22] About half of all American households changed their place of residence during the latter half of the 1950's according to Grier, *The Negro Ghettos and Federal Housing Policy*, 32 LAW & CONTEMP. PROB. 550, 559 (1967). The KERNER COMMISSION REPORT gives the percent of household heads who moved in 1958–60 in urban areas where civil disorders arose in 1967. In greater Grand Rapids, 27.7% white and 45.7% nonwhite moved; in greater Milwaukee, 32.3% white and 52.8% nonwhite moved; in greater Phoenix, the figures are 50.0% white and 40.4% nonwhite; in greater Tucson, 49.0% white and 37.2% nonwhite. Similar percentages are given for the other major cities studied.

ment varies according to geographical areas. This leads to a discussion of the nature of high quality education today. It also leads to questions on differences in the quality of other types of services provided by government and private agencies based on place of residence, and what is to be done about these differences.

1. The Quality of Education

Many families try to move to the suburbs or to more exclusive neighborhoods when their children reach school age, even if this causes considerable financial strain or lengthens the husband's commute. In this way they hope to provide the best educational environment for their children, and to protect them from certain harsh realities of ghetto and big city life. Many of these parents expect their children to go on to college for a liberal arts education (followed, perhaps, by a short stint in the Army).

At this juncture it may not be too late to pose a few questions about

A MAN'S HOME IS HIS CASTLE
PLANNED FOR, PROTECTED, SERVICED, GOVERNED, AND TAXED BY GOVERNMENT AND BUSINESS 24 HOURS A DAY ACCORDING TO ITS LOCATION

PRIVATE DEVELOPER'S SUBDIVISION
INSURANCE COMPANIES' RATING ZONE
FHA LOANING DISTRICT
CITY/REGIONAL PLANNING AREA
MODEL CITY ZONE
PUBLIC PROPERTY IMPROVEMENT ZONE
CITY HOUSING ZONE
STATE HIGHWAY PLANNING AREA
FAIR HOUSING AGENCY REGION
PUBLIC SCHOOL DISTRICT
NURSERY SCHOOL DISTRICT
PUBLIC LIBRARY DISTRICT
JUNIOR COLLEGE DISTRICT
SHOPPING CENTER
SHOPPING DELIVERY SERVICE AREA
APPLIANCE REPAIR SERVICE AREA
TV, RADIO COVERAGE AREA
CULTURAL/ENTERTAINMENT CENTER
RECREATION, PARK DEVELOPMENT AREA
SPORTS ARENA
CHURCH SYNOD
TRADE UNION LOCAL
COMMUNITY CHEST AGENCIES

PROPERTY TAX DISTRICT
INTERNAL REVENUE DISTRICT
SEWAGE DISTRICT
GARBAGE DISPOSAL DISTRICT
MUNICIPAL UTILITY DISTRICT
ELECTRIC COMPANY SERVICE AREA
GAS COMPANY BUSINESS AREA
WATER SUPPLY REGION
WATER POLLUTION QUALITY CONTROL
AIR POLUTION CONTROL AREA
HOUSING CODE INSPECTION DISTRICT
HEALTH DEPARTMENT REGION
HEALTH SERVICE DISTRICT
AMBULANCE SERVICE AREA
PUBLIC HOSPITAL ZONE
COUNTY WELFARE OFFICE
AIRPORT TAX AREA
RAPID TRANSIT DISTRICT
TELEGRAPH ZONE
TELEPHONE COMPANY AREA
POSTAL ZONE

POLITICAL PARTY PRECINCT
ELECTORAL DISTRICT
JURY COMMISSIONERS' AREA
JUVENILE COURT JURISDICTION
CITY COURT JURISDICTION
COUNTY COURT JURISDICTION
FEDERAL DISTRICT COURT JURISDICTION
FEDERAL COURT OF APPEAL JURISDICTION
PUBLIC DEFENDER OFFICE
OEO LEGAL SERVICE OFFICE
LEGAL AID SOCIETY OFFICE

FIRE STATION
CITY POLICE PRECINCT
SHERIFF'S OFFICE
HIGHWAY PATROL AREA
STATE POLICE DISTRICT
NATIONAL GUARD POST
FEDERAL BUREAU OF INVESTIGATION AREA
ARMY COMMAND REGION
CIVIL DEFENSE REGION
ATOMIC ENERGY COMMISSION AREA
LOCAL DRAFT BOARD

the possible effects of such moves. What kinds of books are being used in the best public (and private) schools today? If the pupils aren't reading Dickens' classic tales of the London poor or *West Side Story*,[23] they are likely to be assigned *Children of Sanchez*,[24] *Native Son*,[25] or *Manchild in the Promised Land*.[26] If children are going to do well in school, they must become curious about the kinds of people they meet in these books. Is this better than meeting such people in the flesh in a city school, where Bigger Thomas may sit in the next seat? Do parents really want to protect their children from meeting the likes of Huck Finn? Even if they do, how long can children be so protected?

Suburban children who go to college take courses in sociology, political science, philosophy, economics, and social work, in all of which they study people different from themselves. Is this better than knowing the people described in the textbooks? Which will better prepare them to live in a world most of whose inhabitants are poor people of color? They will study housing as part of "The Urban Problem," and learn that part of the problem is created by many people who live in one place (where they vote, pay property taxes, send children to school, and participate in community decisions), and who work in another place (where they pay no taxes and ignore the school, employment, and housing problems). Some of these students may ask their fathers whether it is fair for them to contribute nothing *as citizens* to the solution of problems in the cities where they spend the better part of each working day. If their fathers are lawyers, architects, bankers, educators, or realtors, they may further ask how their fathers can give good professional advice about urban problems or make sound decisions when they have limited knowledge of and emotional concern about the lives of urban dwellers. Mothers in these professions face the same questions.

As some of these students leave the suburb and college for life in a Haight-Ashbury, they create a new aspect to the problem of urban housing, as well as raising new questions about the wisdom of their parents' move from the city.

If the sons are drafted, or enlist, without a specific skill, they will almost certainly meet and live with some of the people from whom their parents isolated them. It is conceivable that at some point their lives may depend on their ability to become intimate friends with slum dwellers turned soldier.

2. *The Quality of Other Types of Services Related to Place of Residence*

The chart on page 344 indicates the types of services that come into the home, services related to housing, and agencies that serve people in their homes or make decisions according to place of residence.

---

23 Laurents, Sondheim & Burnstein, West Side Story (1958).
24 O. Lewis, Children of Sanchez (1961).
25 R. Wright, Native Son (1940).
26 C. Brown, Manchild in the Promised Land (1965).

The agencies that provide services inside the home are public utilities owned publicly or privately, e.g., gas, electricity, telephone, post office, water, sewage disposal, garbage disposal. Other agencies deliver goods to the home, e.g., dairy products, diapers, cleaning and laundry, shopping center purchases. The fire and police departments provide protection to the home and other government departments provide street lights, repair streets, and build parkways.

These public and private agencies, and others listed on the chart, provide different kinds of service in different areas. For example, mail deliveries are made several times a day in commercial areas, but only once a day in residential areas, although special delivery service is equally fast in both areas. Other differences in treatment cannot be explained on such utilitarian grounds. There are many complaints that it takes longer to get a policeman to answer a call for help from the ghetto than from the hills.[27] I know the sidewalk near my mother's apartment building in Detroit was always kept up until the area was almost completely occupied by Negroes.[28] Few people realize that insurance companies charge different rates in different neighborhoods, and in some urban areas it is difficult to buy property insurance at all.[29] Even food prices are higher in some areas than others, and in inverse proportion to the income of the citizens in the neighborhood.[30] The same is true of rents in the slums.[31] With a higher concentration of children, there are fewer playgrounds and parks.[32] With less money to buy private automobiles, ghetto residents frequently get worse public transportation.[33]

[27] "[T]he residents of a large area in the center of the Negro ghetto are victims of over one-third of the daylight residential burglaries in the city. Yet during the daytime only one of Hartford's eighteen patrol cars and none of its eleven foot patrolmen is assigned to this area. Sections in the white part of town about the same size as the central ghetto area receive slightly more intensive daytime patrol even though the citizens in the ghetto area summon the police about six times as often because of criminal acts." Comment, *Program Budgeting for Police Departments*, 76 YALE L.J. 822 (1967).

[28] Suits have been filed by Negro residents to compel defendant cities to give Negro and white districts equal treatment in street paving, sidewalk and gutter construction, fire hydrants, street lights, water service, sewage and garbage collection. *See, e.g.,* Hawkins v. Shaw, 13 CIV. LIB. DOCK. 171, No. 553 (1967-68); Harris v. Itta Bena, 13 CIV. LIB. DOCK. 171, No. 553 (1967-68).

[29] *See* KERNER COMMISSION REPORT at 305-06. Until July, 1967, the FHA followed a practice of "red-lining" large districts in major cities, refusing to insure mortgages there regardless of the condition of the property or the buyer's ability to make payments.

[30] *Id.* at 141; D. CAPLOWITZ, THE POOR PAY MORE: CONSUMER PRACTICES OF LOW INCOME FAMILIES (1963).

[31] *Id.* at 258. In Newark, for example, the "color tax" on rentals was estimated at well over 10 percent, ranging from 8.1% to 16.8% higher for nonwhites than whites for similar housing units.

[32] *See, e.g.,* KERNER COMMISSION REPORT at 82. *See also Re* Southern Water Co., 13 CIV. LIB. DOCK. 126 (Cal. Pub. Utilities Comm'n 1967-68) (complaint alleged difference in quality and price of water).

[33] This was a common complaint of Watts residents. *See* Robles v. Gilroy Unified School District, 13 CIV. LIB. DOCK. 129, No. 428.1 (1967-68).

3. What Can Be Done To Eliminate Differences in Services

The National Commission on Civil Disorders has documented in considerable detail the racist nature of American society in this time. This racism pervades every aspect of American life where it is not being consciously fought (as some public school systems are finally doing[34]). That it pervades the housing market is well known. The extent to which it touches government agencies and private companies related to housing is less well known.

In other words, the government provides or controls, through franchises, all services to the housing unit, not simply the educational facilities. In this way it controls the quality of life in the neighborhood.

Should prospective tenants ask how quickly the fire department will get to their new home, the nature of the police protection in the area, what kind of tactics the Army or National Guard will use if it becomes a riot area,[35] and whether the local draft board is likely to classify men as conscientious objectors if they qualify for that status?

Should they retain lawyers to sue for every denial of equal protection based on location of dwelling?

E. Is Housing a Public Utility?

1. "Public Utility" Defined

Since every person requires housing to the same degree, since everyone cannot provide housing for himself, and since every housing unit will be used by many users,[36] it seems logical to consider whether housing is a public utility. Certainly public utilities are related to housing: gas, water, electricity, telephones all go into housing units. So do radio and television. Transportation has no function except to go from one housing unit to another, whether the unit is for people or goods.

In fact, housing fits the definition of a public utility in *Black's Law Dictionary*. It is:

> "A business or service which is engaged in regularly supplying the public with some commodity or service which is of public consequence and need, such as electricity . . . Any agency, instrumentality, business industry or service which is used or conducted in such manner as to affect the community at large, that is which is not limited or restricted to any particular class of the community."

[34] For example, the September, 1968 implementation of the Berkeley, California plan for integration of all public schools.

[35] See DEP'T OF THE ARMY, CIVIL DISTURBANCES AND DISASTERS (Field Manual 1968). Cf. Comment, *Kill or be Killed: Use of Deadly Force in the Riot Situation*, 56 CALIF. L. REV. 829 (1968).

[36] See note 22 supra.

Finally we get to Black's dictionary test for determining whether a concern is a public utility:

> "Whether it has held itself out as ready, able and willing to serve the public. . . . The term implies a public use of an article, product, or service, carrying with it the duty of the producer or manufacturer, or one attempting to furnish the service, to serve the public and treat all persons alike, without discrimination."

The last part of the definition has created the problem. While there may not be in existence anything which might be called "the housing industry" in the precise sense in which there is an A.T.&T. Co., and while "the housing industry" may never have held itself out openly as prepared to provide adequate housing for everyone as A.T.&T. may have promised to provide universal phone service to get a franchise from the government, that does not end the matter. Everyone assumes he can obtain housing without building it himself. In other words, tenants (that is, everyone in need of housing, which is everyone) know they need housing and they assume it will be provided for them if they are prepared to pay for it. This was not always true, but it is certainly true at this time in this country.

The more one ponders why housing has not been considered a public utility, the more one concludes that we have not changed our terminology and concepts to fit the facts of transient urban living. Nor have we admitted that virtually every housing unit in this country is today financed in whole or in part, directly or indirectly, with government money (or, at the very least, is deeply affected by government tax, lending and spending policies). If one considered the government (federal, state, and local) as a public utility company in the field of housing, housing would fit the definition in Black's.

2. If So, A Suggested Model Housing Agency

As Professor Powell indicated in the passage quoted above, housing has been subjected to increasing government regulation. Legislative and executive bodies have set minimum standards for decent housing; administrative agencies have had power to inspect private housing units for violations of the housing code as to light, air, fireproofing, number of occupants, and so forth. In war periods rent controls have been established. Plans for new buildings, and even for major remodeling of existing private homes, must be approved. All of these standards are set and actions taken to protect society from the effects of bad housing, to limit the number of fires, the spread of disease, and other social ills.

If housing is a public utility, much further government regulation is permitted or even required. Housing is already treated like a public utility in that it enjoys the right of eminent domain. Under present federal housing laws, private companies as well as public agencies can obtain occupied land and raze existing dwellings in order to construct new units in the public interest. In defining the public interest the need for housing cannot blind us to the need to retain sufficient open space to insure an adequate food supply for an exploding population and for recreational use.

Housing, then, should be subject to the kinds of regulation the government has exercised for decades over other public utilities such as the railroads and electric power companies. Like them, it should be judged by whether it fulfills its function, not by the profit it earns. And it should be subject to the established principle that a public utility may not earn excessive profits.

Imagine a model area in which every vacant housing unit is listed with a government agency. The agency prepares an accurate description of the facilities, promptly inspects the unit and, if necessary, fumigates, repairs, and repaints it to meet current housing standards. If it cannot be rehabilitated, it is demolished. A salaried government employee shows lists of unoccupied housing to prospective purchasers and tenants and takes them to see new and old units they think may be suitable. When the right housing unit is found, the employee discusses financial problems and puts the prospective buyers or tenants in touch with the appropriate government agencies for assistance in obtaining loans, insured mortgages, rent subsidies, or other kinds of financing.

If such a system were adopted, it would serve several immediate purposes that society considers to be of great value. It would prevent discrimination in buying, selling, leasing, and renting housing units on the basis of race[37] or financial condition; it would bring inadequate housing up to standard, creating jobs in the process; it would destroy structures dangerous to the neighborhood and prevent the creation of slum areas; it would permit tenants to share their financial problems with officials knowledgeable in housing law and financing and prevent some unwise purchases which now lead to mortgage foreclosures; it would permit people to fit their housing to their needs, instead of being shoved into inexpensive but inadequate housing.

Even if this be considered an impossible dream, it suggests the kind of regulation the federal government has exercised over many other parts of the so-called private sector of the economy.

Now, keeping in mind this theoretical discussion, let us get down to practice.

III. THE PROPER ROLE OF THE GENERAL PRACTITIONER IN REPRESENTING TENANTS

A. The Typical Role of the General Practitioner With a Housing Case

Let us start with an extreme situation involving government housing in a case[38] decided by the United States Supreme Court in 1967. A man

---

[37] A number of cases have involved realtors and racial discrimination. *See, e.g.,* Chicago Real Estate Bd. v. Chicago, 36 Ill. 2d 530, 224 N.E.2d 793 (1967); Diona v. Lomenzo, 26 App. Div. 2d 473, 275 N.Y.S.2d 663 (1966); Filippo v. Real Estate Commission, 223 A.2d 268 (1966).

[38] Brooks v. Florida, 389 U.S. 413, 88 S. Ct. 541 (1967).

alleged, without contradiction, that he and two other men were housed for 35 days in a unit 6½ feet wide and between 7 and 13 feet long without external windows, beds or furniture, containing a hole in the floor for a toilet. A lawyer was appointed to represent him on a related matter, in which he was unsuccessful. The opinion does not disclose whether he was assisted by counsel in his effort to bring these facts to the attention of the Supreme Court. In any event, the sole result of the litigation was that a confession obtained from the prison inmate while he was in this sweatbox was held not voluntary and the inmate's conviction was reversed.

Did the lawyer appointed by the court have a duty to his client to go any further than representing him (and 12 codefendants) at a criminal trial for causing a prison riot, as a result of which he was placed in this box? If the same lawyer had represented a man on retainer and he had somehow gotten into such a unit of government housing, would the lawyer have had a duty to seek affirmative relief? It would certainly have been appropriate to file a petition seeking a declaration that the operation of such a facility violates constitutional prohibitions against cruel and unusual punishment and is a "shocking display of barbarism which should not escape the remedial action"[39] of the appropriate state or federal court and to seek an injunctive order to close or destroy the facility and delete all prison regulations permitting its use.

Let us take an easier case. In *Habib v. Edwards*,[40] a tenant gave information to city authorities concerning violations of statutes and regulations governing the sanitary conditions in her rented apartment. Her landlord sued to evict her. When she defended on the ground that the cause of the eviction was that she gave such information, the trial judge held that she had a "constitutional right to provide such information to the government" which right "is protected not only against interference by the government but also against interference by private persons."[41] When the matter came before the Court of Appeals for the District of Columbia Circuit, it granted a stay of eviction, and Judge Skelly Wright, in a concurring opinion,[42] pointed out that "every citizen has the right, if not the duty, of informing his government of a violation of the law, and that a court of equity, on a proper showing, may enjoin any interference with that right. . . . Indeed, an interference with such a right may be punishable under the criminal

[39] *Id.* at 415, 88 S. Ct. at 542. *Cf.* Jordan v. California, 13 Civ. Lib. Dock. 109, No. 411.38 (1967-68), in which the court, while denying the requested habeas corpus writ, ordered the strip cells refitted so that inmates would be supplied with at least "the basic requirements which are essential to life."

[40] Edwards v. Habib, 366 F.2d 628 (D.C. Cir. 1965), *cert. denied*, —— U.S. ——, 89 S. Ct. 618 (1969).

[41] Habib v. Edwards, Civil No. LT75895 (D.C. Ct. of Gen. Sess. 1965), reprinted in 2 Civ. Rights & Lib. Handbook 290L (1963, 1966 Supp.), *motion for stay of judgment granted*, 366 F.2d 628 (D.C. Cir. 1965).

[42] Habib v. Edwards, 366 F.2d 628, 629 (D.C. Cir. 1965).

statutes of the United States." With this partial victory, the OEO legal service lawyers for the tenant had to conclude their representation.[43]

If this had been a private client represented by a lawyer in private practice, particularly if it had been an affluent commercial client, would the matter have ended there or would the lawyer have sought some affirmative relief? Would the lawyer, perhaps, have suggested that the tenant consider seeking federal funding to build new housing units that would never be permitted to fall into such disrepair? (This would have been a realistic suggestion only if the tenant could create an organizational client with considerable patience and perspicacity.)

When a tenants' union comes to a sympathetic lawyer for advice on how to obtain fair treatment from a slumlord, the lawyer may help his organizational client prepare a model contract[44] and negotiate with the landlord to get his signature. The lawyer may represent the union in subsequent efforts to get the contract enforced, or to prevent its breach by the landlord.[45] Does the lawyer have a responsibility to spend some of his time learning housing law so he can suggest that the tenants' union might want to seek federal funding to build new housing units, to be run by the union, or to take over and rehabilitate existing units? Who would pay the lawyer for the time he spent reading the Housing Act of 1968, which runs 136 pages in small type and requires frequent references to the previous legislation it amended?

What about a lawyer who agrees to defend a black ghetto resident charged with looting or violating the curfew during an urban disorder. What if, in the process of representing his client, he comes to understand something about the filth of ghetto housing that could cause a person to burn down his own home. Does his responsibility end when the criminal charges are dropped? How will this lawyer get to work in his downtown office during the next civil disorder in his community? Down what street will he drive when the main thoroughfare is clogged with bricks and burning trash, and filled with police or looters? Is this practical question relevant here? Does it affect the responsibility of the lawyer in general practice to work in housing law?

---

[43] OEO legal service offices are frequently not permitted to represent clients in fee-producing cases unless three lawyers in private practice first reject the case. In fact, indigent clients sometimes fail to carry through on referrals when it is complicated to do so. *But see* Barbee v. Crane, 13 Civ. Lib. Dock. 124, No. 423. Pa. 1 (1967-68).

[44] For the text of sample contract between a tenant's organization and a landlord, see the agreement between Chicago's JOIN Community Union and landlord Max Gutman, reprinted in 2 Civ. Rights & Lib. Handbook 290a (1963).

[45] Tenants who signed the contract cited in note 44, *supra*, successfully arbitrated under that agreement to possess the property, collect rent therefor and apply that rent for needed repairs. When the landlord sued, in Sampson v. Davis (Cir. Ct., Cook Co. #66CH 4827), the court held the contract unenforceable. 13 Civ. Lib. Dock. 122, No. 423. Ill. 5 (1967-68).

B.   The Traditional Role of the Housing Lawyer

The lawyer for a large company in the business of construction, management or financing of real estate is expected to study pending legislation on housing and occasionally to prepare testimony for legislative committees. Whether he is a general practitioner on retainer or house counsel, on passage of a housing law he is expected to prepare a memorandum summarizing major provisions of the act and analyzing in some detail those sections relevant to the company's operations. It is assumed that counsel will take time to attend classes and conferences concerning operation of the new housing act and possible tax advantages under it, and to keep up with the literature on the subject.

As a result, he may suggest ways in which the company could operate more profitably under sections of the act, and he will probably be asked to discuss the new act at meetings of the staff and the board of directors. If the board decides to seek funding for a housing project under the act, he will be asked to draft a proposal and to work through the administrative procedures necessary to obtain the funding, perhaps making several trips to Washington in the process. As he becomes more knowledgeable about the operation of the act, he will probably be asked to give speeches to lay and bar groups.

If counsel to such a company did nothing after passage of a new housing act until the president of the company was charged with violation of it (e.g., of the fair housing provisions of the 1968 Civil Rights Act), he would almost certainly be considered derelict in his duty to his client. If he did nothing until it was too late for his company to gain any competitive advantage by obtaining quick federal funding under the new act (e.g., the many programs under the 1968 Housing Act), he would likewise be subject to serious criticism.

The traditional role of the lawyer includes great emphasis on advising and counseling the client and in knowing enough about administrative law and procedure to achieve the client's goal. Frequently this kind of work results in expertise on the part of the lawyer leading to his involvement in company management and sometimes to appointment to government office. Filing and defending law suits plays an insignificant part in his functions.

One basic flaw in recent housing legislation is the unspoken assumption that there are now in existence nonprofit corporations and organizations of poor people prepared to go into the housing business. Another flaw is the assumption that these organizations, like profit-making corporations, have experienced lawyers prepared to give them the necessary advice on how to proceed administratively.

What is the fact?

C.   Representing Litigants

There has been a great increase in litigation on housing in the past few years, due in large measure to the existence of OEO neighborhood legal service offices and fair housing organizations where tenants can come for legal assistance, and to the efforts of the imaginative and determined lawyers working for these agencies. Some tenants have been saved from evictions by private[46] and public[47] landlords because the grounds[48] or procedures[49] were improper. Some tenants have withheld rent in order to repair their apartment buildings.[50] Rent strikes[51] and tenants' unions[52] have brought some fairness to some apartment house dwellers. City and state fair practices commissions have obtained housing for some minority group members through conciliation,[53] public hearings,[54] and litigation.[55] These activities, even when successful, are all defensive in nature. They seek to prevent injustice to tenants of existing housing. They seek fairness in the distribution of existing housing. None of them build or rehabilitate the units needed to solve the housing crisis.

Some affirmative litigation has also been filed. Plaintiffs have sued or filed counter-claims seeking court orders to force landlords to make repairs.[56] A few class suits have been filed: against housing developers to prevent construction of new units that would involve Negro clearance rather than slum clearance;[57] to compel city officials to inspect housing conditions and enforce housing codes as required by state law;[58] to compel public housing authorities to establish fair procedures for selecting tenants and to publicize eligibility requirements.[59] But again, the results do not create new livable fair housing units.

[46] *E.g.*, Edwards v. Habib, 366 F.2d 628 (D.C. Cir. 1965).

[47] *E.g.*, Thorpe v. Housing Authority, *rem.* 386 U.S. 670, 87 S. Ct. 1244 (1967); *rev'd*, —— U.S. ——, 89 S. Ct. 518 (1969); Hiller, *Public Landlords and Private Tenants: The Eviction of "Undesirables" from Public Housing Projects*, 77 YALE L.J. 988 (1968).

[48] *E.g.*, Edwards v. Habib, 366 F.2d 628 (D.C. Cir. 1965).

[49] *E.g.*, Thorpe v. Housing Authority, 386 U.S. 670, 87 S. Ct. 1244 (1967).

[50] *E.g.*, Murrey v. Tinkler, 13 CIV. LIB. DOCK. 120, No. 423. Calif. 10 (1967-68).

[51] *E.g.*, Re 114 Stanton Street, 13 CIV. LIB. DOCK. 123, No. 423. N.Y. 9 (1967-68); Glotta, *The Radical Lawyer and the Dynamics of a Rent Strike*, 26 GUILD PRACTITIONER 132 (1967).

[52] *E.g.*, Cotton, *Tenant Unions: Collective Bargaining and the Low-Income Tenant*, 77 YALE L.J. 1368 (1968).

[53] *E.g.*, Pennsylvania Human Relations Commission v. McIlhinney (Del. Ct. of Common Pleas 1968), Commission news release Mar. 15, 1968 (conciliation after injunction issued preventing sale of house for 30 day period). On file, Meiklejohn Civil Liberties Library.

[54] *E.g.*, Hartfield v. Swinsick, 13 CIV. LIB. DOCK. 165, No. 533. N.Y. 18 (1967-68), 12 RACE REL. L. REP. 524 (1967).

[55] *E.g.*, Henderson v. Wurman, 53 Misc. 2d 979, 281 N.Y.S.2d 198 (1967).

[56] *E.g.*, Gregoriades v. 55 Walker Corp., 13 CIV. LIB. DOCK. 123, No. 423. N.Y. 7 (1967-68).

[57] *See, e.g.*, Norwalk CORE v. Norwalk Redevelopment Agency, 395 F.2d 920 (2d Cir. 1968); Speth, *Judicial Review of Displacee Relocation in Urban Renewal*, 77 YALE L.J. 966 (1968).

[58] *E.g.*, Greenwood v. Detroit, 13 CIV. LIB. DOCK. 122, No. 423. Mich. 3 (1967-68).

[59] *E.g.*, Holmes v. Housing Authority, 13 CIV. LIB. DOCK. 123, No. 423. N.Y. 6 (1967-68); Manigo v. Housing Authority, 13 CIV. LIB. DOCK. 122, No. 423. N.Y. 2 (1967-68).

These cases represent six types of litigation: defending against individual civil suits for eviction, defending individual ghetto residents against criminal charges arising (in part) out of frustration at bad housing, filing individual civil suits to force landlords to make repairs, filing class suits to enjoin construction of the wrong kind of government housing, filing class suits to stop improper practices by government housing and inspection agencies, and filing complaints with fair practices commissions to prevent racial discrimination. None of these approaches meet the creative potential required at this time, although all are necessary and should be pursued with vigor. Few can be undertaken by a lawyer in private practice because they are not fee producing. None prepare a lawyer to help a client construct a housing project.

D.   Creating Paying Clients and Expert Lawyers

What implementation of the 1968 Housing Act requires is the creation of clients who need housing and who are capable of retaining legal counsel and other experts to help them get the government funding to build the kind of housing they need. Clients need to be created because the Act does not provide for the funding of people in need of housing but only of corporations prepared to construct housing.[60]

Some lawyers already have their hands full of housing law problems for tenants. They seem to have followed a single path, although they practice in various areas. Some time ago they started talking about housing problems to everyone—spouses, children, clients, organizations, churches, unions, cooperatives. They studied the housing acts and the fair housing provisions of the 1968 Civil Rights Act, only to discover that housing statutes are a maze still uncharted. They learned that there is no service for lawyers which provides statutes, regulations, administrative and case law (with scholarly commentary) on the federal, state and local aspects of the public and private sectors of the industries concerned with construction, rehabilitation, and financing. They began to study informal agency manuals and handbooks, rather than statutes and regulations. They joined bar committees on housing, attended conferences, read material in part 3 of my bibliography, *infra*, and subscribed to a few housing publications. They read *Jones v. Alfred H. Mayer Co.*[61] and articles[62] discussing its broadest implications. They have thought

---

[60] The role of the lawyer in educating clients, prospective clients, and the public generally, in becoming retained in matters with constitutional law implications, and in developing community organizations must be reconsidered in light of the times, as indicated by Judge Bazelon, 68 COLUM. L. REV. 1012, and Judge Wright, 68 COLUM. L. REV. 1046, and the decisions of the Supreme Court in NAACP v. Button, 371 U.S. 415, 83 S. Ct. 328 (1963), and United Mine Workers v. Illinois State Bar Association, 389 U.S. 217, 88 S. Ct. 353 (1967). OEO legal service offices are already incorporating nonprofit corporations which may decide to seek funding for housing in the ghetto. *See* ABA, 16 COORDINATOR AND PUBLIC RELATIONS BULLETIN (Sept. 1968).

[61] 392 U.S. 409, 88 S. Ct. 2186 (1968).

[62] *E.g.*, Kinoy, *The Constitutional Right of Negro Freedom Revisited: Some First*

about the advantages of new and rehabilitated housing in their own communities. They realize the many positive effects of a housing construction program in an urban center with a large population of so-called minority-group members who actually comprise a majority in the area, and who could work on the houses they would later inhabit and administer.

These lawyers have roots in the community, or are building such roots. They have met leaders in the community who know the housing needs and who can see the possibilities for new projects when they become familiar with the new housing laws and the *Jones* decision.[63] These citizens have organized nonprofit corporations through their existing organizations and they have become the clients seeking construction and rehabilitation of housing.

One experienced housing lawyer recently described his functions.[64] He indicated that the challenge posed to attorneys by our urban ills can neither be properly understood nor adequately resolved by dealing solely with the question of shelter. We must deal with unemployment, underemployment, family and interpersonal relations, community problems, and conflicting value orientations. We must begin to make an impact on the entire environment of a community through a complete rehabilitation of the physical and social scene if we are to achieve any degree of success.

There are several functions for lawyers in representing clients in search of new or renovated housing, he says. One requires expertise on housing law which can be used directly or can be passed on to a second lawyer who has expertise on a particular community, its needs and desires. Another function is as coordinator of the professional team required to carry out a specific housing development. A community-based lawyer, even without expertise on housing law, can fulfill the indispensable function of meshing the requirements of various government agencies with the objectives of his client, the community sponsor of the project.

At the outset, the attorney must know the answer to the question, is this project feasible? In other words, will the cost of construction be so great that the resulting rents will be too high for the tenants sought to be assisted? Will the apartment distribution be suitable for the prospective tenants or the size of homes fit the prospective home buyers? In the early

---

Thoughts on Jones v. Alfred H. Mayer Company, 22 RUTGERS L. REV. 537 (1968).

[63] For a suggestion that the United States Supreme Court promulgate a new rule permitting designation of some cases as "major cases" for which counsel may submit film statements of their arguments, along with traditional briefs, to go into a court-made film on the decisions, and that the Court publish and distribute hundreds of copies of decisions in such "major cases" to all interested public and private organizations, mass media and individuals, see Ginger, *'Dja See What the Supreme Court said the Other Day?,* 1968 YEARBOOK OF THE COMMITTEE ON FREEDOM OF SPEECH OF THE SPEECH ASSOCIATION OF AMERICA (1968).

[64] Letter from Barney Rosenstein of New York, co-chairman, National Lawyers Guild Committee on Housing Law Seminars, August 23, 1968 (on file, Meiklejohn Civil Liberties Library).

stages, the lawyer can help in consideration of proper land re-use and draft the instruments to insure implementation of the re-use plan. With an awareness of the various legal and social tools at his disposal, the attorney must also realize that the administrative determinations made by the various agencies which dictate the framework of a housing project may not be subject to administrative procedure acts and are not subject to adequate judicial review. For this reason they require initial close scrutiny by the organizational client and his counsel.

E. Types of Projects Possible under the Housing Acts

Having touched on the economics of housing and the old and new legal concepts of home ownership and occupancy, having talked about the inadequacy of legal representation of poor people in need of housing and the proper function of the lawyer in r epresenting such clients, what can the lawyer actually do for a client if he is r etained and prepared to go to work?

The 1968 Housing and Urban Development Act provides for a wide variety of programs to assist in housing Americans, some new and many refurbished from previous acts. Congress declared a ringing national goal:[65] "a decent home and a suitable living environment for every American family." Congress found that this goal has not been met and that this is a matter of grave national concern. It also found that the nation is capable of fulfilling this goal. In doing so, "the highest priority" must be given to meeting "the housing needs of those families for which the national goal has not become a reality,"[66] although the Act also includes provisions for government assistance in building "seasonal" housing,[67] that is, vacation homes for the well-to-do.

It is inspiring to read in a piece of legislation that government housing should be of the highest architectural design[68] and should use the latest technological developments.[69]

Under the Act, agencies are authorized to make grants and loans to assist at the counseling, planning, and organizational stages of housing projects.[70] Nonprofit organizations are eligible for such loans,[71] and for other assistance from the Department of Housing and Urban Development.[72]

---

[65] 1968 Housing and Urban Development Act, § 2.

[66] Id.

[67] Id. at § 318.

[68] Id. at § 4.

[69] Id.

[70] Id. at § 107(d).

[71] Id. at § 106(b)(1). If neighborhood organizations develop nonprofit corporations to construct and rejuvenate housing in existing neighborhoods, this should end the practice of removing poor families individually from slums and rehousing them individually, destroying low income neighborhoods and dispersing the collective, affirmative human qualities that provide strength to residents of defined communities at whatever income level. See M. YOUNG & P. WILLMOTT, FAMILY AND THE KINSHIP IN EAST LONDON 121-130 (1957).

[72] Id. at § 106(a).

State and local public bodies and agencies are eligible for grants[73] to carry out three types of programs: clearance, rehabilitation, and code enforcement.[74] Private profit-making corporations may be created to provide housing for the poor.[75]

The Act approves programs: to promote homeownership for poor families[76] through payments to be used on mortgages,[77] and to cause the private insurance industry to assist families to keep up mortgage payments despite temporary lack of income;[78] to build additional low rent public housing,[79] and to assist public housing agencies in financing tenant services;[80] to provide loans for occupant-owned, rental, and cooperative housing[81] with self-help funds for loans and grants to public and private nonprofit corporations;[82] to reduce interest rates on loans to landlords so they can lower rents;[83] to provide money to supplement the amount of money tenants can pay as rent;[84] to guarantee bonds issued by new community developers to help finance projects;[85] to provide mortgage insurance to nonprofit organizations for resale to poor families,[86] even where formal requirements for insurance are not met in "declining urban areas."[87]

The Act recognizes and provides for special needs and problems of servicemen,[88] Indians,[89] seasonal workers,[90] families with many children,[91] and with poor credit ratings.[92]

The Act emphasizes the need to use small builders[93] and local firms[94]

---

[73] *Id.* at § 412.
[74] *Id.* at § 514.
[75] *Id.* at § 901 et seq.
[76] *Id.* at § 107.
[77] *Id.* at § 101.
[78] *Id.* at § 109.
[79] *Id.* at § 203.
[80] *Id.* at § 204. Social workers and lawyers may need to confer about the constitutionality and wisdom of seeking to provide some services to government housing tenants, such as the assistance of resident social workers, which the tenants may consider rather as efforts to violate their right of privacy in a manner possible only because of their low income.
[81] *Id.* at § 1001.
[82] *Id.* at § 1005.
[83] *Id.* at § 201.
[84] *Id.* at § 202.
[85] *Id.* at § 403.
[86] *Id.* at § 101(a).
[87] *Id.* at § 103(a).
[88] *Id.* at § 301.
[89] *Id.* at § 206. Agencies seeking to assist Indians in need of housing may be stung by the experience on Turtle Mountain Reservation, North Dakota, where Indians refused to move into new government housing because of its urban, "un-Indian" design. See photographs in S. Steiner, The New Indians 206(d) (1968).
[90] *Id.* at § 102(a).
[91] *Id.* at § 209.
[92] *Id.* at § 102(a).
[93] *Id.* at § 409.
[94] *Id.* at § 3(2).

in construction programs under the Act, and to create opportunities for training and employing ghetto residents.[95] In other words, the Act permits a sort of return to the situation in which people helped build and manage their own housing, this time with government assistance. However, even this Act does not provide for what some tenants consider the simplest and least expensive approach to one of their major problems. They argue that they would paint, repair, and remodel their apartments and homes if they could go to a government agency where they could borrow tools, instruction books, ask expert advice, and get free or low-cost materials. Many are unemployed or have free time they would like to use to fix up their homes, if assured that the rents would not be raised and that they could get long-term leases when they had finished. If this resulted, in time, in catching up with needed repairs and thus avoiding more expensive and difficult repairs at a later time, the program would be worth whatever it cost. Another approach to this problem, through home maintenance insurance, is also not covered in this Act.

The preamble of the 1968 Act discusses not only the human function of providing housing for the ill-housed and homeless—it also provides[96] that "in the carrying out of such programs there should be the fullest practicable utilization of the resources and capabilities of private enterprise and of individual self-help techniques." A major feature of the Act is government assistance to private corporations which get into the business of housing the indigent, as indicated by the list of programs above. While assisting tenants by providing them with better housing than they could afford from their own resources, the Act also assists private industries to sell, rent, and invest in units that are priced beyond the means of many who need housing. It therefore is deeply concerned with the second, nonhousing function of housing discussed in part one: the effect of activity in the housing and mortgage industry on the national economy.

It would be interesting to analyze what percent of the programs under the Act would primarily benefit the homeless and what percent would primarily benefit private housing, loan, and insurance industries, to see how much the Act increases the mixed private-government economic base in housing, and the percent of profit it contemplates for the private developers. However, the real question is not what programs the Act authorizes but what programs Congress appropriates money for[97] and what programs lawyers and clients actually get funded.

---

[95] *Id.* at § 3(1). *And see* THE HARLEM UNEMPLOYMENT CENTER STORY: BLACKS AND THE CONSTRUCTION INDUSTRY (1968) (2035 Fifth Avenue, New York City 10035).

[96] *Id.* at § 2.

[97] For up-to-date information on the status of future legislation concerning fair housing and appropriations to enforce the provisions of the 1968 Civil Rights Act and similar legislation, see MEMOS, LEADERSHIP CONFERENCE ON CIVIL RIGHTS (2027 Massachusetts Avenue, N.W., Washington, D.C. 20036). And see colorful description by Hannibal Williams of National Citizens' Lobby [for housing appropriation] on March 25, 1969, for Bay Area Chapter. (On file, Meiklejohn Civil Liberties Library.)

It is the burden of this article that there is no way to insure that the goal required of our society and described by Congress will be implemented unless conscientious and imaginative attorneys for determined tenants quickly organize themselves to apply for funds and use their legal knowledge and political pressure to obtain them on a priority basis. Further, the goals of the fair housing legislation will not be implemented unless Congress appropriates sufficient funds for the Assistant Secretary of the Housing and Urban Development Department to enforce the law and educate the public on fair housing, and unless the same determined lawyers and clients demand equal housing and job opportunities at every phase in every housing project funded by any government agency.

F.   Who Pays the Fee, and When

The question of fees is critically important. Without a fee, all that has been said can be criticized as daydreaming during working hours, as morality that won't pay the office overhead. The housing acts, inadequate and cumbersome as they are, do provide assurance that the lawyer who puts together a housing package for an institutional client will be paid, not by the low-income client, but by the federal government, as part of the cost of the project. The fee will be paid nine months to two years from the date the work begins, and will be large enough to make the work worthwhile. However, there is no way to hurry it, and if the project fails entirely, it may not be possible to recoup it. In this respect, perhaps it needs to be called a contingent fee. But determined lawyers around the country have found that they could struggle through from the original idea to the date of closing the deal, and even to the gala opening of the new housing units, despite all kinds of niggling problems never imagined at first.

Anyone who has accomplished this in one unit can be considered an expert. He has learned the statute and the agency procedures. He has selected the federal program closest to the needs of his client and then has obtained approval of minor variances needed at almost every turn.

IV.   CONCLUSION

To possess a legal education and a social conscience can become a curse when one must earn a living and remain aware of the multitude of basic social problems on which one could work constructively but for lack of time. I wish I could set this article aside for six months and then rethink and rework it to make it more meaningful and concise. However, the major problem in housing law is the unwillingness of a sufficient number of citizens and policy-makers to stop expensive programs that do not solve social ills and to use the money now going into such programs in the construction and maintenance of housing and for other affirmative social ends. A second problem is the continued insistence that housing must produce income first and fulfill human needs second. Further work on this article will not assist in changing this condition so I submit it to readers in its present form, hoping that they will think through and carry forward any valid ideas they find here.

V. BIBLIOGRAPHY

The following is a highly selective list of materials, although the selection was not made scientifically and the list undoubtedly omits very useful and significant works. It will at least serve as a good starting point, since each publication lists others. The attorney starting out in housing can simply write to local and federal agencies for material; they will oblige very quickly and voluminously.

A better solution would be for the government to establish practical, on-going training programs, bringing law school graduates into government housing agencies for experience before they move into private practice.

1. DESCRIPTIONS OF HOUSING PROBLEMS

B. Bremner, *The Big Flat: History of a New York Tenement House, 1855-1888*, 64 AM. HIST. REV. 54 (1958).

COMM. ON SOCIAL LEGISLATION, NEW YORK CHAPTER, NATIONAL LAWYERS GUILD, THE HOUSING CRISIS—1968, A CRASH PROGRAM (June 1968) (an editorial for a program of "drastic action").

EDITORS OF FORTUNE MAGAZINE, THE EXPLODING METROPOLIS (Doubleday 1958) (an overview of urban problems—cars v. rapid transit, slums, sprawl, City Hall.) On housing for poor people, see pp. 23-52, 111-132.

D. HUNTER, THE SLUMS, CHALLENGE AND RESPONSE (N.Y., Free Press of Glencoe, 1964) (about forty pages on housing; the rest discusses other aspects of slum problems and stresses their interrelation).

J. JACOBS, THE DEATH AND LIFE OF GREAT AMERICAN CITIES (Random House, 1961) (a celebration of cities as they could be by an anti-park, pro-sidewalk iconoclast).

J. LOWE, CITIES IN A RACE WITH TIME (Random House, 1967) (a witty journalistic history with close looks at particular people (Robert Moses) and places (New York, Pittsburgh, Philadelphia)).

MEYERSON, TERRETT, & WHEATON, HOUSING, PEOPLE AND CITIES (McGraw Hill, 1962) (a primer on shelter, under rubrics of The Consumer, The Producer, The Investor, The Federal Government, The Community).

NAT'L ASS'N MUTUAL SAVINGS BANKS, ANNUAL REPORT: FINANCIAL DEVELOPMENTS LEADING TO MORTGAGE STRINGENCY AND HOUSING DECLINES IN 1966 (1967).

NATIONAL COMM'N ON URBAN PROBLEMS, HEARINGS (GPO 16680-286-819, May-June 1967).

G. STERNLIEB, THE TENEMENT LANDLORD (Urban Studies Center, Rutgers, 1966) (analysis and recommendations based on a survey of owners of 576 parcels of slum land in Newark).

Symposium: Housing. Part I: Perspectives and Problems, 32 LAW & CONTEMP. PROB. 187-371 (1967).

C. B. WURSTER, *The Urban Octopus*, in D. BROWER, ed., WILDERNESS AMERICA'S LIVING HERITAGE 117-122. (Sierra Club 1961).

Generally, see also J. AM. INSTITUTE OF PLANNERS ($8/year; American Institute of Planners, 917 15th Street, N.W., Washington, D.C. 20005) in university City Planning Department libraries.

See also URBAN AMERICA (Publications of General Interest) (1717 Massachusetts Ave., N.W., Washington, D.C. 20036).

2. *BACKGROUND IN FEDERAL RESPONSE TO HOUSING PROBLEMS*

NAT'L HOUSING CONFERENCE, LEGISLATIVE PROPOSALS OF APRIL 9, 1967, in 113 CONG. REC. H4799 (daily ed. Apr. 27, 1967).

PRESIDENT'S ADVISORY COMM'N ON GOVERNMENT HOUSING POLICIES AND PROGRAMS, REPORT (GPO, 1953).

SUBCOMM. ON HOUSING & URBAN AFFAIRS, SEN. COMM. ON BANKING AND CURRENCY, CONGRESS & AMERICAN HOUSING 1892-1967 (Comm. Print 1968, GPO 89-102).

———, PROGRESS REPORT ON FEDERAL HOUSING PROGRAMS (Comm. Print 1967, GPO 77-610)

S. WARNER, PLANNING FOR A NATION OF CITIES (MIT Press, 1966) (essays on urban policy by Myrdal and others.)

Hearings on the Federal Role in Urban Affairs, Before the Subcommittee on Executive Reorganization of the Senate Committee on Government Operations, 89 Cong., 2d Sess. Pt. 1 (1966).

Hearings on the Fair Housing Act of 1967, Before the Subcommittee on Housing and Urban Affairs of the Senate Committee on Banking and Currency, 90th Cong., 1st Sess. (1967) (GPO 83-986).

Hearings on Housing Legislation of 1967, Before the Subcommittee on Housing and Urban Affairs of the Senate Committee on Banking and Currency, 90th Cong., 1st Sess. (1967) (GPO 81-73).

Hearings on Housing Legislation of 1968 Before the Subcommittee on Housing and Urban Affairs of the Senate Committee on Banking and Currency, 90th Cong., 2d Sess. (1968) (GPO 91-619).

Hearings on H.R. 9751 (Housing and Community Development Act of 1964) Before the Subcommittee on Housing of the House Committee on Banking and Currency, 88th Cong., 2d Sess. (1964) (GPO 30-150).

F. Cleaveland, *Congress and Urban Problems: Legislating for Urban Areas*, 28 J. POLITICS 289 (1966).

R. Bartke, *FHA: Its History and Operations*, 13 Wayne L. Rev. 651
(1967).

Low-cost Housing and Slum Clearance, 1 Law & Contemp. Prob.
135-256 (1934).

Housing, 12 Law & Contemp. Prob. I, 205 (1947). *Land Planning in a
Democracy*, 20 Law & Contemp. Prob. 197, 350 (1955). *Urban
Housing and Planning*, 20 Law & Contemp. Prob. 351, 529 (1955).

3. FEDERAL HOUSING PROGRAMS DESCRIBED

W. Roth, Listing of Operating Federal Assistance Programs as
Compiled During the Roth Study (1968) in 114 Cong. Rec.
H5441 (daily ed. June 25, 1968) (highly detailed; includes appropriations, average assistance, application deadlines, approval/dis-
approval time, lead time, probably the most comprehensive list
extant, although unofficial) This is more complete than Catalog of
Federal Assistance Programs, *infra*.

Office of Economic Opportunity, Catalog of Federal Assistance
Programs (GPO 1967, 0-256-044, 1967) (slick and easy to use, but
old).

Office of Information, U.S. Dep't of Agriculture, Federal Programs For Individual And Community Advancement (Agriculture Handbook #312, 1966) (53 pp; marginally useful).

U.S. Dep't of Housing and Urban Development, Assistance for
Urban Planning (HUD IP-2, 1966) (a summary of federal grants
available for comprehensive planning in metropolitan and other
urban areas).

———, Programs of HUD (HUD IP-36, 1967) (fifty pages of brief
descriptions of program scope and requirements, no reference to
statutory authorization or funds available).

———, Publications of The U.S. Department of Health, Education
and Welfare (HUD MP-36, 1967) (essential; get a copy; lists
laws and regulations, statistics, studies, bibliographies; includes
such publications as "How to Develop Rent Supplement Proposals," "Sixty Books on Housing and Urban Planning," mostly
free).

House Committee on Banking & Currency, Basic Laws & Authorities
on Housing & Urban Development Through July 15, 1968 (GPO
89-983, 1969).

Housing, Part II: The Federal Role, 32 Law & Contemp. Prob. 371,
560 (1967).

Note, *Government Housing Assistance to the Poor*, 76 Yale L.J. 508
(1967).

Urban Coalition, Guide to Federal Law—8 Moderate-Income Housing & Community Development Programs (1819 H Street N.W.,
Washington, D.C. 20006).

4. URBAN RENEWAL

C. ABRAMS, THE CITY IS THE FRONTIER (Harper & Row, 1965) (excellent, clear hard criticism of the business economics of redevelopment).

ANDERSON, THE FEDERAL BULLDOZER (MIT Press, 1964) (argument for repeal of urban renewal on financial, social and constitutional grounds).

BELLUSH, HAUSKNECHT (Eds.), URBAN RENEWAL: PEOPLE, POLITICS AND PLANNING (Doubleday Anchor, 1967) (a $1.95 paperback anthology; excellent background).

DOXIADIS, URBAN RENEWAL AND THE FUTURE OF THE AMERICAN CITY (Public Information Service, 1966).

S. GREER, URBAN RENEWAL AND AMERICAN CITIES: THE DILEMMA OF DEMOCRATIC INTERVENTION (Bobbs-Merrill, 1966).

J. WILSON (Ed.), URBAN RENEWAL: THE RECORD AND THE CONTROVERSY (MIT Press, 1966).

Gans, *The Failure of Urban Renewal—A Critique and Some Proposals*, COMMENTARY, April 1965, p. 29.

Gruen, *Urban Renewal's Role in the Genesis of Tomorrow's Slums*, 39 LAND ECONOMICS 285 (1963).

Symposium: Urban Renewal, 25 LAW & CONTEMP. PROB. 631, 812 (1960). 26 *Id.* 1, 171 (1961).

Note, *Urban Renewal: Problems of eliminating and preventing Urban Deterioration*, 72 HARV. L. REV. 504 (1959).

Note, *Urban Renewal: Essentials of the Federal Program*, 48 KY. L.J. 262 (1960).

5. REHABILITATION

FRIEDEN, THE FUTURE OF OLD NEIGHBORHOODS: REBUILDING FOR A CHANGING POPULATION (MIT Press, 1964) (studies of N.Y.C., L.A., & Hartford, Conn.).

MILLSPAUGH & BRECKENFELD, THE HUMAN SIDE OF URBAN RENEWAL (Ives Washburn, 1960) (examples of self-help, private and local rehabilitation projects in Baltimore, Miami, Chicago, and New Orleans).

W. NASH, RESIDENTIAL REHABILITATION: PRIVATE PROFITS AND PUBLIC PURPOSES (McGraw Hill, 1959).

U.S. DEP'T OF HOUSING & URBAN DEVELOPMENT, MINIMUM PROPERTY STANDARDS FOR URBAN RENEWAL REHABILITATION (HUD PG-31, Dec. 1963 as amended).

———, RESIDENTIAL REHABILITATION IN THE HARLEM PARK AREA, BALTIMORE, MARYLAND (1962).

NATIONAL COMMISSION ON URBAN PROBLEMS (Paul Douglas, ch.), RE-
SEARCH REPORT #14, LEGAL REMEDIES FOR HOUSING CODE VIOLA-
TIONS (GPO 1968).

Note, *Preference Liens for Costs of Repairing Slum Property*, 1967
WASH. U.L.Q. 141 (1967).

6. *PUBLIC HOUSING*

U.S. DEP'T OF HOUSING & URBAN DEVELOPMENT, A HANDBOOK FOR FHA
MULTIFAMILY PROJECTS (1965).

———, LOW-RENT HOUSING MANUAL (1967).

———, LOW-RENT PROJECT DIRECTORY (1965).

———, PHILADELPHIA 5000-UNIT "TURNKEY" REHABILITATION AND NEW
HOUSE PROGRAM (1968).

———, PUBLIC HOUSING FACT SHEET (1964).

———, REPORT ON FAMILY LIVING IN HIGH APARTMENT BUILDINGS (1965).

Bauer, *The Dreary Deadlock of Public Housing*, May 1957 ARCHITEC-
TURAL FORUM, p. 140.

Friedmann, *Public Housing and the Poor: an Overview*, 54 CALIF. L.
REV. 642 (1966); also in THE LAW OF THE POOR 318 (TENBROEK ed.
1966).

7. *THE POOR TENANT*

13 CIV. LIB. DOCK. 118-124 (1967-68) (classification #423 describes
recent and pending cases on housing problems of the poor).

NATIONAL COMMISSION ON URBAN PROBLEMS (Paul Douglas, Chairman),
Research Report #4, THE LARGE POOR FAMILY HOUSING GAP.

——— #7, HOUSING AMERICA'S LOW AND MODERATE INCOME FAMILY.

——— #8, MORE THAN SHELTER, SOCIAL NEEDS IN LOW AND MODERATE
INCOME HOUSING.

——— #9, HOUSING CONDITION IN THE URBAN POVERTY AREAS.

U.S. DEP'T OF HOUSING & URBAN DEVELOPMENT, LOW-COST HOMES
THROUGH GROUP ACTION (1967).

———, RENT SUPPLEMENT PROGRAM PROJECT MANAGEMENT OUTLINE
(1967).

———, RENT SUPPLEMENT PROGRAM, PUBLIC INFORMATION GUIDE AND
INSTRUCTION HANDBOOK (1966).

Sax & Hiestand, *Slumlordism as a Tort*, 65 MICH. L. REV. 869 (1967).

Blum & Dunham, *Slumlordism as a Tort—a Dissenting View*, 66 MICH. L.
REV. 451 (1968).

Korb, *Primer for FHA Multi-Family Rental Housing*, 48 MASS. L.Q.
461 (1963).

Krier, *Rent Supplement Program of 1965: Out of the Ghetto, Into
the . . .*, 19 STAN. L. REV. 555 (1967).

Schier, *Protecting the Interests of the Indigent Tenant,* 54 CALIF. L. REV. 670 (1966).

Schoshinski, *Remedies of the Indigent Tenant: Proposals for Change,* 54 GEO. L.J. 519 (1966).

Note, *Oakland Leased Housing Program,* 20 STAN. L. REV. 538 (1968).

Note, *Rent Withholding—A Proposal for Legislation in Ohio,* 18 W. RES. L. REV. 1705 (1967).

Note, *Rent Withholding in New York,* 13 VILL. L. REV. 205 (1967).

URBAN AMERICA, NON-PROFIT HOUSING SERIES (1717 Massachusetts Ave., N.W., Washington, D.C. 20036).

8. HOME OWNERSHIP FOR THE POOR

U.S. DEP'T OF HOUSING & URBAN DEVELOPMENT, BUYING FROM DEVELOPERS (1966).

Note, *Cooperative Apartments in Government-assisted Low-middle Income Housing,* 111 U. PA. L. REV. 638 (1963).

DEP'T OF ECONOMIC & SOCIAL AFFAIRS, UNITED NATIONS, MANUAL ON SELF-HELP HOUSING, UN Doc ST/SOA/53 (1964).

INTERAMERICAN HOUSING & PLANNING CENTER, PAN-AMERICAN UNION, SELF-HELP HOUSING GUIDE (Bogotá, 1962).

9. HOUSING AND RACE

Jones v. Alfred H. Mayer Co., 392 U.S. 409 (1968).

Exec. Order No. 11063, 18 Fed. Reg. 4939 (1962).

13 CIV. LIB. DOCK. 162-167 (1967-68) (classifications ##530-535 describe recent and pending cases on racial discrimination in housing).

Title VIII Fair Housing, §§ 801-819 of 1968 Civil Rights Act, P.L. 90-284, 82 Stat. 81, 42 U.S.C. 3601-3619, § 3631 (penalty).

Cf. Conyers, H.R. 14492 Full Opportunity Act, Title V Adequate Housing, Title VI Fair Housing, 144 Cong. Rec. E 1446 (March 4, 1968).

NAT'L COMMITTEE AGAINST DISCRIMINATION IN HOUSING, TRENDS IN HOUSING (mthly), (323 Lexington Avenue, N.Y.C., N.Y. 10016). $2/yr.

GRIER, OPERATION OPEN CITY: EVALUATION OF AN EXPERIMENTAL PROGRAM IN NEW YORK CITY (1965) (suggested guidelines for other communities).

GRIER & GRIER, EQUALITY & BEYOND: HOUSING SEGREGATION AND THE GOALS OF THE GREAT SOCIETY (Quadrangle Books, 1966) (an updated version of their DISCRIMINATION IN HOUSING—A HANDBOOK OF FACTS).

GRIER & GRIER, PRIVATELY DEVELOPED INTERRACIAL HOUSING, AN ANALYSIS OF EXPERIENCE (U.C. Press, 1960) (a study of the motives—

liberalism, religion, profit—problems, limited success, and future of this rare phenomenon).

NATIONAL ADVISORY COMM'N ON CIVIL DISORDERS, REPORT (1968, GPO 0-291-729) (see especially pp. 133, 147, 215, 252).

U.S. COMM'N ON CIVIL RIGHTS, COMPLIANCE OFFICER'S MANUAL—A HANDBOOK OF COMPLIANCE PROCEDURES UNDER TITLE VI OF THE CIVIL RIGHTS ACT OF 1964 (1966).

——, A TIME TO LISTEN . . . A TIME TO ACT (1967).

——, *Hearings Held in Cleveland, Ohio, April 1-7, 1966*, pp. 18-277.

BUREAU OF LABOR STATISTICS/BUREAU OF THE CENSUS, DEP'T OF LABOR/ DEP'T OF COMMERCE, SOCIAL & ECONOMIC CONDITIONS OF NEGROES IN THE UNITED STATES, 51, 58 (1967).

BUREAU OF LABOR STATISTICS, U.S. DEP'T OF LABOR, THE NEGROES IN THE U.S.—THEIR ECONOMIC AND SOCIAL SITUATION (1966).

Bailey, *Effects of Race and Other Demographic Factors on the Values of Single Family Homes*, 42 LAND ECON. 215 (1966).

Grodzins, *Metropolitan Segregation*, SCIENTIFIC AMERICAN, Oct. 1957, p. 33.

Pearl & Terner, *Fair Housing Laws—Halfway Mark*, 54 GEO. L. REV. 156 (1965).

Sloane & Friedman, *The Ex '·tive Order on Housing: The Constitutional Basis For What It Fails To Do*, 9 HOW. L.J. 1 (1963).

10. COMMUNITY PLANNING

COMMUNITY ACTION PROGRAM, OFFICE OF ECONOMIC OPPORTUNITY, COMMUNITY ACTION AND URBAN HOUSING (1967).

U.S. DEP'T OF HOUSING & URBAN DEVELOPMENT, THE WORKABLE PROGRAM FOR COMMUNITY DEVELOPMENT—FACT SHEET (1966).

——, THE WORKABLE PROGRAM FOR COMMUNITY IMPROVEMENT—A GUIDE FOR CITIZEN'S ADVISORY COMM'S (1966).

——, WORKABLE PROGRAM FOR COMMUNITY IMPROVEMENT—PROGRAM GUIDE SERIES:

    1. CODES & ORDINANCES (1965).
    2. COMPREHENSIVE COMMUNITY PLAN (1966).
    3. NEIGHBORHOOD ANALYSES (1966).
    4. ADMINISTRATIVE ORGANIZATION (1965).
    5. FINANCING (1966).
    6. HOUSING FOR DISPLACED FAMILIES (1966).
    7. CITIZEN PARTICIPATION (1966).

11. PROGRAMS FOR THE PARTICULARLY QUALIFIED

BURSTEIN (Interview), *Doors To Profit Opened Thru Turnkey Program*, NATIONAL NEWS, NATIONAL LUMBER & BUILDING MATERIAL

DEALER'S ASSOC., Apr., 1967 (available in reprint from Bureau of Indian Affairs, Washington, D.C.).

FARMER'S HOME ASSOCIATION, U.S. DEP'T OF AGRICULTURE, FARM OWNERSHIP LOANS (1966).

——, FARM LABOR HOUSING LOANS AND GRANTS (1966).

——, RENTAL & CO-OP HOUSING IN RURAL AREAS (1967).

——, RURAL HOUSING LOANS (1967).

——, SELF-HELP HOUSING FOR LOW-INCOME RURAL FAMILIES (1967).

U.S. DEP'T OF HOUSING AND URBAN DEVELOPMENT, MINIMUM PROPERTY STANDARDS FOR HOUSING FOR THE ELDERLY (1967).

——, SENIOR CITIZEN'S HOUSING, INFORMATION FOR APPLICANT'S ATTORNEY (1966).

——, SENIOR CITIZEN'S HOUSING LOAN PROGRAM (1967).

BUREAU OF INDIAN AFFAIRS, DEP'T OF THE INTERIOR, PUBLIC HOUSING PROGRAM FOR INDIANS (mimeo, 1968).

VETERANS ADMINISTRATION, TO THE HOMEBUYING VETERAN (1964).

——, QUESTIONS & ANSWERS ON GUARANTEED & DIRECT LOANS FOR VETERANS (1967).

12. CONSTRUCTION JOBS AND ON-THE-JOB TRAINING

Manpower Development and Training Act of 1962, 42 U.S.C. § 2584.

Title VII of the Civil Right Act of 1964.

Exec. Order No. 11,246.

13 CIV. LIT. DOCK. 178–182 (1967–68) (Classifications # # 573–575 describe recent and pending cases on racial discrimination in employment.)

Ethridge v. Rhodes, 268 F. Supp. 8 (S.D. Ohio 1967).

FORD FOUNDATION, MANUAL OF ORGANIZATIONAL STEPS AND PROCEDURES FOR THE ESTABLISHMENT OF A MINORITY CONTRACTOR BONDING PROGRAM (1968).

City of Berkeley City Council Resolution No. 42, 268-N.S. (establishing Council policy for affirmative action programs against discrimination on construction contracts) Feb. 20, 1968. (On file, Meiklejohn Civil Liberties Library.)

Aileen C. Hermandez, AN AFFIRMATIVE ACTION PROGRAM: REPORT AND RECOMMENDATIONS TO THE RICHMOND REDEVELOPMENT AGENCY (1968). (On file, Meiklejohn Civil Liberties Library.)

PROSPECTIVE ROLE OF LEGAL INSTITUTIONS IN THE CIVIL RIGHTS STRUGGLE

BY A. A. LENOIR*

IN THE NEXT DECADE the United States must face in the area of slum housing one of the gravest problems brought on by discrimination and rigid segregation. It has continued as an almost insoluble enigma, in spite of legislative, judicial and administrative assault. The following excerpt from the Report of the National Advisory Commission on Civil Disorders indicates the impotency of legal institutions alone in solving or making even the slightest inroad toward a solution to this problem.

> "Thousands of landlords in disadvantaged neighborhoods openly violate building codes with impunity, thereby providing a constant demonstration of flagrant discrimination by legal authorities. A high proportion of residential and other structures contain numerous violations of building and housing codes. Refusal to remedy these violations is a criminal offense, one which can have serious effects upon the victims living in these structures. Yet in most cities, few building code violations in these areas are ever corrected, even when tenants complain directly to municipal building departments.
>
> "There are economic reasons why these codes are not rigorously enforced. Bringing many old structures up to code standards and maintaining them at that level often would require owners to raise rents far above the ability of local residents to pay. In New York City, rigorous code enforcement has already caused owners to board up and abandon over 2,500 buildings rather than incur the expense of repairing them. Nevertheless, open violation of codes is a constant source of distress to low-income tenants and creates serious hazards to health and safety in disadvantaged neighborhoods."[1]

This is not to suggest that efforts of legal institutions should come to an end. Quite to the contrary, there are still many areas where legislation, administrative orders and judicial interpretation can be extended and expanded to render nugatory practices and procedures which now tend to perpetuate slum and substandard living accommodations. Since most of the inner city is now owned or controlled by absentee landlords, it would appear that a fruitful source of attack on the problem could be legislation directed at the landlord-tenant relationship with all of its archaic vestiges from feudal times. The need for action in this area is imperative because the effects of such denials of civil rights develop and ferment in these blighted areas. Statistics indicate that the high percentage of crime, corruption, anti-social attitudes and pov-

*A. A. LENOIR. A.B. 1939, Xavier University (New Orleans); LL.B. 1942, Lincoln University; Dean, Southern University School of Law.

[1] REPORT OF THE NATIONAL ADVISORY COMMISSION ON CIVIL DISORDERS 259 (1968).

196

erty combine in these slum areas to make of them virtual time bombs. Add to the foregoing the high rates of illiteracy and unemployment and you have the ingredients of a volatile situation. These conditions in most instances can be attributed to lack of enforcement of existing local building codes. A contributing cause is the failure on the part of the courts to interpret laws imaginatively in light of present realities. The result is that they frequently become bogged down in the quicksand of case precedents established hundreds of years ago when the concept of feudal tentures was in effect.

The courts have failed to embrace fully the theory that the United States as well as the respective states have a positive duty in the whole field of civil rights. The Bill of Rights and the several amendments to the Constitution are essentially negative. Out of this negativism the courts adopted the "state action" theory. It would appear that a proper interpretation of the Bill of Rights and the 14th amendment could include application not only to state action in denying rights but also to a state's failure to insure and protect the rights of its citizens. This protection of citizens in the exercise of their civil rights should indeed include the right of the citizen to have an opportunity to earn a decent living and to live in a decent house, whether the denial results from action or failure to act and whether by the state or by the private sector. The United States Supreme Court has recently come very close to adopting this view.[2] Certainly this theory is not new even though it would seem to rearrange the rights of citizens in a more positive sense than has in the past generally been regarded as within the prerogative of government.[3]

Archibald Cox says that a new political philosophy has exerted a profound influence upon constitutional decisions.[4] The court was probably wise, in the interests of preserving the continuity of the legal system, to work out the decisions in terms of the familiar 14th amendment power to enact legislation necessary and proper to assure the enjoyment of settled rights against interference by the states. However, it is suspected that the opinions upholding Congressional power in several cases are equally attributable to the various courts' awareness that the 14th amendment, under conditions of modern life, has come to impose upon the states affirmative duties which cannot be satisfied by inaction but whose scope and proper implementation can be defined by legislation better than through adjudication.

The Congress took an imaginative step in the Civil Rights Act of 1968.

---

[2] Jones v. Alfred H. Mayer Co., 392 U.S. 409, 88 S. Ct. 2186 (1968).

[3] Note, *Decent Housing as a Constitutional Right—42 U.S.C. 1983: Poor Peoples' Remedy for Deprivation*, 14 How. L.J. 339, 340 (1968):

"It seems fair to assert that the fourteenth amendment guarantees a living environment fit for human habitation. That shelter is an obvious necessity of life needs no argument. The Supreme Court has pointed out that not only is the right to purchase, sell or lease property a civil right, but, also, that inherent in any such right is the right to enjoy a proprietary interest."

[4] Cox, *Foreword: Constitutional Adjudication and the Promotion of Human Rights*, 80 HARV. L. REV. 91, 114 (1966).

Particular reference here is made to the fair housing provision.[5] By applying the 14th amendment the courts have been equally imaginative, ruling that the right to purchase and live on property is a constitutionally protected right instead of basing its decision regarding restrictive covenants on the inability of a state to be a part of such private discrimination.[6] In fact, as long ago as 1879 the Court did use comprehensive enough language in interpreting the provisions of the 14th amendment.

"The Fourteenth Amendment makes no attempt to enumerate the rights it was designed to protect. It speaks in general terms and those are as comprehensive as possible. Its language is prohibitory, but every prohibition implies the existence of rights and immunities, prominent among which is an immunity from inequality of legal protections either for life, liberty, or property. Any *state action* that denies this immunity to a colored man is in conflct with the Constitution."[7]

The Supreme Court now has in the *Jones* case[8] a more recent precedent for holding that all of the civil rights of citizens can be protected under the 14th amendment provisions. It is recognized that the *Jones* case dealt with injunctive relief against a private concern to prevent implementation of a plan for a new subdivision which would restrict sale and occupancy in the subdivision to whites. Nonetheless, the Court's application of section 1982 of Title 42, United States Code, and sections 1 and 2 of the Civil Rights Act of 1866 in ruling that petitioners were entitled to the injunctive relief sought said:

"In its original form, 42 U.S.C. § 1982 was part of § 1 of the Civil Rights Act of 1866. That Section was cast in sweeping terms:
'*Be it enacted by the Senate and House of Representatives of the United States of America in Congress assembled*, That all persons born in the United States and not subject to any foreign power, . . . are hereby declared to be citizens of the United States; and such citizens, of every race and color, without regard to any previous condition of slavery or involuntary servitude . . . shall have the same right, in every State and Territory in the United States, to make and enforce contracts, to sue, be parties, and give evidence, to inherit, purchase, lease, sell, hold, and convey real and personal property, and to full and equal benefit of all laws and proceedings for the security of person and property, as is enjoyed by white citizens, and shall be subject to like punishment, pains, and penalties, and to none other, any law, statute, ordinance, regulation, or custom, to the contrary notwithstanding.' The crucial language for our purposes was that which guaranteed all citizens 'the same right, in every State and Territory in the United States, . . . to inherit, purchase, lease, sell, hold, and convey real and personal property . . . as is

[5] 42 U.S.C. §§ 3601-3631 (1968).
[6] Shelley v. Kraemer, 334 U.S. 1, 68 S. Ct. 1087 (1948).
[7] Strauder v. West Virginia, 100 U.S. 303, 310 (1879).
[8] Jones v. Alfred H. Mayer Co., 392 U.S. 409, 88 S. Ct. 2186 (1968).

enjoyed by white citizens. . . .' To the Congress that passed the Civil Rights Act of 1866, it was clear that the right to do these things might be infringed not only by 'State or local law' but also by 'custom, or prejudice.' Thus, when Congress provided in § 1 of the Civil Rights Act that the right to purchase and lease property was to be enjoyed equally throughout the United States by Negro and white citizens alike, it plainly meant to secure that right against interference from any source whatever, whether governmental or private.

"Indeed, if § 1 had been intended to grant nothing more than an immunity from *governmental* interference, then much of § 2 would have made no sense at all. For that section, which provided fines and prison terms for certain individuals who deprived others of rights 'secured or protected' by § 1, was carefully drafted to exempt private violations of § 1 from the criminal sanctions it imposed. There would, of course, have been no private violations to exempt if the only 'right' granted by § 1 had been a right to be free of discrimination by public officials. Hence the structure of the 1866 Act, as well as its language, points to the conclusion urged by the petitioners in this case—that § 1 was meant to prohibit *all* racially motivated deprivations of the rights enumerated in the statute, although only those deprivations perpetrated 'under color of law' were to be criminally punishable under § 2.

"In attempting to demonstrate the contrary, the respondents rely heavily upon the fact that the Congress which approved the 1866 statute wished to eradicate the recently enacted Black Codes—laws which had saddled Negroes with 'onerous disabilities and burdens, and curtailed their rights . . . to such an extent that their freedom was of little value. . . .' *Slaughter-House Cases*, 16 Wall 36, 70, 21 L. Ed. 394, 406. The respondents suggest that the only evil Congress sought to eliminate was that of racially discriminatory laws in the former Confederate States. But the Civil Rights Act was drafted to apply throughout the country, and its language was far broader than would have been necessary to strike down discriminatory statutes.

"That broad language, we are asked to believe, was a mere slip of the legislative pen. We disagree. For the same Congress that wanted to do away with the Black Codes *also* had before it an imposing body of evidence pointing to the mistreatment of Negroes by private individuals and unofficial groups, mistreatment unrelated to any hostile state legislation. 'Accounts in newspapers North and South, Freedmen's Bureau and other official documents, private reports and correspondence were all adduced' to show that 'private outrage and atrocity' was 'daily inflicted on freedmen. . . .' The congressional debates are replete with references to private injustices against Negroes—references to white employers who refused to pay their Negro workers, white planters who agreed among themselves not to hire freed slaves without the permission of their former masters, white citizens who assaulted Negroes or who combined to drive them out of their communities."[9]

[9] *Id*. at 419-423, 88 S. Ct. at 2197-2201.

Certainly it cannot now be contended that the right to purchase property without discrimination which was the issue in the *Jones* case is the only civil right embraced in the provisions of the 14th amendment. In light of what has just been stated the 14th amendment must be construed to mean no state shall do or permit done any act that would deprive another citizen of his constitutionally protected right, whether by government, or by private citizen.

The history of every American social institution, at least up to the present era of the civil rights struggle, indicates that a major concern in the ordering and structuring of society—politically, economically and socially—has been the maintenance of the minority (Black) community in its condition of dependence and oppression. This has been directed not only toward the individual Black by the individual white man, but against the Black communities as total acts of the establishment. To repeat the warnings of the findings of the Commission on Civil Disorder, this is a racist society. Racism carries with it an assumption of superiority which has been so deeply engrained in the structure of our society that it infuses the entire functioning of the society and has become so much a part of it that it is taken for granted and is frequently not even recognized.

The slow and gradual pace with which the Administration, the Congress and the Court have come to recognize this in some small measure and to take feeble steps to correct these inequities accounts for much disenchantment and frustration. Even with these small advances and partial understanding of the cause, the application by our national government of legal techniques for solving the plight of the minorities has not yet produced a national commitment.

These de jure gains have met with massive opposition and evasive techniques. The tortuous progress is best illustrated by the 14-year delay in implementing the 1954 *Brown* decision.[10] The Supreme Court in the school desegregation cases has passed from a period in which it enunciated general principles of educational equality, to one in which the Court has shown an increased willingness to involve itself in details of desegregation plans. Thus, in *Goss v. Board of Education*[11] and *Watson v. City of Memphis*[12] the Court has acknowledged the long delays in the desegregation process. Furthermore, in three 1968 cases[13] the Court has struck down the challenged plans of integration as applied and suggested that geographical zoning might serve as the basis for acceptable plans. There is, however, little evidence that court decisions will substantially speed up the process. And

10 Brown v. Bd. of Educ., 347 U.S. 483, 74 S. Ct. 686 (1954).

11 373 U.S. 683, 83 S. Ct. 1405 (1963).

12 373 U.S. 526, 83 S. Ct. 1314 (1963).

13 Green v. County School Bd., 390 U.S. 936, 88 S. Ct. 1689 (1968); Monroe v. Bd. of Comm'r, 390 U.S. 936, 88 S. Ct. 1700 (1968); Raney v. Bd. of Educ., 390 U.S. 936, 88 S. Ct. 1697 (1968).

it may well be, as suggested by Mr. Justice Black in a recent television interview, that the "all deliberate speed" formula was a mistake.

With the passage of the 1964 Civil Rights Act and the vesting of authority to implement the *Brown* decision in the Health, Education, and Welfare and the Justice Departments, the practical significance of a Supreme Court desegregation decision changed considerably. The role of private suits in the school area is placed back where it was before the decision, that of innovating and pushing forward in situations where government, for one reason or another, does not act. In *Rogers v. Paul*,[14] after quoting from *Bradley v. School Board*,[15] the Court said that delays in desegregating public schools are no longer tolerable, and it ordered prompt admission of Negro children to a high school from which they had been excluded because the district's desegregation plan had not yet reached their grades. This re-emphasizes the necessity of a case by case approach to the problem which delays the realization of the full right. This same slow progress with resistance has obtained in all aspects of civil rights dating back to the Emancipation Proclamation, including voting, public accommodations, housing and jobs. With the advent of peaceful non-violent demonstrations, the minorities engaged in prayerful pleas to the existing traditional legal institutions to *do something now*. Though in some quarters these pleas were heard, the urgency was not fully understood, nor did these institutions have the independence and machinery to get the job done. The minorities became restive and impatient and then suspicious—in fact, mistrustful—of traditional institutions. This mistrust spawned a new breed of activists and militants. It need not be repeated here that a crisis has gripped America since that time.

The more moderate of these activists are seeking a Black identity, a coalition of all Blacks in America to establish their own institutions, their own communities, their own culture. This represents a turnabout from the early struggles for complete integration to a theory of nonlegally enforced segregation and limited integration of the Black minorities for the purpose of restoring pride, of which they had been robbed by centuries of humiliation.[16] This Black identity, if attainable in peaceful ways, would involve the Blacks in establishing their own institutions, which would give them muscle to deal from a posture of strength for the fulfillment of the promises of democracy. The movement contemplates progress within the present framework of the law but with constant use of newly found power to change the law when in the interest of the Black minorities and of benefit to society in general. Indeed to be otherwise would be anarchy and self-destructive.

It may very well be that the importance of legal institutions in the civil rights movement will be tied to the role that the government assumes in other areas of vital concern to the nation. The central issue may not be whether

---

[14] 382 U.S. 198, 86 S. Ct. 358 (1965).
[15] 382 U.S. 103, 86 S. Ct. 224 (1965).
[16] FORTUNE, Jan. 1968, at 146.

the federal government is to play a role in such fields as education, consumer affairs and urban problems, but how much the structure of government itself may undergo a change where domestic affairs are concerned, particularly in the broad area of federal-state relations. Newer kinds of programs involving broad cooperation between government and private enterprise may develop. Such programs may rest on tax incentive and other programs less oriented to governmental bureaucracy. The extent of their success, however, will depend on the extent to which there is a dedication as a matter of national policy to the eradication of the variety of evils plaguing our domestic life.

There must be a reversal of approach on the national scale from one of reaction to dislocations to one of planning for future growth. This will involve an inducement to promote more institutional businesses and community-oriented action into a massive effort to deal with the problems of minorities. In this sense, the approach may become more community-oriented than institutional. However, traditional legal institutions must continue to set the tone for such developments. The courts must constantly reflect constitutional idealism and judicious enforcement in problem areas. The legislature must become more responsive to future developmental needs. The executives must address the best of government and business brains to dealing with the problems in the manner in which a business would anticipate consumer trends. Only to the extent that an enlightened approach is made will the pressures from extremists be abated.

Index

Administration of justice, 24, 29
Amendments. *See* Federal legislative action
Attorney
  education for civil rights work, 180, 182, 187 ff.
  fees for work on fair housing, 182 ff.
  role of general practitioner in representing tenants, 177 ff.; representing defendant tenants, 181, 182; representing plaintiff tenants, 181, 182
  role of lawyers specializing in housing: traditionally, 180 ff.; since 1968 act, 182, 184, 185

Bill of Rights. *See* Federal legislative action
Black Muslims, 27
Black power, 52
Brown v. Board of Education, 20, 25-31, 39, 59-82, 200

Civil Disorders, National Commission on (Kerner), 161, 175, 196, 200
Civil Rights, Commission on, 29, 31, 32, 36-39, 41, 44, 94
Civil rights activism
  black militancy, 201
  CORE, 27
  freedom riders, 35
  march on Washington, 36
  sit-ins, 33-35, 37, 85, 86, 88
  SNCC, 27
  voter registration, 35
Civil rights acts. *See* Federal legislative action; State legislative action
The Civil Rights Cases, 13, 93
Commerce power. *See* under Public accommodations
Community Relations Service, 43
Constitutional guarantees. *See* specific article or amendment under Federal legislative action

Defense, Department of, 97, 102, 104, 105, 107, 108, 109, 111, 118, 119, 120, 121, 122
Discrimination. *See* specific manifestation

Economic Opportunity, Office of
  legal services offices, 179
Education
  correlation of level with: conduct, 56; economic position, 56; employment opportunities, 56; exercise of franchise, 56
  effect of: community control, 83; defacto v. dejure segregation, 16, 25, 26, 30, 31, 39, 50, 67, 68, 73, 81, 82, 83; freedom-of-choice plans, 49, 72, 79; loss of federal funds, 72
  executive activity in: duty to balance races, 67; duty to forbid segregation, 63, 64; duty to require integration, 65, 66; HEW guidelines, 79, 183
  integration: inadequacy of separate but equal, 57; rate of, 39; right to, 63 ff.; standard for, 75 ff.; value of, 56-58, 61
  judicial activity: *Brown v. Board of Education*, 20, 25-31, 39, 59-82, 200; *Bell v. School Board of the City of Gary, Indiana*, 65 ff.
  legislative activity: Elementary and Secondary Education Act of 1965, 48
  rate of progress toward integration, 70 ff.
  segregation: books, 83; courses of study, 83; effect, 56 ff.; faculty placement, 49, 79; geographical zoning, 79; inadequacy of library facilities, 56, 57, 66, 83; physical plant, 59; pupils, 70 ff.; schools, 16; school buses, 79; state and local action, 50; teacher certification, 83
Emancipation Proclamation, 55, 201
Employment
  Discrimination in: facilities for Negro employees, 103; rate of promotion, 100, 106, 111, 114 ff.; status of Negro employees, 100
  discrimination within government, 19, 22, 24
  effect of federal action: Civil Rights Act of 1964, 101 ff.; Equal Em-

DATE DUE

31 87			